REINVENTING THE
HEART
LAND

HOW ONE CITY'S INCLUSIVE APPROACH TO INNOVATION AND GROWTH CAN REVIVE THE AMERICAN DREAM

NICHOLAS LALLA

HARPER HORIZON

Published by Harper Horizon, an imprint of HarperCollins Focus LLC.

Any internet addresses, phone numbers, or company or product information printed in this book are offered as a resource and are not intended in any way to be or to imply an endorsement by Harper Horizon, nor does Harper Horizon vouch for the existence, content, or services of these sites, phone numbers, companies, or products beyond the life of this book.

Design by Neuwirth & Associates, Inc.

ISBN 978-1-4002-4902-2 (eBook)
ISBN 978-1-4002-4900-8 (HC)

Library of Congress Cataloging-in-Publication Data
Library of Congress Cataloging-in-Publication application has been submitted.

Printed in the United States of America
24 25 26 27 28 LBC 5 4 3 2 1

To Mama:

For a lifetime buttoning up my overcoat.

CONTENTS

INTRODUCTION

Split in two by a highway—as communities of color often are—the Greenwood District of Tulsa, Oklahoma, was once known as America's Black Wall Street. At the start of the twentieth century, Greenwood was home to one of America's most affluent Black communities, including a notable density of doctors, lawyers, bankers, and entrepreneurs. I didn't fully appreciate the neighborhood's significance when I pulled up to the Greenwood Cultural Center during my first visit to Tulsa in January 2019. With its quiet streets and empty parking lots, Greenwood seemed like so many of the places I'd been to before. But small commemorative plaques on the sidewalks where businesses once stood hinted at an overlooked and extraordinary history.

I was there because the George Kaiser Family Foundation (GKFF) had invited me to town to consider working with them on an economic development project. GKFF is a multibillion-dollar philanthropy that combats intergenerational poverty in Tulsa, making it one of the largest foundations in the United States dedicated to improving lives in a single city. At the time, I was living in Manhattan and leading the cornerstone of Mayor Bill de Blasio's jobs plan—Cyber NYC, an initiative of the New York City Economic Development Corporation (NYCEDC). The *New York Times* called this public–private partnership "among the nation's most ambitious cybersecurity initiatives,"[1] and GKFF reached out to gauge my interest in helping Tulsa develop its own cyber ecosystem.

My trip happened to coincide with a visit by former New York mayor Michael Bloomberg. He was in Tulsa to award the Greenwood Cultural Center a million-dollar grant for a public arts project depicting the 1921 Tulsa Race Massacre that destroyed Black Wall Street. I arrived before the event and wandered around the center, browsing the photographs and news clippings from the tragedy: a White mob attacked Black residents, burned down more than a thousand of their homes, and ruined nearly two hundred businesses. I was horrified by the images of charred houses, dead bodies, smoke billowing in the air, land scorched and flattened, rubble drenched by fire hoses. The mob killed some three hundred Black Tulsans, devastating what legendary sociologist W. E. B. DuBois called the most "highly organized" Black community he'd ever seen.[2] It was America's worst episode of racist violence in the twentieth century, and its impact lingers to this day.

Understandably, the event at the center had a religious solemnity to it. There were prayers for the victims and moments of silence. Speakers reflected on all that was lost in 1921 and again during the period of urban renewal when, in the late 1960s and early '70s, the community was torn apart for a second time by I-244, the highway that runs through Greenwood today. At the center, there were pleas for neighborhood investment, hope of revitalization, and murmurs about reparations. Speeches reminiscent of Sunday sermons joined with the political rhetoric of local elected officials, such as City Councilor Vanessa Hall-Harper and Mayor G. T. Bynum, who had just authorized a search for unmarked graves to determine the massacre's total number of victims.

Juxtaposed against these grim remarks were the flashing cameras, news media, and public excitement that accompany the presence of not just one but two of America's wealthiest men. Mayor Bloomberg was joined that day by another billionaire, George Kaiser, a lifelong Tulsan and the founder of GKFF. The mix of Black trauma and White philanthropy created a peculiar vibe in the event space, at once somber and thrilling, mournful and hopeful. The dramatic tension in the air mesmerized me, and it caused me to wonder about how Black trauma is often portrayed as spectacle; how White philanthropists relate to the diverse communities they seek to serve; how Greenwood reflects the contemporary effects of past injustice; and what it would take to create economic opportunities for Tulsa's Black, Indigenous, and White working-class citizens.

The event helped me see a cultural kinship that I hadn't expected, one that would begin pulling me inexorably toward Tulsa. Listening to Tulsans talk about racism, poverty, and trauma, the need for Greenwood's redevelopment, and the city's broader desire to change economic course transported me back to my childhood in New Orleans—growing up in a White working-class family with a single mom, wrestling with feelings of alienation, and living through Hurricane Katrina. I was a stranger in Tulsa, but I felt at home. For me, Greenwood could have easily been the Lower Ninth Ward. I gravitated toward Tulsa's trauma because it resembled my own, and I understood the city's need to reckon with it because I had undergone a similar journey myself.

I sensed that both Tulsa and I had chips on our shoulders. Underestimated, we both had something to prove, and I realized that this underdog city had so much more potential than people gave it credit for. A few months later, in September 2019, I packed up my life on the Upper East Side and again lit out for the territory of northeast Oklahoma—this time for more than just a visit.

IN JANUARY 2020, right before COVID-19's emergence in the United States, I founded Tulsa Innovation Labs (TIL) with GKFF's support. Our organization kicked off a citywide effort to build Tulsa's innovation economy from the ground up. Like too many places, Tulsa had become complacent with its economy, relying on its oil and gas legacy without investing in a tech ecosystem that could create start-ups or more durable jobs. For decades, Tulsa struggled to reverse the spiral of economic decline and brain drain initiated by postindustrialism, and it became isolated from the US innovation system—a network of tech companies, venture capital (VC), and research and development (R&D). And with automation projected to displace one in four jobs by 2030, disproportionately affecting Black and brown Americans, Tulsa needed to act immediately if it wanted to stay relevant in the twenty-first century.[3]

Tulsa was far from alone in this predicament; most of its midsized-city peers are facing the same challenges. But what made Tulsa unique was the unprecedented ambition to chart a new path forward.

At the same time, Tulsa provided an unlikely case study of economic transformation for another reason: it's America in miniature. Indeed, when modern-day Don Drapers want to test a product's national appeal, they get out of Manhattan and head to Tulsa. Tulsa's mix of demographics and its cultural ambiguity—is it the Midwest or the South?—have made the city ideal for piloting new products for decades, from soft drinks to laundry detergents,[4] pizza to draft beer.[5] Reporting on research that found Tulsa's demographics "match national averages more closely than any other city," a 1993 article in the *Oklahoman* asks a curious question: "Toss the United States into a blender, crank it up and what do you get?" The answer, the article says, is a "big Tulsa puree."[6]

Of course, the country has changed a lot since the '90s—economically and demographically. Over those years, Tulsa diversified as did America writ large, and the city became majority minority in 2021.[7] The city's present racial makeup demonstrates America's own demographic evolution. Oklahoma represents the sad conclusion of the Trail of Tears, and Tulsa serves as the meeting point for tribal nations—the Osage, Muscogee, and Cherokee. The legacy of 1921 holds special resonance for the city's Black communities. And a more recent influx of Asian and Hispanic residents has helped Tulsa maintain its status as one of the most representative cities in America.[8]

If the city that embodies the American mosaic mirrors the country's changing demographics, it also functions as a microcosm for a less positive pattern: Tulsa has fallen out of step with the innovation economies that have bloomed on the coasts, exemplifying a larger trend in the region of which it is a part—the American Heartland.

The Heartland is a political and economic organ that transcends geography, an idea shaped by our own worldviews. Calling "place" a projection, the midwestern novelist Jonathan Franzen asserts that the Heartland is "an idea that exists in a duality with the coasts," with each representing what the other isn't.[9] For some coastal residents today, the Heartland may be a reactionary void, backward in thinking with nothing to offer the nation. For those who associate with the Heartland, they may see it as embodying community, faith, and humility. Cable news shows air dueling narratives about which is the "Real America." But in recent years, there may be a shared understanding that the coasts offer an abundance of opportunity while the Heartland increasingly doesn't.

What I discovered in Tulsa was that the Heartland encompasses the great middle of the country—not only in geographic terms but in societal, cultural, and even spiritual ones. For me, the Heartland represents midsized cities like Tulsa, middle-class citizens, and those striving to reach the middle class. "Whether the mythical heartland is celebrated or reviled," historian Kristin L. Hoganson writes, "it fosters the perception that there is a gulf between the center and the edges, between the heart and the national body."[10] No matter its definition or borders, this perception is real: the Heartland does, indeed, represent a divide. We typically think of people lacking opportunities as marginalized, operating on the edges of society. But the Heartland rightly shows us that the metaphor is inverted—those on the margins of economic opportunity represent the vast middle, while coastal tech hubs, through their concentrated wealth, are in the minority and yet firmly in power.

Every city wants to become a tech hub, but only a handful on the coasts rule America's innovation system—and that's a problem. The Brookings Institution found that between 2005 and 2017, 90 percent of growth from the country's innovation sector came from just five coastal metros.[11] And from July 2022 through July 2023, six coastal cities accounted for almost 50 percent of all US job postings in generative artificial intelligence (AI), which is the cutting edge of today's tech industry.[12] Through the clustering of talent, industry, and capital and the agglomeration economics that result, big coastal cities like New York, San Francisco, Los Angeles, Seattle, Boston, and Washington, DC, have monopolized innovation and its myriad benefits. This narrow geographic distribution of the innovation economy leaves Heartland cities out and restricts opportunities for most of the population.

Consequently, the American Dream—the notion that through hard work everyone has an equal opportunity to lead a good and decent life so that successive generations are better off—is moving further out of reach for more people. In 2023, citing rising income inequality, the Harvard economist Raj Chetty said, "If we look at what has happened over time, we see a dramatic fading of the American Dream such that for children born in the middle of the 1980s and the 1990s who are entering the labor market today, it's now become a coin flip, a 50-50 shot, as to whether you're going to do better than your parents."[13] These are unacceptable odds that undermine faith in American democracy and capitalism, and they're only going to get worse unless Heartland cities act with urgency to reset their economies.

Heartland cities like Tulsa can and must be actors in the innovation economy, which, despite its inequitable access, remains the best opportunity for long-term job and wealth creation. But they don't need to compete with the big coastal hubs. Middleweights are in a class of their own, and they should strive to become the best version of themselves.

Midsized cities like Tulsa, with metropolitan statistical area populations between one and three million people,[14] already have the foundation to support a tech ecosystem: population density, cultural amenities, as well as a relatively low cost of living that can de-risk entrepreneurship. Pandemic workforce trends have highlighted these advantages, as members of the creative class can now more easily search for a better quality of life and move away from coastal cities, where growth and equity too often work in opposition.[15] Established tech hubs are driving out even the well compensated, and this cohort of mobile talent is finding benefits in unassuming places like Tulsa. This influx of talent creates an opportunity for any city that can attract and retain them.

Despite possessing many of the key elements for a tech ecosystem, too many Heartland cities have also shut themselves out of the innovation economy by clinging to outdated notions of economic development, by underinvesting in their communities, or by holding on to a nostalgic sense of culture—an aversion to change that has led to counterproductive policies that turn off outside tech talent and investors and do nothing to foster home-grown ecosystems. While most change happens organically over time, skyrocketing domestic inequality[16] and widening geographic disparities in tech have brought us to an inflection point as a country. Heartland cities need to pivot with intention and haste—or risk dying out.

THIS BOOK IS a call to action for the United States to address one of society's defining challenges: expanding opportunity by harnessing the tech industry and ensuring gains spread across demographics and geographies. The middle matters, the center must hold, and Heartland cities need to reinvent themselves to thrive in the innovation age.

That enormous project starts at the local level, through place-based economic development, which can make an impact far faster than changing the patterns of financial markets or corporate behavior. And inclusive growth in tech must start with the reinvention of Heartland cities. That requires cities—civic ecosystems, not merely municipal governments—to undertake two changes in parallel. The first is transitioning their legacy economies to tech-based ones, and the second is shifting from a growth mindset to an inclusive-growth mindset. To accomplish both admittedly ambitious endeavors, cities must challenge local economic development orthodoxy and readjust their entire civic ecosystems for this generational project.

Urban reinvention is both a singularly inward-facing process and a definitively collaborative one—an uncomfortable, yet exciting experience of change from within a city, supported by a wider community of regional and national partners. It goes beyond revitalization, which suggests improving what already exists. Reinvention is about building on what exists today to create a new, more vibrant world. It means taking what makes a city special, harnessing the Heartland's enduring strengths, and leveraging them to compete in the twenty-first century. It's not too dissimilar from innovation itself, which often takes existing products and builds on them or applies technologies in new ways, rather than creating something from nothing.

Every midsized city can find its place in the innovation economy and establish its own tech identity. But it should not be under any illusions about how difficult it will be. Political scientist Dan Breznitz cautions against "purveyors" of the myth that any city can become a tech hub. "The religious believers of techno-fetishism," he writes in *Innovation in Real Places*, "have a feeble understanding of the big picture of global production and innovation . . . they have not noticed—or will not tell you—that there is a significant obstacle to creating the next VC hub in Oklahoma or Ohio."[17]

Not to kink-shame, but I am no techno-fetishist. I do not pretend that building an innovation hub is easy anywhere, much less in Tulsa. I know how hard it is because I've done it myself. Nor do I see tech as a panacea—quite the opposite, in fact, which is why I focus so heavily on inclusive growth. Rather than "Tulsa the triumphant," this book is about Tulsa the imperfect model; it addresses the city's structural impediments, analyzes the costs and benefits of my approach, reflects upon my own strengths and weaknesses as a leader, and teases out lessons learned from both the city's successes and its failures.

In doing so, this book chronicles the initial phase of Tulsa's historic effort to prove that catalytic change can happen anywhere, and it aims to inspire other cities to begin their own process of reinvention.

TO GET OFF the roller coaster of oil booms and busts, shake off its malaise, and create a path toward steady, sustainable, and inclusive growth in tech, we established a vision that would diversify Tulsa's economy, prepare its citizens for the jobs of the future, widen access to opportunities, and grow from the inside out.

Over four years, Tulsa Innovation Labs (TIL) built the city's first tech-led economic development strategy and raised more than $200 million in public, private, and social sector capital that it is now currently deploying through multiple initiatives. This success has spurred additional investments. Since TIL's launch, several new organizations—supported by GKFF—have been established to help the city transition to tech—the first time in American history a city has dedicated itself in such a concerted way to becoming a player in the innovation economy.

While long-term outcomes are yet to be determined, people now widely recognize Tulsa as a city on the ascent. Remote workers flock to the area, new direct flights connect Tulsa to the world, downtown development is accelerating, start-ups are relocating to the city, and the region is winning major federal grants for innovation infrastructure. The GKFF-backed effort aims to catalyze at least twenty thousand tech jobs over the next decade, a third of which are attainable without a bachelor's degree.[18] TIL's initiatives are expected to account for half of these totals.[19]

Drawing on this real-world experiment, a new kind of pilot, my book establishes an action plan for reinvention over an initial five-year time frame that other Heartland cities can adapt and adopt. Instead of recipes, the following pages articulate a bold vision for urban reinvention and a realistic plan for achieving that vision. Bringing together various Tulsa threads under a unifying architecture, the action plan spans the full civic ecosystem, offering readers a set of tools to build a tech hub in the Heartland so that all their citizens have the opportunity to achieve the American Dream.

Reinventing the Heartland can help civic leaders and all those working in the innovation economy position themselves as impactful change agents. Each chapter covers a core plank of the action plan, organized in three sections:

I. ESTABLISHING A TECH IDENTITY

1. Build an industry cluster strategy to find your city's tech niche.

2. Enable good troublemakers, leaders who can challenge the status quo.

3. Coordinate across your ecosystem and inspire collective action.

II. BUILDING AN INNOVATION ENGINE

4. Establish a remote-worker incentive to attract outside tech talent.

5. Upskill incumbent talent to grow your city's tech clusters.

6. Create diversity, equity, and inclusion (DEI) initiatives to support the underserved.

7. Reorient universities toward technological innovation and talent production.

8. Connect start-ups with existing corporations to foster a culture of innovation.

III. FUELING THE FUTURE

9. Partner with philanthropy to raise capital for economic development.

10. Forge urban–rural alliances and compete as a region for federal funding.

I explain this multipronged approach through the context of Tulsa, but I explore other cities as well, proving that Tulsa is not an outlier but a leader.

Why should America care about Tulsa? Because if we can get Tulsa right, we can get America right. And we might even teach big coastal cities a thing or two about inclusive growth in the process.

Throughout the action plan, this book engages timely issues affecting American society at large and shows how national and global forces play out in a little corner of northeast Oklahoma—from the pros and cons of remote work to the political consequences of the urban–rural divide to the need to stay competitive in an increasingly dangerous world. The book also shows that learning from the past is a painful, yet integral part of urban reinvention, and that neighborhoods like Greenwood must be part of the innovation economy.

Unlike a lot of books about cities, this one takes you inside a community undergoing change, with real people, real problems, and real solutions told from a practitioner's—not a theorist's—perspective. Taking you inside Tulsa's journey, I'll introduce you to a cast of characters who are all making a positive difference. You'll meet Kian Kamas, who transformed the city government's economic development system; Tyrance Billingsley II, who, inspired by the legacy of Black Wall Street, founded the nonprofit Black Tech Street; Garrison Haning, a West Point and Wharton alum, who founded an energy tech start-up; and Raymond Redcorn, the former assistant chief of the Osage Nation who championed an early investment in drones—to name just a few.

Further, as a gay millennial from a working-class background, I share an approach influenced as much by my personal upbringing as by my success in Tulsa.

Blending the personal with the practical, this book reveals the messy, complex, yet fundamentally hopeful realities of the struggle to catalyze change and create shared prosperity. The action plan for reinvention this book offers can demystify what it means to build a tech hub and help you create your own path toward inclusive growth with clear, pragmatic eyes.

Anthropologist and author Zora Neale Hurston writes in *Their Eyes Were Watching God*, "There are years that ask questions and years that answer."[20] During my four years in Tulsa, I got answers to many of the questions I had been stewing over about America and her future. I also experienced milestones in my personal life and in the collective life of our country, including marrying my husband and surviving a pandemic—all of which provided further perspective on what I value and what the American Dream means to me. My experience in Tulsa gave me a rare gift, something even more valuable than answers: I found clarity. Having rediscovered my own Heartland roots, I better understand the path forward for America. And I'm determined to see it applied not just in Tulsa but in any city ready to take its fate into its own hands and embrace the future.

SECTION I

ESTABLISHING
A TECH IDENTITY

CHAPTER 1

FIND YOUR TECH NICHE

(INDUSTRY CLUSTER STRATEGY)

Although I had spoken to George Kaiser a few times, I didn't know what to expect when I went before his foundation's board of directors to pitch my vision for Tulsa. It was the fall of 2019, and I was excited to share my ideas about how to transform the city's economy. I could sense this presentation would be my shot at a once-in-a-lifetime opportunity. Heading into the meeting, I had envisioned a scene straight from HBO's *Succession*: A downtown skyscraper crowned with a helipad. A billionaire and his kids sitting at a dark wooden table in a large conference room. Executives and lawyers clad in Ermenegildo Zegna and Brunello Cucinelli suits. An air of tension and formality, with power politics pulsing through terse conversation.

To my surprise, pitching to the George Kaiser Family Foundation's board was nothing of the sort. The meeting was held in a modest room in one of their grantees' buildings; members of the board, including two of Kaiser's three children, chatted freely between sessions. The atmosphere was relaxed, and it was clear most of them had known each other for a long time. Affable yet shrewd, Kaiser commanded the room with a humble and understated gravity. His eyes came to rest on me, and with a smile, he invited me to begin.

I called my presentation "Transforming Tulsa into a Cyber City," but my goal was much more ambitious than even the title suggested. It had been a few months since my first visit to Tulsa, and in that time, I had researched how GKFF could structure an investment in Tulsa's cyber ecosystem. Their interest in cyber was based on a belief among Tulsa civic leaders that the University of Tulsa's (TU) cyber program—one of only a handful of programs recognized for excellence by the National Security Agency (NSA)—was an underutilized gem. In the time since GKFF had reached out to me, I had come to realize that investing in cyber alone wasn't going to move the needle meaningfully. What GKFF really needed to ask was: How could Tulsa become a hub for technological innovation, and how could that economy create opportunities across all of Tulsa's neighborhoods? And: Preconceptions about Tulsa's strengths and weaknesses aside, what were the most promising opportunities for inclusive growth? In short, Tulsa needed to find its **Tech Niche** and develop it to the fullest.

TECH NICHE: A city's tech niche represents the strongest opportunities for tech-led and inclusive economic growth in that metropolitan region. It is a city's own place within the innovation economy. You know you've approached defining your tech niche in the right way if it has these four elements: (1) it should **build on your city's legacy industries** to best facilitate the transition to tech; (2) it should **represent high-growth emerging tech clusters** that offer the most promise for long-term opportunities; (3) it should **provide jobs requiring a range**

of educational attainment levels to ensure pathways are as inclusive as possible; and (4) it should **give your city the opportunity to lead** in these clusters, not just serve as a supporting player. The genuine potential to be a leader in an industry cluster because of existing assets is known as your "right to win."

Cyber, however, would be my Trojan horse. I started with an outline of how I would structure a cyber investment but then pivoted to the core of my presentation: a blueprint for how to build an inclusive innovation economy in a city that didn't have one. As Tulsa's core industries stagnated, the city needed to catch up with the twenty-first-century economy or risk falling into a self-perpetuating cycle of decline. These city leaders recognized that, but accomplishing urban reinvention is an entirely different ball game.

The trick was to take a systems approach to developing cyber while connecting it to opportunities related to the city's legacy industries, tying them together through complementary investments—the approach at the heart of clustering. Made famous by Harvard Business School professor Michael Porter, "clusters" is a rebrand of the old concept of agglomeration and refers to "geographic concentrations of interconnected companies and institutions in a particular field."[1] Leading urbanists, such as Richard Florida, consider clustering to be the best way to generate innovation and growth—and it's also why a few big cities dominate tech.[2] My idea for a city's tech niche builds upon the concepts of agglomeration and clustering and applies them to today's need for cities to locate their sweet spot in the innovation economy. If cities can develop a strategy that is attainable, builds on local strengths, and galvanizes the partners necessary to succeed, they can catalyze inclusive growth in tech.

While cyber could be the base of a multi-industry strategy, it could not succeed if isolated from Tulsa's present industries; investing in a few other clusters directly related to Tulsa's existing employers and developed in a coordinated way could lead to a sustainable tech-based economy. From the research and stakeholder interviews I had conducted, I hypothesized that some combination of health-care informatics, energy technology, aerospace, and cyber made sense because they built upon Tulsa's current industries. Think of it as connecting cyber—a horizontal play since it functions across industries—with existing industry verticals.

Some may warn of overspecialization, but focusing on a handful of the strongest opportunities will enable cities to create the clustering of activity necessary for growth. And while some may wring their hands that establishing a tech niche precludes other opportunities, it doesn't. What it means is that most economic development efforts (say, 80 percent) should go into developing the most promising clusters, leaving cities the ability to engage in opportunistic pursuits. The entire point, though, is to avoid shiny-object syndrome. As many stakeholders told me, Tulsa had long taken a scattershot and disordered approach to economic development. Establishing the city's tech niche called for a data driven and focused strategy.

Before Tulsa made any investments, I continued, we would need to kick the tires on potential opportunities by conducting an industry cluster strategy. After we identified the strongest clusters, we would then curate a set of investments to catalyze growth, akin to my work at the New York City Economic Development Corporation. Cyber NYC was a public–private investment, but it wasn't a singular, siloed investment. The sweeping initiative aimed to grow the city's cyber cluster while supporting New York's financial services industry, which has made cyber a top priority. Cyber NYC did so through interconnected initiatives that, when combined, were greater than their individual parts. Talent fuels start-ups; academic research powers innovation, leading to new start-ups; and capital grows businesses, which, in turn, lead to more jobs. This virtuous cycle was why Cyber NYC included new degree and credentialing programs, a training boot camp, an academic-based start-up accelerator, and a growth-stage start-up accelerator. In my pitch, I suggested Tulsa should take a similarly holistic approach to developing their clusters.

Before my presentation, someone warned me that a few board members had expressed concern that economic development was unnecessary mission creep for the foundation. Kaiser and GKFF's priority had long been on combating intergenerational poverty through early childhood interventions. This mission is rooted in Kaiser's belief that in the United States who you were born to dictates too much of your life's trajectory. As he often says, "No child is responsible for the circumstances of his or her birth." Who your parents are affects your educational attainment, who your friends and neighbors are, how much wealth you accumulate, even how long you live.

I grew up in poverty, while Kaiser grew up in wealth, yet we both understand how impactful a child's first years are. We both know that everyone is capable, especially if given the opportunity, of living the American Dream. Kaiser is quick to acknowledge his privilege and honest about racial and socioeconomic disparities. He has said he feels a "moral responsibility" to reduce inequality. Knowing all this, I pointed out during my presentation that to fight poverty, it's not enough to support the child. You need to support the parents too.

As I saw from my own mother, who worked tirelessly to provide for my brother and me, parents are crucial to a child's success. But parents need skills and education to get the income and health care they need to provide for their families. To make the case that Tulsa needed to build an inclusive innovation economy, I suggested that the foundation should broaden how it understands its mission and help by connecting parents to the "jobs of the future"—jobs that pay well and are resilient. Doing so could help lift children out of poverty and reduce the city's racial inequality: the median household income for White Tulsans is $68,408, while for Black Tulsans, it's $42,994.[3]

To give GKFF a sense of the scale I thought we needed, I said I wanted to "build a gathering place for innovation"—a reference to the GKFF-funded $500 million park by that name that had opened in 2018. Designed to aid child development, the Gathering Place has won several design awards and generated local pride. With more than a million plants and six thousand trees, the park embodies the region's verdant setting. Rather than the tumbleweed-strewn desert landscape I first imagined Tulsa to be, the city is lush with trees, for Tulsa sits near the base of the Ozarks; this is why locals call the area "Green Country." I closed by asking the board to imagine an innovation community in which all Tulsans could come together, grow together, and thrive together.

Looking back, I didn't realize that my theory of change represented a paradigm shift for both GKFF and Tulsa. GKFF had brought me in to talk solely about cyber, and yet I was recommending that the foundation not only change how they thought about their own mission but go all in on building an innovation economy. By connecting economic development to more familiar antipoverty initiatives, such as those that GKFF funds, I presented a solution to a problem they hadn't raised, defining inclusive growth in a way that could resonate with them while challenging them to widen the scope of what they needed to do and what they could achieve. To use Ohio-born novelist Toni Morrison's phrase, I wanted to inspire Tulsans to "dream tall" and spark their own renaissance. Ambition in tech shouldn't be reserved for big cities or White start-up founders.

To expand opportunities in tech—from north Tulsa to downtown—the city would need to go from checkers to chess, from opportunistic to strategic investments. A knowledgeable Tulsan shared this analogy with me: "George made his money by drilling at one oil well and then another and then another. He takes the same approach with his philanthropy." For GKFF, projects were funded through one-off decisions based on their own merits. But as I demonstrated, GKFF needed an economic development strategy that linked investments.

Cities looking to find their place in the innovation economy need to conduct an industry cluster strategy that locates their tech niche. Properly executed over time, an industry cluster strategy with coordinated investments can establish a more dynamic and inclusive economy.

Thankfully, most of the board seemed excited by my vision. The foundation's general counsel was enthusiastic, as was a local investor, whose son had graduated from TU's cyber program. Kaiser chimed in about the opportunities he saw in emerging tech and what companies they may try to attract. Another board member spoke of the need for an "air traffic controller" to unify and synchronize the city's disjointed economic development work. There appeared to be consensus that if GKFF didn't act now, then Tulsa was going to be further left behind. The room was buzzing. With a rush of adrenaline surging through my body, I tried not to sweat through my suit. Although the board doesn't vote up or down on matters, it was clear to me that we were moving in a positive direction, a feeling that we were at the start of something momentous.

LOOK IN THE MIRROR

Bob Dylan once said, in his characteristically cryptic and cheeky way, "All I can do is be me, whoever that is."[4] Understanding your core competencies and brand isn't important just for individual leaders or companies; it's critical for cities too. When it comes to innovation economies—particularly in midsized cities led to think that they don't have a place in tech—many cities don't clearly understand their assets and strengths. Bits and pieces may be spread out across town, but cities don't typically leverage them to their full extent. Blind spots exist in every city. And many cities acknowledge the need to transition to innovation but don't know where to start. The first step, then, is to understand who you are—or, more precisely, who you can be. And that requires conducting an industry cluster strategy.

Well into the twenty-first century, Tulsa hadn't found its spot in the nation's innovation system, and warning lights were flashing. Tulsa's primary legacy industry, energy, had been seesawing for decades, and by that point it was well past its prime. Tulsa was no longer the "Oil Capital of the World," and the energy companies that had provided strong employment and wealth for generations began to see the writing on the wall: climate change, renewables, and digitization were going to cause continuous disruption. Many of the once solid middle-class jobs that oil and gas provided were now susceptible to automation. (More on Tulsa and oil in chapter 8.) The same could be said for Tulsa's manufacturing and service jobs—they were at high risk of being automated as well. And Tulsa had been struggling to retain a demographic key to an innovation economy: the twenty-five- to thirty-four-year-old population with bachelor's degrees.

Of course, Tulsa wasn't the only city facing this conundrum, and certainly not the first—cities are always looking to turn themselves around. In 1989, filmmaker Michael Moore documented to comedic effect the efforts of Flint, Michigan, to become a tourist destination following layoffs from General Motors. That's as if gambling became illegal in Las Vegas and the city suddenly decided to become a hub for AI. Indeed, many think the solution for older, manufacturing-based cities in decline is "tech": a mystical source of jobs, investment, and rebirth. But cities can't transform with a snap of their fingers and certainly not in response to a prompt as vague as "tech." Nor can they just wait for conditions to evolve in their favor. Every medium-sized city can participate in the innovation economy by identifying their current resources and carving out a niche for themselves.

The key thing to understand is that an industry cluster strategy is based on what a city has, not what it doesn't have. In *The Death and Life of Great American Cities*, famed urbanist Jane Jacobs writes that "cities contain the seeds of their own regeneration,"[5] which I take to mean all cities have assets ripe for growth and development. Heartland cities should adopt that as their mantra. Expanding upon Jacobs's work, John McKnight and John Kretzmann formulated the asset-based community development methodology (ABCD) at Northwestern's Institute for Policy Research. ABCD saw local assets as the building blocks of development and encouraged civic leaders to focus on those positives rather than allow challenges to define their communities, sap hope, or delay investment.[6]

Heartland cities need to identify their assets, nurture them, and grow their legacy industries into more tech-based clusters. Mayor G. T. Bynum, who is the fourth member of his family dating back to 1899 to serve as Tulsa's mayor, put it this way: "The cities that will thrive in the twenty-first century are those that are relentlessly focused on the growth of new businesses and industries. One of the best ways to do this is to tap local expertise in one industry that can translate to the evolution of an entirely new one."[7] For Tulsa, that meant going from oil and gas to tech, built on tangible assets that already existed. But for other cities, it will be different.

CASE STUDY: PITTSBURGH REIMAGINED

Although many Tulsans didn't know what their city *could* be, they had models for what they wanted their city to be like. Pittsburgh, Pennsylvania, and Austin, Texas—the best-known tech hubs outside the coasts—enamored many stakeholders. They represent the eastern and western edges of the Heartland, respectively, and both have progressed significantly in building their innovation economies over the past three decades. Other literature has extensively covered these cities, and we'll explore Austin's strength in engineering talent in chapter 5. But a primer on Pittsburgh's tech identity helps illustrate how a midsized city should think about its own niche.

From 2013 to 2014, I worked as the analyst to the CEO and chief content officer of the Urban Land Institute. I had the pleasure of sitting across the hall from my colleague Tom Murphy, mayor of Pittsburgh from 1994 to 2006. I remember listening intently as Mayor Murphy described biking the Great Allegheny Passage, a 330-mile-long trail stretching from Pittsburgh to Washington, DC. Mayor Murphy served on Tulsa Innovations Labs's advisory council and has visited Tulsa to see our progress firsthand. Given TIL's work, he's told me that he sees parallels between where Tulsa is today and where Pittsburgh was ten years ago. Coincidentally, Alejandra Y. Castillo, assistant secretary at the US Economic Development Administration (EDA), also told one of my TIL colleagues that Tulsa reminds her of Pittsburgh. Given its transformation since then, Pittsburgh serves as a useful benchmark.

For decades, Pittsburgh was an international powerhouse in steel. But the collapse of the city's steel production threw Pittsburgh's identity into crisis, creating a rust belt that stretched across the industrial Heartland. Today, however, Pittsburgh is well known for a new industry altogether: robotics. Mayor Murphy explained Pittsburgh's transformation in a 2018 interview in *Site Selection* magazine: "After the steel mills closed down, we lost

500,000 people from 1970 to 1990. . . . When I became mayor in 1994, we had just been managing decline. South Side Works was a steel mill. My father worked there for 51 years. When it closed down, we had to reimagine Pittsburgh."[8] This required transitioning Pittsburgh to a more tech-based economy. "The problem at the time was that we had no entrepreneurial culture," Mayor Murphy continued. "They weren't accustomed to innovation."[9]

As Jacobs and the ABCD methodology instruct, Pittsburgh leveraged two of the city's strongest assets to build an innovation economy: the University of Pittsburgh and Carnegie Mellon University (CMU), whose applied research gave birth to the city's robotics cluster. Building on its machinery and manufacturing know-how, Pittsburgh is now able to design industrial robotics. And thanks to the allure of strong academic assets (talent and innovation) and city leaders actively engaging venture capitalists, Pittsburgh saw an influx of capital that helped fuel the robotics cluster. Between 2012 and 2021, VC and private equity firms invested $3.3 billion in Pittsburgh-based robotics companies; as of 2021, the region's robotics cluster supported seven thousand jobs, not to mention forty-five thousand tech workers in related fields—a growth of 300 percent over a ten-year period.[10]

CMU's Robotics Institute, the largest robotics research institute in the world, has spun off thirty start-ups and counting, serving as an essential asset to this cluster's development.[11] By building on existing research capacity, Pittsburgh was able to carve out a niche for itself in robotics, which has helped attract Google, Apple, and Intel to the city.

Mayor Murphy explained the choice cities face in his admirably blunt way: "Are you, like Pittsburgh, willing to embrace the future, or will you settle for managing decline? You can either continue to manage decline or reach for the future. I hope you kick the door down."[12]

Like Austin and San Francisco, Pittsburgh may have kicked the door down for those educated and skilled enough to position themselves within its tech sector. Yet the city struggles to create far-reaching opportunities. Pittsburgh's poverty rate has steadily increased over the past few decades. In 2022, the city's poverty rate (19.4 percent) is about seven points higher than the national average.[13] And research from the Pittsburgh Foundation revealed that systemic racism and the poverty that results from it affect "about 30% of the regional population, with 18% of children under age 18 living in poverty."[14] These sobering statistics are proof positive that the city's innovation economy is benefiting too few people. As Andrew Carnegie was building his steel empire during the Gilded Age, political economist Henry George observed: "material progress does not merely fail to relieve poverty—it actually produces it."[15] Today, it isn't enough to build an innovation economy: you must deliberately design it for inclusive growth.

After an initial run of success, Pittsburgh is now at an inflection point. According to Jason Griess, the former ecosystem and research director at InnovatePGH, a public–private partnership that runs the Pittsburgh Innovation District, "That era inflated expectations, which we had to work through when we didn't see the massive, immediate growth we expected. We've cut some of the noise and are reaping the benefits of doing the tactical work—putting together meaningful partnerships, deploying programs to increase the pipeline of high-growth entrepreneurs, and helping connect the corporate sector with start-ups to improve their chances of success."[16] Now that Pittsburgh has built a thriving robotics cluster, Griess, who recently joined CMU's CityLab, sees AI and biotech as good fits to build on that foundation, and he also urges the city to better engage diverse constituencies to create a more inclusive future.

While there's room for improvement, Pittsburgh demonstrates that former industrial cities can reimagine themselves and build innovation economies. There are second acts for American cities.

And third acts and fourth acts, too, because cities are capable of constant evolution. Cities should learn from exemplars like Pittsburgh, working to replicate successes while avoiding the mistakes. For your city to become the best version of itself, however, it must find its tech niche based on its own, special assets. To lead this effort of self-discovery, your city must get to know itself and its regional neighbors inside and out.

MAP YOUR ASSETS

The best way to familiarize yourself with a place is to identify and engage with all its key players. As a newcomer to Tulsa, I brought fresh eyes and useful ignorance to this endeavor. Everything about the city, and everyone in it, was new to me. I spent six months meeting with dozens of folks. Tulsa's insularity is both a blessing and a curse, but when it comes to networking, it's a blessing. From the start, it was easy to identify local leaders, and I found most everyone was eager to chat with me.

When mapping a city's assets, it's worth outlining the six main segments of your tech ecosystem: innovation, community, talent, employers, capital, and underrepresented voices. In essence, those segments represent the **Innovation Flywheel**, a concept first developed by Jim Collins in his book *Good to Great* (see below). The Innovation Flywheel is a framework to catalog, organize, and understand your city's tech ecosystem. When these segments are working effectively with one another, the flywheel can spin and generate growth. Within each segment, ask yourself the following:

INNOVATION: Which organizations, people, or other assets are producing, or could help produce, research and innovation that could be commercialized? These assets may include universities, start-ups, corporate R&D teams, entrepreneurs, start-up accelerator and incubator programs, infrastructure, Big Data sets, and equipment.

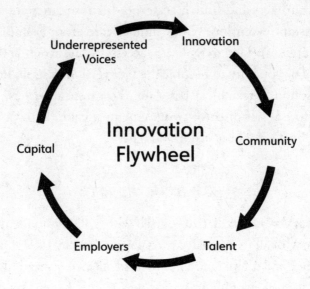

COMMUNITY: What social networks, meeting places, buildings, or professional associations bring people together? It's important to consider coworking spaces, parks, incubators, entrepreneurial support groups, industry networks, and real estate developers.

TALENT: Which organizations are producing or supporting tech talent? Look into four-year colleges, universities, community colleges, talent coaches, wraparound services, training boot camps, and other educational service providers that may already exist. Also consider large incumbent employers who can attract and develop talent.

EMPLOYERS: Who are the companies in your community that can serve as clients, customers, investors, mentors, or employers? Think small and medium-sized businesses, start-ups, nonprofits, major corporations, military bases, and local governments.

CAPITAL: Where are the potential sources of capital that could fund R&D, start-ups, and other economic development initiatives? Funding is a major component, so go deep and explore venture capital firms, family offices, community and private foundations, local, state, federal, and tribal governments, university-based innovation funds, and publicly supported risk capital funds.

UNDERREPRESENTED VOICES: A valuable twist in asset-mapping that goes beyond Collins's original concept is to ask yourself: "Who doesn't usually get a seat at the table?" Who are the nontraditional, overlooked, or underestimated assets? These could include veterans' associations, health-care clinics, reentry programs, LGBTQ+ centers, or public libraries.

In T-Town, I quickly put the Innovation Flywheel approach to work, meeting with presidents, deans, and professors from the University of Tulsa, Oklahoma State University–Tulsa, the University of Oklahoma–Tulsa, and Tulsa Community College; Mayor Bynum and his chief of economic development, Kian Kamas; corporate executives, especially from oil and gas; start-up founders; Mike Neal, the CEO of the Tulsa Regional Chamber; venture capitalists; real estate developers; representatives from the Osage and Cherokee governments; and leaders from the Schusterman, Lobeck Taylor, and Coretz Family Foundations. These meetings helped me understand what stakeholders could offer and what barriers they encountered. They also surfaced recurring themes and patterns that I was sure to note. Not only was this the beginning of the discovery process, but it also gave me an indication of potential partners. As I continued this work, I brought these folks together and regularly briefed them on our progress.

GET THE DATA

Just as I was learning new things about Tulsa's tech world, I was also getting acquainted with my new community. When I moved to Tulsa, some of my New York friends acted as though I were David Rose, the gay television character whose rich family lost all their money and was forced to live in a small town called Schitt's Creek. This says more about New Yorkers than it does Tulsans. But Tulsa didn't seem like the middle of nowhere to me. Far from it—one major aspect that drew me there was that exciting things happened all the time. And the opportunity to totally remake a city's economy didn't exist in New York. Though I did feel somewhat exiled from my former Manhattan bubble during my first few months, I became so immersed in my work that I didn't have time to miss my old neighborhood. Tulsa quickly proved to be a nice change from New York's frenetic pace.

My new home in Tulsa's Arts District had its own charm. The Arts District, which is part of downtown, has seen a billion dollars in investment over the past decade or so; it used to be a place no one would go to, I was told, but by the time I got there, it was bustling. I first lived in an apartment above Antoinette's, a bakery with irresistible orange chocolate chip cookies. Artist studios, cannabis shops, cocktail bars, breweries, and restaurants pepper the neighborhood, most in redbrick buildings no more than a few stories high. Almost everywhere I looked, colorful murals at street level cut through the neighborhood like rainbows. Down the block, former warehouses had become the homes of the Woody Guthrie and Bob Dylan Centers, both across from the Guthrie Green Park. Each morning, I'd walk around the corner to meet my team at Gradient (then known as 36 Degrees North), a coworking space for entrepreneurs.

Tulsa Innovation Labs started with just me. But in a short time, I'd built a team. Like Danny Ocean assembling his eleven-person squad, I was looking for talent—especially those who had experience in the region, subject matter knowledge of legacy industries, and the skills to build economic development programs. I hit the jackpot with a wonderful crew.

My first hire was Kastle Jones, who had been born and raised in Muskogee, Oklahoma, less than an hour outside Tulsa. His dad had been an entrepreneur in Tulsa's oil and gas industry. Kastle is a bright guy who as a teenager had an urge to explore the world. His wanderlust first took him to a university in Korea, then to Baltimore, where he finished college at Johns Hopkins. He was then off to the London School of Economics for his master's degree, winding up in New York, where he worked at an innovation organization, Endeavor, which would go on to set up an office in nearby Bentonville, Arkansas. Kastle would ultimately lead TIL's energy tech portfolio and then manage one of the initiatives that spun out of it.

My second hire was Jennifer Hankins. A graduate of Oklahoma State University and the University of Oklahoma's Economic Development Institute, Jenn was a vice president at the Tulsa Regional Chamber and previously worked at the Greater Oklahoma City Chamber. Her dad was the mayor of a suburb of Kansas City, Missouri. Given this background, she was a perfect fit to be TIL's head of partnerships. Jenn knew the region well and was respected for getting shit done, having successfully directed a start-up initiative in town. She would help me manage stakeholder relationships and avert (or resolve) crises with partners. TIL has since grown to a team of more than fifteen, but I remember those early days fondly.

What the three of us soon realized once we started working together was that, especially in comparison to the sophisticated databases and economic models I enjoyed at NYCEDC, the most pressing gap in Tulsa's economic development capabilities was a lack of data. My TIL team wouldn't have the capacity to get the data we needed, much less the time to analyze it as thoroughly as

I'd want. We reached a conclusion many cities dread: we needed a consultant.

THE POWER OF ANALYTICS

As a former strategy consultant myself, I know the value consultants can bring to clients, but I also know their limitations. TIL set out to find the best partner possible to meet our needs. Given strong local relationships and a forward-thinking proposal, McKinsey was the front-runner. As I later told Kaiser and the board, the higher quality the data, the better the decision-making. After all, this strategy would help us shape the entire city, so it was well worth the investment. Kaiser was most concerned that industry studies weren't action plans, which was music to my ears. I gave him my commitment that I would shape the strategy to be as action oriented as possible, and I did.

We were lucky to have the resources to hire a consultant who could bring to bear huge amounts of data to guide our decision-making. McKinsey's proprietary datasets helped us forecast which industries were prone to automation and other disruptions, and their independent analysis instilled confidence in our findings. But not every city needs to hire a high-priced consultant to help identify their tech niche. There are many affordable, quality firms and independent consultants out there. No matter your budget, it's advantageous to leverage a third party to help manage the process and mitigate the perception of bias.

In fact, with the rise of Big Data, AI, and machine learning, cities may not require consultancies to get the data and analytical insights they need to make economic development decisions. The *New Yorker* provocatively asked in a recent article, "Will A.I. Become the New McKinsey?"[17] Maybe. But what is for certain is that as data becomes more available and AI more user-friendly, cities should become more adept at aligning their assets with market conditions and supply chains and identifying opportunities for growth.

Moreover, publicly available data will get you to most of the answers you're looking for, so gathering the data and analyzing it in-house is a viable path if you have staff capacity. As you'll see, my original hypothesis for Tulsa's tech niche proved fairly accurate—and that was a result of desktop research and conversations with local leaders. There are many free sources that can provide the data you need. But regardless of where your numbers come from, you need three main buckets of data to identify your niche:

PUBLICLY AVAILABLE DATA SOURCES		
Category	Publicly Available Source	Sample Offerings
Economic & Labor Trends (City, State & National)	US Bureau of Labor Statistics	Labor force size, employment, unemployment, and employee earnings, including by race, gender, and age as well as location quotients, a statistic used to gauge the concentration of industries and occupations in certain locations.
	US Department of Commerce's Bureau of Economic Analysis	Gross Domestic Product and personal income, with industry detail.
	US Census Bureau	Population, sex, age, poverty status, educational attainment, and computer and internet access; all by race.

PUBLICLY AVAILABLE DATA SOURCES		
Category	Publicly Available Source	Sample Offerings
	Hiring Lab by Indeed	Real-time, aggregated job posts.
Tech & Innovation Trends	US Patent and Trademark Office	Number of patents granted each year by county, state, and country, with detailed technology classification.
	Small Business Innovation Research & Small Business Technology Transfer	Number of awards granted for federal R&D with the potential for commercialization to a city's small businesses.
Venture Capital Flows	National Venture Capital Association	Quarterly reports on venture capital activity in the entrepreneurial ecosystem.

Quantitative data is essential to building a fact base. But it's crucial to remember that this data should go hand in hand with qualitative inputs and that outside consultants work best in tandem with clients who build local capacity through their own organizations. My team and I laid out the vision, set the research questions, conducted stakeholder interviews, and, using our economic development experience, translated McKinsey's insights into Tulsa-based actions. While the consultants brought hard data, the TIL team contextualized it and identified takeaways that resonated with the community—you can't find that information by downloading reports, crunching numbers, or googling. The perspective of local leaders, with community knowledge and implementation responsibility, is more important than the Compound Annual Growth Rate of a particular cluster.

SELECT YOUR CLUSTERS

Having assembled a constellation of data, we were now ready to begin the analysis. We first cast a wide net, considering the full universe of options—all the major segments of the global innovation economy. From there, we did a deep dive into six specific clusters: agriculture technology, aviation, cyber, educational technology, energy technology, and health innovation. Next, we identified opportunities within those six clusters that were most relevant to Tulsa's existing assets. That left us with twenty-five subclusters, specific parts of each cluster's value chain, such as agriculture analytics, educational delivery innovations, and health informatics—far too many on which to build a focused strategy. It was time to prioritize, because cities must make thoughtful choices.

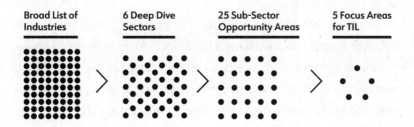

To whittle the twenty-five subclusters down to an optimal three to five, TIL and our consultants developed a weighting system. We assigned a value to the factors that mattered most to us and analyzed each subcluster based on them. This process was more art than science. An inclusive innovation economy can happen only by design, but there's no perfect answer, and spreadsheets can be easily manipulated. We landed on three criteria:

IMPACT: How big is the potential impact we could make within each subcluster?

FEASIBILITY: What are the chances of making such an impact?

INCLUSION: How inclusive is each subcluster?

This last criterion merits a double click. Inclusion is one of TIL's core values. Although people give the idea a lot of lip service today, the US's lack of progress in decreasing inequality only goes to show how little priority it is given (and how hard it is to positively impact). Further, emphasizing this value was good for business, mission aligned with our philanthropic funder, and a way to differentiate Tulsa from competition like Austin. Ensuring we properly prioritize inclusion within our strategy, and not leave it as an afterthought, would also help us mitigate future side effects of an innovation economy.

To do so, we utilized a proxy: the share of jobs within each subcluster attainable without a bachelor's degree. Statistics about people of color in tech, as well as related data, can be hard to find and disaggregate, so using this proxy helped surface opportunities more accessible for Tulsans with limited education.

Finally, we examined the remaining options through the lens of a collective. Cyber NYC's power had been its interlocking initiatives that fed into one another. I wanted to ensure that Tulsa's clusters could similarly work together. For example, would ag tech support the growth of ed tech and vice versa? Could we design initiatives to enable both at once? Did those clusters have similar talent needs? To answer these types of questions, we coupled this analysis with the weighting exercise to determine the strongest permutation of clusters. The result was five "right to win" opportunities, which I coined "Tulsa's Tech Niche."

TULSA'S TECH NICHE

In June 2020, well into the pandemic, TIL released the first tech-led economic development strategy in Tulsa's history. We positioned it as answering the underlying question "What should the city's tech identity be?" After rigorous analysis and more than one hundred stakeholder interviews, our answer was clear: virtual health, energy tech, advanced air mobility (AAM), and cyber and analytics (see below). For TIL, this would be the city's new brand that we'd promote and invest in aggressively.

Tulsa's Tech Niche		
Virtual Health	Energy Tech	Advanced Air Mobility
Cyber		
Analytics		

More specifically, we identified three vertical subclusters: virtual health and remote-care solutions; automation, analytics, and operational technology (OT) for energy; and drone operations and testing in agriculture and energy. There were also two enabling horizontals: cyber, with an emphasis on applied research and talent, and advanced analytics talent. We released a thirty-two-page executive summary to the public, which outlined each cluster and subcluster and presented our strategy for developing them:

VIRTUAL HEALTH. Virtual health popped as an opportunity even before the pandemic began. But in the wake of COVID, it was obvious there was a dire need in this area, especially in Oklahoma, which has one of the nation's worst health outcomes.[19] Oklahoma rates high for suicides, adult obesity, and drug abuse, and in the rural areas outside of Tulsa, people find it difficult to access health care. By decentralizing health care and enabling technologies that connect rural and Native communities to the care they need, TIL could make first, second, and third order impact (economic, health, and social). Local assets included the Saint Francis Health System, the School of Community Medicine at OU–Tulsa and TU, and OSU–Tulsa's Center for Health Sciences and telemedicine practice. By accelerating academic research in tools such as remote glucose monitoring, as well as supporting its commercialization, TIL could position Tulsa as the urban–rural gateway for virtual health.

Key Stats from 2020: Virtual health is growing fast, especially because of COVID, with a 10–15 percent projected compound annual growth rate for 2017–21 and a 39 percent investment compound annual growth rate from 2014 to 2019; virtual health is also contestable, with 72 percent of companies located outside traditional "tech hub" states.[20]

ENERGY TECH. The pandemic intensified the city's sense of urgency to diversify the economy, especially the energy sector. Tulsa saw how volatile the energy industry is when gas prices tanked during the pandemic, displacing hundreds of jobs. TIL discovered that Tulsa's strong suit was in the enabling technologies of analytics, automation, and operational technology, stemming from local oil and gas companies such as ONEOK, Williams, and Helmerich &

Payne. OT systems manage and secure industrial operations and often involve industrial control systems and supervisory control and data acquisition systems. If we invest in those enabling technologies only for oil and gas operations, Tulsa would still be reliant on oil and gas, but analytics, automation, and OT are also relevant to the emerging renewables sector as well. Through university and start-up partnerships, energy companies could adopt new technologies to enhance their OT and data analytics while taking advantage of renewables and energy efficiency initiatives. TIL also confirmed that Tulsa lacked a start-up scene in the sector, so the city's strong corporate base didn't have experience working with new firms. To become an energy tech hub, we'd need to focus our efforts on connecting new firms to our corporations in addition to developing these other technological systems.

Key Stats from 2020: Energy tech is highly contestable, with 71 percent of companies located outside of major tech hubs, and early-stage investment into monitoring and automation companies has grown by 33.5 percent over the last five years.[21]

ADVANCED AIR MOBILITY. Tulsa's value proposition in drone operations and testing had been growing for years, but no one had fully realized it. Aviation is undergoing its greatest period of innovation in decades, brought about by the maturation of technologies that will enable safer, more sustainable flight. The growing drone market was ripe for Tulsa. Regional agriculture and energy companies flew drones to monitor crops and oil and gas pipelines, respectively, and soon, drones could deliver medicine to rural communities. Aviation also had a strong presence in

Tulsa, albeit in manufacturing and maintenance, repair, and overhaul, through companies such as Spirit Aerosystems and American Airlines. Notably, a drone testing facility owned and operated by the Osage Nation came to our attention, called Skyway36. It also turned out that Oklahoma State University has one of the best aerospace engineering departments in the country and conducts research on unmanned aerial systems. Our job at TIL would be to unite and leverage these regional assets.

Key Stats from 2020: The drone market is experiencing strong growth, with a projected 12 percent compound annual growth rate over the next few years and a market size of $23 billion by 2024, about half of which is in commercial and consumer applications.[22]

CYBER AND ANALYTICS. To civic leaders' relief, the cyber hypothesis was validated. Tulsa had cyber and data analytics capabilities in energy, aviation, manufacturing, and health care. Partners like TU and critical, vulnerable infrastructure in the energy sector proved this cluster was a "right to win." The study also uncovered a major shortfall in Tulsa's production of cyber talent, which was stalling innovation and growth. TIL would need to focus on talent development if we wanted to build the virtual health, energy tech, and advanced air mobility clusters. The good news was that many cyber and data analytics roles didn't require bachelor's degrees, so there was an opportunity to upskill Tulsans not currently participating in tech.

Key Stats from 2020: The cyber market continues to experience rapid growth at ~10 percent per year, with five hundred thousand open cyber jobs across the United States. And analytics is seeing healthy growth across all industries (for example, in the last five years, 68 percent growth of health-care data and analytics platforms).[23]

Now, just because you identify certain tech clusters at the start of the process doesn't mean they're set in stone. While you *must* give the strategy enough time to bear fruit, cities should note that developments in the market and the ecosystem—not to mention necessary political compromises—may require you to recalibrate your approach. At TIL, these have been surgical refinements, not wholesale changes. For example, given the increasingly blurry distinction between cyber, blockchain, Big Data, machine learning, and AI, as well as their similar workforce needs, TIL eventually subsumed analytics under cyber to create one portfolio. And while we focused on drones at first, we soon broadened our engagement to advanced air mobility, which includes innovations in electrification, vertical takeoff, and autonomy, to better align with regional partners.

It's also worth acknowledging that some of your city's clusters will inevitably progress more quickly than others. Ultimately, if just one of them truly takes off, then that means success. Given how quickly tech evolves, cities should formally reevaluate their strategy every five years to ensure that they're giving themselves the best chances of this happening.

PLAN FOR ACTION

Once TIL identified Tulsa's tech niche, we then outlined the initial investments necessary to make the opportunities we had uncovered real. These investments took the form of economic and workforce development initiatives, designed to fill gaps in the ecosystem and catalyze growth. I wanted to develop each cluster comprehensively and sync initiatives to support start-ups, spur academic innovation, and train talent aligned to each.

Your city should identify one high priority initiative for each focus area. The following questions can help you select which to pursue:

PROBLEM: What is the primary barrier to growth in the cluster?

SOLUTION: Have you identified a solution to overcome that barrier?

PARTNERS: Do you have buy-in from key stakeholders to pursue this solution?

FUNDING: Have you identified funding sources for the initiative?

TIMELINE: Can the initiative launch within one year?

In our public report, TIL included an action plan, with a set of priority initiatives and a timeline of next steps. In virtual health, TIL suggested an academic-based start-up incubator to commercialize research. In energy tech, we proposed a venture fund to attract and support start-ups and help corporations innovate. In advanced air mobility, TIL identified an R&D facility to expand innovation and better utilize the drone testing facility at Skyway36. And in cyber and analytics, we recommended an applied cyber research center as well as a boot camp to help Tulsans pivot to in-demand careers in data analytics.

Aligning on these initiatives enabled us to move forward with tempo once we completed the study, saving us time and effort by accelerating the initiative design process. Alignment also gave stakeholders an understanding of what to expect, and it primed them for the support TIL would need down the road. Not surprisingly, TIL ended up evolving our initial wave of investments. Designing investments with our partners necessitated changes to programmatic and budget models—most of which made initiatives more viable and impactful. After all, TIL didn't have every answer, and economic development initiatives must be codesigned with partners, so cities should anticipate the need for agility. Including a flexible action plan, laser focused on your industry cluster strategy, will give you a head start and signal that you mean business—think "acta non verba" (actions, not words).

The illusive nature of a city's identity is a function of how it changes over time. Though some may think Tulsa's glory days are over, the city may one day reign as the tech capital of the Heartland, enjoying a generations-long renaissance. Just as Tulsans struck oil, so, too, could the city produce a unicorn. Or, through a series of wise investments, a cluster or two could provide sustainable growth. Only time will tell. But by positioning Tulsa and other cities for inclusive growth, no matter what the future holds, they'll be prepared to meet the challenges full on. This can happen, though, only if the community and its key stakeholders embrace a tech identity and seriously invest in it over the long term.

TIL's strategy gave the community the focus it needed to start transitioning its economy. And it gave the city hope and encouragement that there were exciting assets on which to build. As I was fond of saying, Tulsa represented a "blue sky of opportunity," and TIL had proven that sentiment through our strategy.

But success can't happen without leadership. An individual, a team, and an organization charged with and empowered to deliver the strategy are all required to drive reinvention. For Tulsa, that was TIL and me. I was the rookie quarterback, an outsider bent on disrupting the status quo. It was the first role of its kind in my career, and along the way, I knew I'd make mistakes. What I didn't fully understand was that building the strategy and implementing it required different skill sets: to achieve TIL's mission, I needed to learn how to become a leader.

ACTION PLAN SUMMARY		
REINVENTION *What needs reinventing?*	**GROWTH** *How do you catalyze growth?*	**INCLUSION** *How do you advance inclusion?*
Too many cities rely upon economic development strategies that don't prioritize tech or inclusion, or that don't sufficiently build upon local assets. As a result, cities haven't found their tech niche, their special place in the innovation economy, and are suffering from a slow economic decline.	Cities must identify the strongest opportunities for inclusive growth through an industry cluster strategy. As part of this process, they must map their assets, leverage data and analyze how those assets fit within larger trends, and then select a subset of the strongest clusters to focus their investments.	Inclusion must be factored into the strategy on the front end, not left as an afterthought. Using proxies, such as the share of jobs attainable without a bachelor's degree, cities can identify which tech clusters offer the most accessible opportunities for their citizens.

CHAPTER 2

ENABLE (GOOD) TROUBLEMAKERS

(LEADERSHIP)

"That's just not the Tulsa way."

A local real estate developer said this to me back in early 2020, when I was still fresh on the job. He had been pitching me on a new project for months, and in the hope of winning support, he brought a delegation of Tulsa civic leaders, me included, to Boston to visit an organization that runs start-up accelerators around the world. He wanted the George Kaiser Family Foundation to fund their presence in Tulsa and for the new organization I was building to manage the project. As a real estate guy, he was keen to see Tulsa's economy grow and his properties increase in value. His interests, therefore, extended widely throughout Tulsa, including to my work strengthening the city's tech ecosystem. Tulsa has quite a few of these businesspeople, whom I admire for their entrepreneurial spirit, breadth of curiosity, and civic boosterism. Yet many of them were accustomed to working a certain way, and they wanted me to play ball.

After the visit to Boston, however, I wasn't sold on the project. As I explained to the developer, Tulsa Innovation Labs was still formulating its strategy. We didn't yet know the clusters we'd be investing in or their programmatic needs, so it was premature to sign a contract with an operator. I was inclined to pursue an open and competitive process to build partnerships, ensuring that we were matching the right partner with the right opportunity and getting the strongest deal possible. Moreover, I was concerned that multi-national accelerator businesses create networks designed to benefit them but not necessarily their host cities. The ubiquity of these companies means it can be difficult for cities to differentiate themselves and to retain start-ups once they complete the program. I was more interested in exploring bespoke solutions for Tulsa than supporting a one-size-fits-all franchise.

This was not what the developer wanted to hear. This was not the Tulsa way. Incredulous that I would tell him no, he gave me an impassioned lecture. But the Tulsa way wasn't working—one-off investments, emotional decision-making, and lack of coordination had resulted in poor growth for a decade. The status quo was leading Tulsa toward decline, and if we wanted to course correct the economy, then the way of doing business in Tulsa would need to change. Joining with like-minded others, I saw my job as charting a new path. This is the same road many Heartland cities need to embark upon posthaste, breaking from their habit of business as usual: of doing things the way they've done them for years. Indeed, the hard reality is that, if you're a midsized city looking to pivot to tech in 2025, then your city's economic development practices probably haven't been working as well as they could either. I understand it may be unpleasant to hear from an "outsider." But the cities that will successfully reinvent their economies will acknowledge what isn't working, seek out new perspectives, embrace disruption, and celebrate change.

> Change requires leadership, and that means com-
> munities need to welcome new perspectives and build
> new organizations; they need leaders who can chal-
> lenge the status quo and take a systems approach to
> establishing their city's tech identity.

As dynamic as cities are, their institutions often have a powerful inertia, with bad habits, toxic cultures, and special interests
calcifying over time. Without fresh leadership and new ideas,
organizations can atrophy to the point that they prioritize control over competence and power over professionalism—all of
which comes at the expense of impact and progress. Control is
the opposite of leadership, and it causes stasis and bitterness in
communities, especially when paired with a lack of results. In his
book *Big Bets*, Rockefeller Foundation president Rajiv Shah offers
succinct advice applicable to anyone supporting change makers:
"give up control."[1] Disruptors will need to learn how to succeed
in urban environments designed to maintain control and to shut
out new leaders.

In Tulsa, I played the role of disruptor. That's the real reason
why GKFF recruited me—not to manage decline but to change
the city's trajectory by taking a new, more strategic approach to
economic development. In some respects, I was the best person
for the job, and in others, I was the worst. I wasn't "of Tulsa," so I
could look dispassionately at the city, make hard choices, and not
let one group or another control me. But, also, having no affiliation with Tulsa meant I had no friends, no allies, no long-standing
partners. I'd have to build support from the bottom up, allay
Tulsa's sense of stranger danger, and learn how to lead. While the
developer I skirmished with would greet me kindly at a wedding
for a colleague a few years later, I would continue to ruffle feathers.

Tulsa wasn't ready for me, and, as it turned out, I wasn't ready for Tulsa. The experience changed my sense of what a leader needs to do to bring cities into the future and gave me new insight into my own skills and capabilities.

RECRUIT LEADERS WHO
SEE CITIES FROM THE OUTSIDE

I've spent most of my life on the margins, on the outside looking in. An introvert by nature, I'm most comfortable off center, away from the crowd. In New Orleans, our cramped little house I grew up in was just a few blocks from the Mississippi River and surrounded by fast-food chains like Chubbie's Chicken and Domino's Pizza. Our working-class neighborhood was diverse, and because my Black and Latino neighbors lived in similarly difficult circumstances, poverty bonded us where race could have divided us. Crossing the river from the city's west bank, I'd commute to a private Catholic high school in the Garden District, a wealthy part of New Orleans, with fulsome trees, antebellum mansions, and a streetcar line running up and down St. Charles Avenue. Thanks to a scholarship and a work-study program, I got a good education and excelled academically; but I could never shake the difference in upbringing between my peers and me.

When I was admitted to Northwestern for college, I was catapulted to the North Shore of Chicago and the middle class all in one fell swoop. This phenomenon is often called "escape velocity," and in some ways I never looked back at my previous social class until I came to Tulsa. At Northwestern, which people like to say offers an Ivy League–caliber education without the East Coast pretense, I was one of just a few hundred recipients of Federal Pell Grants in my class,[2] financial aid that goes to low-income students. I felt the campus's class divide acutely. One memory stands out: there was a rumor on campus that Warren Buffett's grandson was a year or two ahead of my class, and there would be whispers at parties and phantom sightings.

Sure enough, according to a 2017 study of economic mobility in higher education, about 14 percent of Northwestern students came from the top 1 percent of household incomes, compared to just 3.7 percent from the bottom 20 percent. This helps explain why a mere 1.7 percent of Northwestern students moved from the bottom to the top income quintiles later in life.[3] While I may never be rich, my future was bright, and my own mobility came with anxieties and challenges. I was growing accustomed to shifting between worlds, caught in an uncomfortable limbo in which my present belied my background and signaled my future social status.

My queer identity only added to the vulnerability I felt growing up poor. Before I came out, and even a good decade afterward, I often felt out of my body, as if I were a documentary filmmaker trying to report on and understand how life worked rather than actually living it. I wondered how everyone seemed to fit in so well.

Almost anywhere I went, I felt like a trespasser or a poseur. I sensed, in my own way, what Ta-Nehisi Coates calls "the great barrier between the world and me" and recognized the unique and intransigent barriers facing other people.[4] But because I was White and educated, I could pass through them with relative ease, entering worlds where I didn't really belong—even if, when I was in those worlds, my own perspective and pathologies would cause varying degrees of trouble. I itched to make mischief, to upset the balance of power, to disturb the equilibrium just a little bit, like going to a library and feeling the urge to make noise. But I still wanted to be in the library, not outside with a bullhorn. I wanted to make change from within institutions because I thought upending them was impractical.

As I grew up, my mother inspired me to imagine better, and so my instinct was to question, to challenge, to not accept what is. Still to this day, a part of me resents those who were born on third base and think they hit a triple, who enjoy the "affirmative action of intergenerational wealth," but who are oblivious to the challenges everyday people face.[5] The chip on my shoulder was forged over many years. For me, authority needed to be questioned, and wealth wasn't admirable; much less was proximity to power. All this combined to make me ill-suited to kiss anyone's ring. As I settled into my new role in Tulsa, however, I'd need to learn to adjust. I'd have to balance showing respect for local culture and building relationships with the establishment while pushing back against "the Tulsa way" when it threatened to hold back progress and necessary change. I was a foil for the city's legacy institutions, and I didn't have to tell people what they wanted to hear.

This is a useful, though stressful, role to occupy. Folks too ingrained or too worried about rocking the boat struggle to disrupt cities. Insiders have different motivations than change makers: insiders work to preserve systems and institutions, but to change those systems and institutions, disruptors need to speak their mind and have people listen. Fortunately, I was in a privileged position to do so, thanks to the backing of GKFF.

Heartland cities working to build an innovation economy need to hire leaders who can cause "good trouble," a term brought to life by civil rights legend John Lewis. Good trouble leads to productive and sustainable change. This doesn't necessarily mean hiring an outsider like me but rather someone who can step back and see the ecosystem from the outside, who can analyze it critically and who can build solutions. I like to think that my ability to see the big picture and take a systems approach results from my personal background. Elevating people from diverse upbringings to leadership positions is important: they have a knack for seeing a city's deficiencies because they've often experienced them personally.

WELCOME TO TULSA

At a conference a few years ago, I spoke to a fellow attendee about my work in Tulsa. She was a policymaker from Chicago, and the first question she asked me about Tulsa was, "Were you welcomed?" It was a trenchant question. Obviously, she had seen this movie before: outsider moves to new town wanting to make change. The truth is that most Tulsans warmly welcomed me. Some in the city's establishment, however, considered me a carpetbagger and city slicker, and in working with these individuals, my honeymoon proved to be short lived.

On the one hand, my education and New York City background cast me as an elitist threat. (One lesson I learned: I should have shared my New Orleans upbringing sooner and more candidly than I did.) On the other, I didn't belong to Tulsa high society. I wasn't a member at the Summit Club, the exclusive haunt of the city's old money power brokers; nor was I the son of an oil baron. What Tulsa revealed to me was that, fifteen years since moving away for college, I had become a coastal elite myself. But in Tulsa, that meant I wasn't the right *kind* of elite, and my wariness of the well-heeled combined to make this an odd fit.

When it became clear I wasn't going to follow the Tulsa way, things took a turn. At the point I tried to turn talk into action, the gears of the city began to try and slow me down. As one stakeholder told me about the establishment: "They know they can't control you—you're not dependent upon them, and that scares the shit out of them." Everything I did proved to be disruptive. It almost felt like a bait and switch, where they hired me to do a job and then resented me for doing it. It put me in a continuously combative posture because every issue—big or small—proved controversial. They sabotaged plans, reneged on decisions, upended deal terms, and moved goal posts without explanation. There's an expression I've heard: "Move at the speed of trust." Well, I was moving fast and making decisions that required political capital and trust I hadn't yet earned—and even worse, I hadn't yet realized I needed them in the first place. At the same time, though, it was clear that some civic leaders weren't aware of what it would take for me to deliver on TIL's mission or weren't as serious as I was about pulling Tulsa into the twenty-first century. That meant that when I took what I saw as necessary steps, they didn't understand what merited such big swings or such breakneck speed. "Lead, follow, or get out the way" doesn't apply to everyone, I discovered. Some people merely want to block progress.

But I'm scrappy, and I fight for the things I believe in. I wanted to catalyze as much change as possible in a short time. Admittedly, I wasn't playing a long game, which meant I moved more aggressively than I would have if I saw my engagement as a ten-year project. Besides, I didn't think Tulsa had ten years to get its act together. We required a step change, and to make that happen, I needed to be a cross between, as I saw it, Jane Jacobs and George Patton: I wanted to set a direction and move at battle speed toward it. Many times, however, being a bit more like the diplomatic Ike would have served me better. While I never started fights, I didn't shirk from them either. I made the case for my theory of change, and I wasn't going to let anything stand in the way.

ATTRIBUTES OF URBAN LEADERSHIP

My point isn't to flaunt my battle scars: I want you to benefit from my hard-earned experience in the trenches, avoid my mistakes, and absorb my lessons. After all, there's no way around conflict if you want to get the job done—today's leaders must challenge the status quo because the status quo isn't working.

A Tulsa stakeholder is fond of saying that "anyone can do economic development." But economic developers are professionals, and they should have a specific skill set. Cities need competent urbanists to lead change. So, to be a good troublemaker, you'll want to cultivate a dynamic set of characteristics to effectively navigate a city, its institutions, and its politics, which have a special ability to grind progress to a halt and wear down aspiring change makers. You'll need to be able to drive progress forward without pissing too many people off or pissing off the wrong people too much.

Urban disruptors should have a few attributes you might not expect. An effective troublemaker:

Listens with Humility. By being outspoken in working to change Tulsa's trajectory, I unintentionally put the old guard on the defensive. Instead, I should have listened more. Cordell Carter is the former executive director of the Aspen Institute's Socrates Program, a forum for leaders learning from leaders. He recommends change makers become "humble listeners" to help build relationships, which they can then "leverage for proximate credibility," as he puts it. "Once the old guard understands that the new guard isn't trying to repudiate their years of work, they will have the quiet, behind-the-scenes conversations with others in the community such that 'proximate credibility' is the result," he told me.[6]

Prioritizes the Right Problem. Disruptors need to be able to solve the right problem with a scalable solution. Communities face countless challenges, and leaders can't tackle them all at once. Being strategic in your priorities will set you up for success. That requires identifying the most important gaps in your ecosystem, the most critical impediments to growth. For instance, as I'll show in chapter 5, Tulsa faced serious shortfalls in tech talent, particularly midcareer professionals. To fill this gap and develop the talent our clusters needed to grow, Tulsa had to rapidly upskill talent near the labor market, not try to fix the K–12 system as some had urged.

Doesn't Bullshit. Tom Wolfe writes in *The Bonfire of the Vanities*, "Bullshit reigns."[7] Cities have an abundance of stakeholders who hedge their bets, try to make everyone happy, and never take a firm stand on anything. Communities respect folks who don't bullshit, who have a clear point of view, communicate it, and stick to it. They don't need people pleasers; people pleasers are why they're in this rut in the first place. Being a straight shooter who can follow through will help build allies and get initiatives over the finish line.

Speaks Truth to Power. It takes a distinct and rare ability to constructively tell someone with authority that they're wrong. I hire for this skill when I'm building my own teams: I always ask candidates to tell me about a time they disagreed with their boss on something important. In working with high–net worth individuals, elected officials, and others in power, I've found that they can cocoon themselves from criticism and that their staffs begin to think like them, failing to question their beliefs. Groupthink becomes real, causing blind spots and leading to poor decisions. I am paranoid about that happening to me, and every other leader should be as well. Explaining to others why they're wrong requires some degree of courage, but good leaders seek critical input and can share it themselves.

Leverages Relationships for Action. Relationships are essential to getting anything done, but leaders must leverage them to achieve—not delay—progress. In *The New Localism*, esteemed urbanists Bruce Katz and Jeremy Nowak observe that "leaders must be adept at creating and stewarding horizontal relationships rather than issuing and executing hierarchical mandates."[8] In hindsight, much of the disruption I caused resulted from my executing on my mandate and implementing our strategy before I had built the necessary relationships. But you may not have five or ten years to build relationships, so you'll need to quickly form alliances. It's also important to avoid the bad version of this, which I discovered within Tulsa's civic class, where close familiarity had led to a culture of nice. People avoided upsetting others or making controversial decisions. If deference for an old friend prevents action being taken or a good decision being made, then it's up to you to find another path forward.

Moves with Urgency. It's so easy to never get anything done. Emails go ignored. Contracts languish in legal review. Partners get cold feet and vacillate. That's why disruptors can't let people off the hook. Cities need to hire a leader who can move on concurrent tracks, who sets deadlines and follows up. Complacency gets cities in distress. An effective disruptor should orchestrate action and generate momentum that inspires people, that gets the flywheel moving. Especially in emerging tech, where industries change so quickly, the winners are often the cities that get there first, so there isn't a second to spare.

Possesses Moxie. Can you believe in yourself, your ideas, and your team when others don't? In *Greater Than Ever*, Daniel Doctoroff, the former deputy mayor of New York under Bloomberg and the former CEO of Sidewalk Labs, writes, "A successful urban leader must be willing to endure a sizable contingent of doubters."[9] You can say that again! Disruptors must have the self-belief and determination to press on even if they're alone. They need moxie, a self-confidence and steadfastness, which will serve them and their communities well.

Exudes Kindness. The process of transforming cities can often get heated, and sometimes it feels personal. But a leader needs to be able to advocate for their point of view while still expressing empathy. Showing kindness goes a long way toward easing tensions and building goodwill. You can, in fact, disagree without being disagreeable. Good troublemakers must be thoughtful, team focused, and sensitive to others. Emotional intelligence and intelligence quotient aren't mutually exclusive; they should inform one another, helping leaders make smart decisions while creating the buy-in needed to succeed.

One colleague who showed me how to lead with greater finesse and effectiveness was Kian Kamas, who grew up in rural Oklahoma. Kamas is the former executive director of PartnerTulsa and one of the few people I know in Tulsa whom everyone *really* listens to when they talk. Her deep roots in the region and her understanding of Oklahomans have made her an impactful leader. Kamas said her parents "did the whole Okie thing in the '80s," bought some land, and started their own trucking company.[10] After the trucking company, her dad designed and built a piece of farm equipment called a rotary harrow while her mom managed the Love's Country Store in Kingfisher, about fifty miles northwest of Oklahoma City. To pay for a car, Kamas worked summers mowing lawns or grading grain during harvest. She graduated first in her class at the University of Oklahoma, then earned a master's in comparative public policy from the University of Edinburgh.

In her professional life, Kamas has become the consummate partnership builder. Where so many well-meaning partners create problems, Kamas solves them. She is a disruptor but has a special gift for not making people *feel* disrupted. Within Tulsa's economic development world, Kamas identified inefficiencies and lack of alignment and, aiming to address this, led the transformation of the city government's economic development system, merging five entities into one new organization, PartnerTulsa. PartnerTulsa engages in economic and workforce development, development finance, and strategic investments—from real estate and asset management to community development, which includes housing. Through her patience with partners and her ability to understand where they were coming from, Kamas showed me how to work with legacy institutions, especially when we were collaborating on federal grant proposals.

But when it comes to importing good troublemakers, it takes two to tango, and it's just as important how a city's institutions treat those they've brought in to make change. My experience and the overall success of TIL would depend, in part, on how well legacy institutions supported me and my new organization. So how should cities empower their economic development leaders?

First, don't hire someone unless you align on what they'll be doing. If you have a decent sense of the scope of work and agree, even in broad terms, on what success looks like, then you can give your good troublemaker wide latitude to do their job. You don't need to manage or, worse, micromanage them. As an employer, manager, grantor, or investor, it's your job to empower your team and partners and set them up for success. Too many nonprofit leaders, start-up founders, or public servants feel their creativity or autonomy stifled by their superiors. "It doesn't make sense to hire smart people and tell them what to do," Steve Jobs famously said. "We hire smart people so they can tell us what to do."[11] Change makers will likely need to actualize that maxim themselves by following through on their convictions and building support for their vision, not waiting for folks upstairs to see the light—but that doesn't mean cities should ignore their own part in this relationship.

Second, good troublemakers should be high-capacity individuals, and they should have insights about a host of subjects. Just because they may ask tough questions or disagree with you doesn't mean you should shut them out. You need to stretch your disruptors, so fully utilize them—throw them your thorniest problems. That will require organizations to be comfortable being uncomfortable—not easy for an institution that's never really been challenged. You need your change makers uncovering blind spots and testing your assumptions.

Finally, disruptors and their ideas *should* create conflict. In Tulsa, the tolerance for conflict is low, so people often avoid tough conversations—all of which limits what leaders can do and slows the pace of progress. Indeed, as a society, dissent itself seems under attack—whether it's on college campuses or social media, those who have a contrarian point of view can sometimes be unfairly ostracized. I worry that by the time students get to the workplace, no one's trained them to speak their minds, ask pointed questions, and really scrutinize. Change makers, however, must sow healthy conflict, and their employers should anticipate this and have their back, as GKFF did for me.

BUILD A NEW ACTION ARM

Once GKFF's board approved my blueprint, the questions now revolved around how we would put it into action. What should the delivery vehicle be? What legal structure would this work take? Would it be a new program or division within the foundation? Would it be a separate organization? These were important questions because they asked, in effect, "Who would be the voice of the Tulsans of tomorrow? What would channel their dreams and make long-term investments to create new opportunities?"

Two things were clear and should be clear to Heartland cities pursuing a new approach to economic development. One: hiring a single leader isn't sufficient; good troublemakers need a team, infrastructure, and capital to deploy, which means an organizational apparatus. And two: the delivery vehicle should be new. Typically, as an institutionalist, I caution against creating new programmatic structures; I'd much rather build on existing infrastructure than reinvent the wheel. But since this marks a new direction for your city, take the opportunity to start fresh and create a new organization to spearhead your city's transformation. While your city may have a regional chamber of commerce, a government office of economic development, a philanthropy, or economic development–related nonprofits, it's best to start outside these, if possible. This will allow you to work across sectors and make an impact without having to fit a new leader or entity into an existing organization, with all the political baggage, cultural maladies, legacy staff, and frustrating policies that may exist. In Tulsa, no one was doing tech-led economic development, so starting new was appropriate. If a new organization isn't feasible, then the head of your program should report directly to as senior an executive as possible to mitigate bureaucracy and to fast-track decisions.

When standing up a new economic development venture, social entrepreneurs and their funders should first carefully define the mission and operating model. I've seen too many instances where people create a new organization with a half-baked sense of itself. When missions or operations evolve, sometimes painfully over time, it can confuse the ecosystem and strain the ability for partners to productively collaborate. It's good to have a clear lane from the beginning, thoughtfully deconflicted from the missions of existing organizations; this will help you establish your own brand. Moreover, it's better to define your core competency and stay lean as an organization, ensuring you're executing on the mission before expanding scope or staff.

Next, you should match your mission and operations with the right governance structure. If there are multiple donors, as in an industry consortium, a 501(c)(3) nonprofit may make sense, or its close cousin the 501(c)(6), which business or membership-based organizations use. A 501(c)(3) can receive tax-deductible donations and can apply for nearly all federal grants. On the other hand, one-third of funding must come from the government, corporations, or the public, compelling 501(c)(3)s to have multiple capital partners. The law also prohibits them from serving private economic interests, which could exclude VC funds. If there's a single backer, then a limited liability company may be a better fit. TIL is a subsidiary LLC of GKFF and enjoys the benefits of its parent company's nonprofit status. In practice, TIL acts more like a nonprofit grantee than a division of GKFF proper. Since TIL's launch, GKFF has funded at least a half dozen new LLCs working in the economic development space, which we'll explore in the next chapter.

As I was designing TIL as an organization, I struggled to find good examples of the type of cutting-edge economic development nonprofit I envisioned, especially one in the Heartland. Given the lack of models in peer cities, and maybe because of recency bias, I modeled TIL after my previous employer, the New York City Economic Development Corporation's industries division, which makes programmatic investments in emerging tech and innovation.

TIL's organizational structure (see the next page) reflected our industry cluster approach because a city's tech niche should be the organizing principle on which all efforts are based. At TIL, we built small teams dedicated to each of our clusters. This represented our initiatives division, the core driver of our work. A subject matter expert, paired with a more junior associate, led each cluster team. For example, Shawna Khouri, a biomedical engineer and start-up founder, directed TIL's virtual health portfolio, with support from Sahee Abdelmomin, who had conducted health-related research while an undergrad at Washington University in Saint Louis. Our other division was public affairs, which encompasses our partnerships, grants, and policy team; it enabled TIL's work through fundraising, advocacy, and governmental relations. We also had marketing and operations professionals that served as shared resources for the entire organization.

TIL Org Structure and Governance

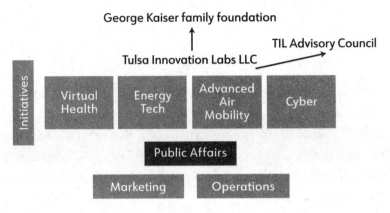

Despite TIL's intentional organizational design, there wasn't a defined reporting structure or decision-making process per our funder's culture. I engaged GKFF's executive leadership team and needed their consensus for most major decisions. And our funding, both annual operating expenses and bigger initiative budgets, required GKFF board approval.

Importantly, TIL also created an advisory council of local and national leaders—one for each of our four clusters plus an executive council—to help guide and promote TIL's work. Council members included chief executives, start-up founders, investors, academics, technologists, and economic developers. We would hold meetings with the council every quarter to get their advice. As they do at council member Cordell Carter's Socrates Program, I found it to be a great opportunity for leaders to learn from other leaders.

I've often said that TIL is the best economic development team on the planet, and it is. Working with them brought me endless joy. A lot of leaders I speak to don't like managing people, but I do. It gives me energy, and I think I'm good at it. The hard parts about my role were managing partners, navigating the founder–funder relationship, and steering a new organization in a nascent and highly fluid ecosystem. All of this presented me with leadership challenges and numerous teachable moments.

DEVELOP URBAN LEADERS

It doesn't matter how brilliant your strategy is, or how thoughtfully designed your organization, if you can't step into your new leadership role. Since leaving TIL in 2023, I've spent a lot of time analyzing my development as a leader. In my job as TIL's managing director, I felt like all my strengths and weaknesses were laid bare. Learning in real time, I built a new organization, assembled a team, raised money, designed initiatives, and tried to lead a citywide effort. These types of roles expose who you are as a leader—and provide you the opportunity to grow into a better one.

Leadership is a skill, and it took me two decades in the workforce to fully realize it. Unfortunately, this means I've been consciously building this skill only for a few years. If you're like me, you probably didn't have any formal leadership training until you were well into your career, if at all. When I was younger, I didn't take advantage of opportunities like Next City's Vanguard Conference, an experiential learning program for emerging urban leaders, or the Coro Fellowship in Public Affairs, a similar program popular among my New York and LA friends. But as a managing director, it felt like the right time to get some professional training. I knew I needed to shift from doing excellent work to influencing ecosystems, from "being a doer to becoming a leader," as Tulsa-based executive coach Tracy Spears wisely says.

So, midway through my tenure in Tulsa, I enrolled in an executive leadership program at Dartmouth's Tuck School of Business. My cohort was talented and diverse; it included the soon-to-be general counsel of the Rockefeller Foundation, the future COO of the JF Maddox Foundation, the head of banks for the Dominican Republic, and the chief policy officer of the Greater Houston

Partnership, among other leaders looking to strengthen their skills. In bucolic Hanover, New Hampshire, we analyzed case studies, participated in group projects, and reviewed 360-degree assessments, which, together, helped build a useful leadership framework applicable to our various careers.

LESSONS FROM A FIRST-TIME LEADER

If not for Tulsa, I wouldn't be the leader I am today: flawed, but always learning; impatient, but determined; a troublemaker, but for good. After reflecting on my time in Tulsa and the kind of leader I want to be in the future, I came up with these **Lessons from a First-Time Leader** that should be useful for anyone looking to contribute to their city's reinvention:

1. **Understand the Baggage:** When I got to Tulsa, I faced an environment tangled with politics and personalities that, quite frankly, I wasn't equipped to handle. I had to learn, often the hard way, a range of interpersonal and interorganizational dynamics, which were almost always outside my ability to influence. Before beginning in their roles, disruptors should gain as much historical, cultural, and political context as possible to understand their city's present idiosyncrasies. This will help them anticipate challenges, tailor messaging to partners, and chart complex waters.

2. **Find Mentors:** For the first two years, I found Tulsa lonely in a certain respect. Outside my team, I didn't have peers. And I didn't have a boss or manager to give me advice. To my detriment, I was slow to find mentors, too focused on the work to realize that I needed support. After recognizing this, I reached out to previous managers, local leaders, and TIL advisory council

members more regularly. One important coach for me was Robert Thomas, GKFF's former chief investment officer. Widely respected in Tulsa, Thomas is the rare civic leader not to have been born there. He came from the Gates Foundation and showed me how to make new ideas happen within Tulsa's conservative civic culture. There's a reason why start-up accelerators prioritize offering successful mentors to founders. Building a new organization presents a gauntlet of tests, and mentors who have seen and done it all before can share their wisdom and guide you through these obstacles.

3. **Lead with Positivity:** I'm not a glass-half-full kind of guy. I'm a guy who sees a half-empty glass and figures out how to fill it. My instinct, therefore, is to identify problems and fix them. This posed a communications challenge for me. I was too critical, too early, too often in Tulsa. I should have spent more time painting a positive vision for what we could accomplish together instead of trying to fix what I, but not everyone, saw as problems. I failed to remind some stakeholders enough of TIL's vision. Leading with the positive will set you up for success and lay the groundwork for when you need to tackle the hard problems.

4. **Explain Your Thinking:** Because I'm fast paced and decisive, I tend to set a direction without explaining it sufficiently. It's a bad habit. Walking people through your logic and reasoning will help bolster your argument and build support for your decision. Especially when it comes to introducing new concepts and ideas in a place unaccustomed to tech-led economic development, be explicit about what you're doing and *why*. It'll help bring your stakeholders on the journey with you. Think of it as

showing your work. The process and logic are often more valuable for stakeholders and teammates to hear than the answer, which, when presented without a full explanation or context, or without discussion, can unintentionally shut out collaboration and input.

5. **Proactively Disarm:** I drastically underestimated how threatening my presence would be to some. I failed to realize that an outsider with new ideas can unwittingly upset people. And I mistakenly attributed unprofessionalism from some of these folks as malicious behavior when, more likely, insecurity or, frankly, incompetence drove it. It's important to show compassion and empathy. I'm not proud to admit it, but, on occasion, when I knew I threatened someone and they exhibited poor behavior as a result, my ego would kick in and I'd lean into the conflict, making matters worse and leaving their behavior unchanged. As a good troublemaker, you should assure anxious stakeholders that you're on their side, highlight shared goals, and work to understand their needs.

6. **Manage Emotions:** I wear my heart on my sleeve. People always know where they stand with me, and this transparency has its benefits. But when I'm frustrated—especially by incompetence, BS, or deception—I tend to react, not respond. I can be abrasive in these moments. Compartmentalizing emotions is tough, but leaders must take a pause before responding. Even saying out loud "I'm frustrated" is better than *acting* frustrated. We tell children to "use your words"; adults need to do so as well. Disciplining yourself to check your emotions will help you stay grounded so you can contribute to a solution.

7. **Own Mistakes:** Anytime I screw up, almost like a tick, Vonda Shepard's theme song to *Ally McBeal*, "Searchin' My Soul," plays in my head. In the song, Shepard sings that she's made mistakes that she can't hide, but by acknowledging those mistakes, she can redeem herself and get back to living and enjoying life. We're all human. I'm a flawed human and a flawed leader. Quickly acknowledging your mistakes, taking responsibility, and learning from them earns respect. Don't let pride or ego cause you to shift responsibility. Some self-deprecation goes a long way to buying grace.

8. **Love Yourself:** I know that I'm my own worst critic, and sometimes negative thoughts and self-doubt interfere. When you own your mistakes, you should put them in context and embrace your fallibility while recognizing your essential goodness as a human. As the Jane Jacobs of drag, RuPaul, says, "If you don't love yourself, how in the hell you gonna love somebody else?" In other words, how can you lead people if you don't see the good in yourself? How can you support your teammates if you don't have self-compassion and self-forgiveness? Loving yourself also means caring for yourself and taking time off to recharge, something I didn't do enough of.

9. **Maintain Ecosystem Awareness:** Leaders must balance quality of work with big-picture awareness. My favorite case study at Tuck was about a Japanese telecom company that consistently won awards for quality and efficiency. Their internal processes were strong, and their products well made. But because the company focused on internal quality at the expense of innovation and staying aware of the industry, they lost market share and eventually went out of business. Urban leaders must constantly be aware

of their ecosystem and work to configure it to their benefit. My work products earned confidence from stakeholders, but, over time, I became too focused on designing initiatives and lost awareness of how my partners felt and how other organizations were developing. I would need to pivot my attention, hire more staff, delegate more, and evolve my role to focus on strategic and ecosystem matters.

10. **Stick the Landing:** There's no shortage of good ideas or sound strategies. Ultimately, results are what counts. Despite any misgivings about me, people started recognizing that TIL was on to something when we consistently produced strong work, treated partners with respect, and did what we said we would do. Outsiders who deliver suddenly don't seem so scary; TIL was generating excitement, building trust, and unlocking funding. To achieve outcomes, however, TIL's initiatives had to work in practice. The success or failure of Tulsa's broader project will also come down to the blocking and tackling of execution—and the same will be true for you, no matter what city you're working in.

In Tulsa, I stretched myself in ways I couldn't have imagined. For the first time in my professional life, making a reasoned argument wasn't sufficient. I had to build support and influence people unaccustomed to economic development and predisposed to mistrust me. Having grown up in New Orleans and having lived in New York, I thought I was tough. But I wasn't ready for local politics. I had to outmaneuver certain troublesome stakeholders, anticipate mines, recover from their blasts when I stepped on them, mend fences when I erred, and take microaggressions on the chin. Funnily enough, I needed to toughen up and not take things personally, because it wasn't about me. This wasn't just the Tulsa way; this was the difficult process of making change in any city. My job as a leader, it turned out, was helping guide Tulsa through this change—not just setting a new direction but bringing the community along with me.

Leadership can, and should, be disruptive, and change makers must empower themselves to make good trouble. But leaders can't solve every problem or instantly fix systemic shortcomings, and just like no one leader can do it all, one organization can't do it all either. To establish a tech identity and reinvent a city, it takes collective action. A good leader should bring the ecosystem together around a shared vision and work to align partners—or else they risk watching a hundred horses all pulling in different directions ruin a community's promise.

ACTION PLAN SUMMARY		
REINVENTION	GROWTH	INCLUSION
What needs reinventing?	*How do you catalyze growth?*	*How do you advance inclusion?*
It takes fresh leadership and new organizations to upend economic development orthodoxy. Cities need leaders who can establish a positive vision, develop a strategy, and guide the community through the process of making change.	By embracing disruption (good trouble), cities can get on a path toward stronger and more inclusive growth. They'll need to design a new economic development organization built for the moment, enable leaders who continuously learn, and gain the support of legacy institutions.	Elevating leaders from diverse backgrounds is important for civic reinvention, as these leaders are often able to see communities from the outside, understand gaps in systems, and build solutions that make lasting change.

CHAPTER 3

INSPIRE
COLLECTIVE ACTION

(ECOSYSTEM COORDINATION)

I f you want live music in Tulsa, you go to Cain's. Built in 1924, Cain's Ballroom is a renowned concert venue that helped popularize western swing. Bob Wills, Hank Williams, and Merle Haggard played there, as have Patti Smith, Elvis Costello, and Bob Dylan. At the center of the ballroom is a "maple, spring loaded dance floor," lit by a "four-foot neon star and a silver disco ball."[1] It's an intimate, historic, and lively setting. Right before the holidays in 2019, I took the stage at Cain's—but certainly not to perform with any legends of country music. No, that night a different lineup was in store. Billed as the "center of gravity" for Tulsa's tech world and organized by a local entrepreneur who liked to call me "Bubba," this was an event designed to kick off the start of a citywide effort to build Tulsa's innovation ecosystem.

In front of a who's who of the city's tech, investment, and economic development worlds, I announced the creation of Tulsa Innovation Labs, which I had been incubating ever since my pitch to GKFF. Explaining my theory of change, I outlined the organization's guiding principles: inclusion, focus, and collaboration. And I boldly declared that TIL would help foster "the nation's most inclusive tech community" in Tulsa.

When I gave that speech, I was still a stranger to Tulsa, a young leader trying to establish TIL, then in its early, abstract stage. And I knew that TIL couldn't do it alone; I'd need more than GKFF's support for the city to succeed. In that spirit, I took the opportunity to invite the audience to join TIL in our work. I previewed some ways businesses could contribute, such as funding student scholarships, hiring interns, and conducting pilots with start-ups. Six months later, when TIL released our strategy, I followed up with an op-ed in *Tulsa World*, the city's daily newspaper, in which I asked for community support in building our tech clusters.

I realized that night at Cain's, amid the live band and white Christmas lights, that several promising efforts were working to grow Tulsa's innovation ecosystem in addition to ours. Among the other speakers were Devon Laney from Gradient and Libby Ediger from the Atlas School (then called the Holberton School), a program that trains software developers. But the problem was that there was no unifying strategy, nothing to connect us all. It wasn't readily apparent how we should work together, and there certainly wasn't the infrastructure in place to facilitate coordination.

Successfully developing a city's tech identity requires collective action. You'll need to coordinate across your ecosystem, building a diverse coalition of partners and aligning them around your industry cluster strategy.

While the Tulsa ecosystem hadn't yet figured out how to collaborate, the event at Cain's was a promising start. Looking out into the crowd, I saw so many excited faces, and I felt confident that if I could bring the ecosystem together, if we could sing the same song, we could turn Tulsa into the tech hub it aspired to be.

VALUE RESILIENT ECOSYSTEMS

Collective action in a dynamic urban ecosystem is hard to pull off, even in a midsized city like Tulsa. Not everyone will share your view of the world or find motivation in the same things you do. I, for one, mistakenly assumed that people knew what "ecosystem coordination" meant and saw the same benefits of it I did. (My use of such jargon wasn't helpful either.)

For instance, I grabbed a drink one evening with a stakeholder from the nonprofit sector. We were at Valkyrie, an elegant cocktail lounge in the Arts District, and TIL had just won a major federal grant. As I sipped on a frosty penicillin, he toasted me and said, "Congratulations on finally establishing your own fiefdom." It was a telling moment because it revealed to me that not everyone understands cities as the ecosystems they are or prioritizes collective effort over selfish interests as they should. And it threw into relief the broader Tulsa culture I was encountering—a disconnected civic ecosystem in which key institutions often felt as though they were competing with one another rather than collaborating, and where some stakeholders mistook power for success. My goal, however, was never to secure a lifetime job or to assume control; I was here to change the city as quickly as I could. To do that, I'd need to convince people to work together, not build my own silo. A key part of civic reinvention is shifting from siloed thinking to an ecosystem-based mindset.

At its most fundamental, an ecosystem is an interdependent network or system. We use the term in multiple contexts—innovation, business, urban planning, and ecology—but the concept is the same. An innovation ecosystem includes start-up founders, venture capitalists, technologists, academics, and more—all the actors identified in the Innovation Flywheel, which describes the virtuously beneficial relationship between actors in an ecosystem when it's working well. It is critical for each player to understand that they are one part of a greater whole. And some players, like economic developers, can help design and connect these ecosystems from a bird's-eye view—a unique position that leads sometimes to accusations of having a God complex. To build the ecosystem and get the flywheel spinning, economic developers and other leaders need to foster cross-sector partnerships, help build the capacities of local organizations, provide services to the community that enable economic activity, and help facilitate growth at the intersections of previously disconnected or undiscovered businesses. TIL designed its initiatives to achieve these objectives.

It's imperative to build and coordinate an urban ecosystem because traditional business sectors are disappearing. This shift is disrupting markets, economies, and societies, making for much more fluid ecosystems that reward those who have strong partnerships and supportive networks, while punishing those who try to go it alone. In *The Ecosystem Economy*, Venkat Atluri and Mikos Dietz demonstrate how borders are quickly falling in the business world, especially in tech, where market segments and domains are blurring. (Another reason why your city's tech clusters should work together and not as silos.) This breakdown isn't happening just within the private sector; it's also happening among the public, private, and social sectors themselves, where interests increasingly cross over, necessitating more collaborations.

Such interconnectedness means that disruptions in markets, climates, and politics have ripple effects. Therefore, we should build innovation ecosystems for resilience to future shocks and stresses; and a key feature of resilience is a diversified economy. In

The Resilience Dividend, Judith Rodin writes that urban ecosystems are affected by the twenty-first century's three signature factors: climate change, urbanization, and globalization.[2] (I'd add a fourth: technological innovation.) Rodin writes, "Because everything is interconnected—a massive system of systems—a single disruption often triggers another, which exacerbates the effects of the first, so that the original shock becomes a cascade of crises."[3] Tulsa's reliance on oil and gas, for instance, doesn't make for a resilient economy; it makes for a vulnerable one. Think back to Pittsburgh and the collapse of the steel industry—industry failures lead to job losses, followed by out-migration, which leads to loss of property value, lower tax revenues, less funding to invest in new opportunities or support basic services, and so on. Most Heartland cities face a gradual decline rather than a dramatic collapse, but the point stands.

To excel in this new paradigm, organizations of all kinds must build ecosystems and foster collaboration within them. Doing so can yield greater value for the collective than would ever be possible if each element operated discretely. The solution, then, is targeted and linked interventions sustained over time that expand and strengthen the ecosystem itself, not one-off initiatives that create temporary islands of excellence or opportunity. Moreover, having a close-knit ecosystem also allows for the recycling of good ideas and good talent—it allows a start-up founder to teach lessons to their peers, an executive confronting layoffs to refer their talent to another company, and a technologist in a stuffy corporate environment to meet and be inspired by entrepreneurs. The connective tissue among partners and economic development initiatives—the connectivity that allows for such flow—can be as valuable as the initiative itself over the long run.

ASSEMBLE A COALITION

A fundamental truth of our modern era is that we live in a global economy in which many factors, from the internet to supply chains to politics, have upended our classic conceptions of international borders. But on a more pragmatic and everyday scale, this global, borderless economy plays out at the local level. Today, economic developers must work with increasingly diverse organizations, many of whom defy traditional categories and have multiple bottom lines. For anyone attempting to build an inclusive innovation economy, assembling key stakeholders, synchronizing efforts, and putting the collective into action are your next arduous steps.

Recognizing this, I positioned TIL as a nonpartisan organization that could work at the nexus of the public, private, and social sectors. In doing so, TIL has been able to convene partners from across the ecosystem and design initiatives that can really move the needle. Bruce Katz and Jeremy Nowak write, "If cities, in short, are to be the world's problem solvers, municipalities must grow new sets of leaders and invent new intermediaries and institutions that align with this disruptive era and its heightened importance."[4] I conceived TIL to be this new type of organization, one equipped to create solutions for twenty-first-century challenges, working to build a unifying strategy for growth and a diverse coalition to propel the city forward. This design, backed up by GKFF's capital, gave us the ability to shape the ecosystem.

Traditionally, economic development has been a collaboration between local businesses, government, and their economic development organizations (EDOs). Scholars have rightly paid much attention to public–private partnerships, which are critical to getting most kinds of urban projects completed. But what's interesting about Tulsa is that the public or private sectors aren't driving tech-led economic development. Nor does an established EDO spearhead the effort. Instead, the social sector primarily leads Tulsa's transformation, through the massive investments of the George Kaiser Family Foundation, TIL-led strategic initiatives, and the important work of other nonprofits. While aligning the public and private sectors on your city's industry cluster strategy is important, Tulsa's particular ecosystem gives us the opportunity to focus on an adjacent topic: coordination between economic developers, ecosystem builders, and the wider social sector.

No matter your city's contours, your fellow economic developers and ecosystem builders will represent a core part of your coalition. Considering that they have similar missions, governance structures, and the need for external funding, however, you may find that working with this part of your ecosystem is especially fraught because you are, in some ways, competitors as much as partners. I often found it easier to work with the private sector—where the market created clear distinctions between priorities—than with peer organizations. Yet your ability to influence and align with your peers will ultimately determine if only your organization succeeds or whether you'll catalyze ecosystem-wide change. Your objective should be to build as large and diverse a tent as possible with partners committed, at various degrees, to support the development of your city's tech identity. The more you can align partners, the better and quicker you'll be able to grow your tech clusters, which rely upon a concentration of activity and investment.

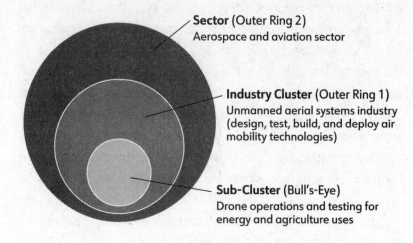

Sector (Outer Ring 2)
Aerospace and aviation sector

Industry Cluster (Outer Ring 1)
Unmanned aerial systems industry
(design, test, build, and deploy air
mobility technologies)

Sub-Cluster (Bull's-Eye)
Drone operations and testing for
energy and agriculture uses

THE CONCENTRIC CIRCLES COMPROMISE

Although you've made the business case for your industry clusters, some important stakeholders likely won't entirely buy into such a narrow focus or will believe the focus should be elsewhere. Even among economic development–related entities, some stakeholders may hesitate to commit or may not be able to pivot completely to this new strategy, because of their priorities or their mission statement.

Also, some organizations may be able to partner on your strategy but will require flexibility and patience on your part to figure out how. If that's the case, as I encountered, then consider using what I call the **Concentric Circles Compromise** (see above). Perfect alignment across the board isn't realistic. The aim is to get as many partners as possible rowing in the same direction, without duplicating efforts or creating unnecessary competition. The flywheel needs to spin together, not rattle, clank, and sputter about. Customizing partnerships rather than trying to force everyone to fully adopt your plan is a win, and securing agreements at the industry or sectoral level will help drive activity and investment that will benefit your strategy, even if it is in adjacent areas or different segments of the value chain.

TIL identified subclusters representing Tulsa's "right to win" opportunities; these are our bull's-eye targets in the graphic. For example, for advanced air mobility, the target was drone operations and testing for energy and agriculture uses. When we couldn't secure agreement with an organization to step up their work in that space, we looked for partnerships in outer rings. This is the Concentric Circles Compromise: broadening your strategic focus can help you enlist more partners and drive more activity that will benefit your city. And sometimes, rather than seeking wholesale strategic alignment, you can partner at the project level. In Tulsa, our strategy led some organizations to totally reorient their approach to align with our clusters, shifting their priorities or service offerings, while others made modest but symbolic pivots.

But not everyone was interested in coordination and alignment. TIL struggled to align with one venture capital firm. This VC didn't share TIL's incentives or desired outcomes, nor was it interested in collective action. They were purely ROI driven, which meant they evaluated opportunities case by case. I felt strongly that such an approach was shortsighted and led to missed opportunities, even if I understood how the singular goal of a financial return might have led them to it. In my mind, this VC should have prioritized investing in Tulsa's clusters and worked to secure deals that helped bring to town new start-ups in those areas. TIL's work to develop the clusters would contribute to their mission by making deals more likely and start-ups more successful, thereby increasing their returns. Despite my best efforts, though, I couldn't get support for a double bottom-line approach that would marry our respective organizations' goals (their ROI with TIL's social and growth impact).

While TIL wasn't the only organization struggling to partner with this VC, in retrospect, my focus on our subcluster targets came off as more rigid than intended. I could have worked earlier on to secure agreement with this firm at the industry or sectoral level. Even though this relationship was frustrating, self-interested VCs are exactly the kind of ingredient necessary to making an ecosystem grow—these are the types of battles one should expect to have. That said, as TIL notched wins and our approach bore fruit while other organizations floundered, this VC began to prioritize our clusters, particularly advanced air mobility, getting to the result of the Concentric Circles Compromise.

Although you'll want everyone to come together around your strategy, such kumbaya isn't going to happen. Don't waste time trying to secure agreements with unwilling parties. Build a coalition of the willing and move on. When you're successful, folks who previously dismissed you will reconsider. As I learned, it's worth taking this approach early in the coalition-building stage so that it can help foster horizontal relationships and widen your tent of partners, signaling your flexibility and giving other organizations more options to contribute and benefit.

THE GKFF COALITION

Identifying partners and assembling your economic development coalition is one-half of the equation. The other half is designating roles and responsibilities so each member of the coalition knows what to do and how they support the broader effort. It's incumbent upon every partner to understand what their core competency is and to execute on it. Urban coalitions need to define and codify these roles and responsibilities and ensure folks stay in their own lane. Taking a close look at the GKFF-backed coalition in Tulsa offers lessons applicable to other Heartland cities as they work to expand and harmonize their ecosystems.

GKFF's economic development universe is impressive in its scope and scale, and it's just now starting to take shape. At the time of TIL's founding, however, it was very much in flux, operating as clumsy checkers rather than carefully deployed chess pieces. Tulsa Remote, an incentive to attract remote workers, began in 2018. I was hired in 2019 and officially launched TIL in January 2020. Then, a series of other organizations launched in quick succession through 2023. Built ad hoc, these new organizations were almost always meant to fill a perceived gap; as you might expect, some worked better than others, and some fit into the overall picture better than others. Here are the entities GKFF supports, which, together, drive the bulk of the city's tech-led economic and workforce development:

\ GKFF'S ECONOMIC DEVELOPMENT–RELATED ENTITIES			
Organization	Flywheel Category	Function	Description
Atento Capital	Capital	Funder & Ecosystem Builder	Early-stage venture capital firm deploying GKFF funds to support underestimated founders at various stages, including direct investments and fund of funds.
Atlas School	Talent	Operator	Training boot camp that offers software engineering and development programs.
Build in Tulsa	Underrepresented Voices & Talent	Ecosystem Builder & Service Provider	Entrepreneurial support organization dedicated to Black founders, offering a range of start-up accelerator programming.

	GKFF'S ECONOMIC DEVELOPMENT–RELATED ENTITIES		
Organization	Flywheel Category	Function	Description
Business Attraction (not a separate LLC, but more of a business unit operating across the coalition and includes GKFF leadership)	Employers	Service Provider & Funder	Informal business attraction unit that identifies, pitches, and secures deals with prospective companies to relocate to Tulsa, offering a wide range of financial and in-kind incentives.
Campus Tulsa	Talent	Service Provider	Summer internship program that recruits college students to Tulsa and matches them with local employers.
Experience Tulsa	Community	Service Provider	Shared-services program to GKFF and its LLCs that coordinates and leads tours and experiences for outside visitors. Experience Tulsa also serves as the umbrella brand that unites the entire coalition.
Gradient*	Community	Ecosystem Builder & Service Provider	Entrepreneurial support organization and coworking space that offers services to founders from all stages and types of companies.

* Gradient is also supported by the Lobeck Taylor Family Foundation.

GKFF'S ECONOMIC DEVELOPMENT–RELATED ENTITIES

Organization	Flywheel Category	Function	Description
inTulsa	Talent	Service Provider	Talent-matching service that works with employers to locate the talent they need in Tulsa.
Tulsa Innovation Labs	Innovation & Talent	Strategist, Initiative Designer & Ecosystem Builder	Tech-led EDO that designs economic and workforce development initiatives to catalyze inclusive growth in Tulsa's virtual health, energy tech, advanced air mobility, and cyber ecosystems.
Tulsa Remote	Talent	Service Provider	Remote work incentive program that offers cash to attract remote workers to Tulsa.

Given the Tulsa ecosystem today, here's how I think these organizations *should* work together, and this picture can give you an idea of what a collaborative ecosystem in the Heartland might look like. **Tulsa Innovation Labs** invests in city assets to develop Tulsa's most promising tech industries, launching new initiatives in select clusters. The **Business Attraction** unit leverages those local assets to pitch new companies to move to Tulsa, offering them a suite of incentives. **Experience Tulsa** curates meetings and experiences for visiting companies and individuals to show off Tulsa and its assets, while also serving as the umbrella brand for the coalition. Those new companies often need talent, so **inTulsa** helps fill their talent needs by matching openings to individuals, drawing upon the software developers trained at the **Atlas School** or talent trained through TIL's industry-specific initiatives. Some of those new firms are start-ups and may need space, so they work out of **Gradient**. Those start-ups may also require follow-on funding and can go to **Atento Capital** to explore investment opportunities; Atento can also refer relevant deal flow to TIL and other partners. All the while, **Tulsa Remote** enriches the ecosystem by attracting remote workers, many of whom are in tech. **Campus Tulsa** is matching summer interns to local employers and building the talent pipeline, and **Build in Tulsa** is supporting Black start-up founders, who may also need space at Gradient, capital from Atento, or industry-specific opportunities through TIL. At its best, all of these organizations support one another, creating the interdependence of a thriving, resilient, and impactful ecosystem.

Benjamin Franklin supposedly said, "Never confuse motion with action." I'd add that cities should never confuse action with coordination. Except for occasional coalition-wide meetings to bring everyone up to date, there weren't formal efforts to align this coalition strategically. I found this deeply frustrating, but my pleas were ignored, proving the limits of my leadership. To the extent it could, the coalition gelled over time from the bottom up, through LLC leaders working together to hammer out ways to support one another and coordinate. We'd get in a room and whiteboard processes, workflows, and initiative relationships. One wider lesson from this struggle is that you need to figure out the incentives that motivate your coalition partners and try to structure a system in which organizations play to their strengths and get what they want out of the partnership.

Being in the thick of this coalition was both rewarding and stressful. I found the ambiguity and fluidity anxiety producing; the tendency to create a new organization every few months without first setting the big picture and establishing a coordinating mechanism concerned me. Tulsa's coalition reflects the organic nature and disorderliness of urban ecosystems—some may say the beauty of cities themselves—but it also demonstrates the need to coordinate strategically. While I would have defined an overall vision and architecture first and then worked methodically to build it out, Tulsa's ecosystem grew in fits and starts, mostly at the tactical level.

As you'd expect, the coalition finally grew so unwieldy that GKFF had to bring this confederation of LLCs under a loose governance structure. They decided to put TIL's industry cluster strategy at its core, giving all the organizations a plan to solidify around. They created an internal operating structure—a unifying legal entity—and leveraged an external-facing umbrella brand for the coalition, Experience Tulsa. This umbrella includes a set of shared services, such as public relations, that the LLCs can use. Overall, GKFF's goal is to create at least twenty thousand tech jobs over the next decade, with half attributable to TIL.

Every city will have a different answer to who has the authority and standing in the community to encourage alignment across the ecosystem. For Tulsa, it was GKFF, but for other cities, it might be a community foundation, corporation, university, economic development organization, mayor, or high–net worth civic leader. While there are trade-offs in every system, Tulsa is lucky that there's a single funder who can serve as the backbone organization and encourage, even compel, alignment between entities. Barring such an institution, cities should look to civic pride, local influencers, and cash to help bring people together.

This coalition's development and the city's maturation as an innovation ecosystem have occurred because of and in parallel to GKFF's evolution. I spoke to Ken Levit, GKFF's executive director since 2006, about this enormous project. Before heading GKFF, Levit served as the president of the University of Oklahoma–Tulsa and was previously counsel to CIA director George Tenet. During his time at GKFF, Levit's understanding of what economic development means for a philanthropy changed a great deal. "It's not just about injecting philanthropic money into the systems; it's alignment of the systems to get better results, breaking down the silos, and getting people to point to shared goals," he said. Levit realized that communities needed to set collective goals that GKFF's partners could align with and then work together to achieve them. "I think that TIL has kind of catalyzed that discussion," he continued. "And this shared-services effort that GKFF is putting together will aspire to be a collective impact organization around economic development."[5]

Although Tulsa's economic development coalition comprises mostly GKFF-funded organizations, TIL didn't limit its partnerships to them: we also worked with the city, including their new economic development organization, PartnerTulsa; the state's department of commerce; and the Tulsa Regional Chamber. TIL got OU–Tulsa and the region's Comprehensive Economic Development Strategy (led by the Indian Nations Council of Governments, the regional metropolitan planning organization) to adopt much of our cluster strategy. It's safe to assume that you, too, will need to work with a motley crew of organizations, with varying capacities and interests, to align with your city's tech niche.

Here's a final recommendation I believe holds true no matter the particulars of your coalition, and it's one that most people won't tell you: don't do too much. In economic development (and philanthropy, for that matter), people tend to privilege outputs over outcomes. New programs and ribbon cuttings generate enthusiasm and get good press, but you need to carefully consider who in your coalition is doing what, when, and why.

In Tulsa, there's the real risk of doing too much too soon. Remember that every economic or workforce development initiative will need funding, staff, mentors, and likely industry partners—this unintentionally strains partners' ability to engage, pulling your corporations in a thousand different directions and leading to fatigue. It also risks performance and management issues because so many efforts can spread oversight and funding too thin. That's why policing the swim lanes—ensuring organizations are not deviating from their core competency—is important, as is ensuring each initiative can strongly influence the development of your clusters—otherwise you probably shouldn't be doing it.

I believe that despite their noble missions, there are way too many nonprofits in the United States, and many of them (and their communities) would benefit from merging or consolidating efforts. Tulsa, I think, is at the point where the coalition needs to focus on implementation and limit new things, because outcomes must reign supreme. Reorganizing GKFF's economic development coalition, as Experience Tulsa has begun, would offer the foundation the opportunity to assess what's working and to clarify goals.

After an era of experimentation and expansion, GKFF's economic development coalition is now contracting. In the fall of 2024, multiple sources told me that Atento and inTulsa will sunset as standalone entitles. There are plans, I'm told, for a slimmed down inTulsa to be absorbed into Tulsa Remote and Atento's functions potentially to be assumed by GKFF itself. There are also plans to merge the Business Attraction unit into TIL. The continued fluidity of the ecosystem suggests that this coalition remains somewhat fragile. Ultimately, the project's success will depend upon GKFF's ability to unify these organizations, empower their success, and continue to fund their work. GKFF's economic development project can't truly scale or sustain itself until the coalition stabilizes with clear roles and responsibilities—even while recognizing this endeavor will always be a bit iterative.

The truth is that urban reinvention doesn't happen through fixed master plans executed exactly as conceived from an authority on high, no matter the influence of Robert Moses, the longtime New York City planning commissioner with a reputation for top-down planning. Tidy frameworks and universally endorsed plans simply aren't realistic. (I still must remind myself of this sometimes.) A coalition is inherently unruly. Left to their own devices, organizations tend toward entropy rather than strategy.

But while it's good to create some structure in an ecosystem, as I've just been describing, you can also overdesign ecosystems, stifling the creative forces that give cities their dynamism. This point occurred to me at dinner one night with former Tulsa mayor Kathy Taylor and an executive from the University of Tulsa. We were at Polo Grill in Utica Square, one of my go-tos, and I was getting their advice. At the time, the Oklahoma Cyber Innovation Institute at TU, which TIL codesigned, had stalled, and I was looking for a game plan to move things forward. Taylor said, seeing my approach to economic development, she thought I was a trained engineer. I studied literature in college, not engineering, and I took this as a polite and fair suggestion not to try and overengineer the ecosystem—especially as we discussed how legacy civic organizations preferred to work in frustratingly fluid ways.

Still, your assets should flow into one another, and you should configure the members of your economic development coalition to reinforce and support one another, not fight or compete. The job of a leader is to build, influence, and align coalitions. The degree of your success, though, is as much about relationships as it is about clarity of roles, and that requires trust.

FOSTER TRUST

We've made great strides in Tulsa, but unifying the ecosystem isn't simple, and despite the strong sense of community I felt there, the city faces a stark trust deficit, publicly acknowledged by Tulsa leaders across sectors. With a history of racist violence and more recent economic stagnation, it's little wonder why various pathologies fester and trust has broken down. But every city has "muck" of some kind, as visual artist Kara Walker says, and unfortunately, trust is eroding across the nation—it is one of the key barriers standing in the way of not just Tulsa but the United States as a whole.

According to Pew Research Center, trust in the US government has steadily declined since 1964, precipitated by the Vietnam War and then Watergate.[6] Besides losing trust in government, the media, and other institutions, Americans also trust one another less.[7] And, as Robert Putnam proved in *Bowling Alone*, community and social capital continue to deteriorate. Thus it is nearly impossible to solve pressing problems. Without collective action, challenges like inequality and climate change are doomed to persist.

We need collective action to generate inclusive growth and trust and social cohesion to build partnerships that drive that growth. Throughout my tenure in Tulsa, I noticed consistent distrustfulness between various segments of the ecosystem—particularly between communities of color and local institutions as well as between local civic institutions themselves. Given this environment, I needed to more intentionally and proactively work to build trust.

THE TRUST EQUATION

At TIL, I simply tried to do strong work and respect my partners, which I figured would cultivate relationships, earn trust, and produce results. I subscribed to an idea often attributed to Ernest Hemingway: "The best way to find out if you can trust somebody is to trust them." While I got burned more than once, I think this is good advice.

But how can organizations instill trust in their communities? A few years ago, Stanford's Nonprofit Management Institute invited me to speak on a panel on how communities build trust. This forced me to stop and think how I and TIL built trust in Tulsa, which later became the **Trust Equation**. I wrote down a few things

I thought we were doing effectively. The following principles became something of a mental model for me:

ENGAGEMENT: TIL proactively sought input from a diverse array of stakeholders, especially those with local credibility. We codesigned initiatives with partners, engaging in structured and unstructured ways to envision, scope, and design initiatives. And we were good about following up. TIL leadership also constantly met with members of the business community, and we held quarterly meetings with our advisory council, composed of local and national leaders, to ensure we gained input and insights from a variety of people. Where TIL fell short was on traditional community engagement, such as tabling events, town halls, or other forums open to the public. We engaged in a more targeted way with industry leaders and civic institutions.

TRANSPARENCY: Transparency and inclusion when it came to decision-making was a challenge. In the old days, people spoke of the smoke-filled room where power brokers made decisions. In Tulsa, I often felt as though I didn't have a seat at the table . . . until I realized there was no table. Decisions weren't deliberated; worse, a handful of old friends, the proverbial "Good Ol' Boys" network, made them through informal conversations. TIL worked to change that by consistently engaging the business community, adhering to a thoughtful methodology for initiative design, and by making our strategy open to the public, with the data, analysis, and plans posted on our website; we did this with all reports, requests for proposals, and other important documents.

ACCOUNTABILITY: TIL was responsible to its funder, not to the public. But we knew that we would succeed only if we aligned with our ecosystem and met local needs. Our advisory council held us accountable but so did our partners, the local corporations and universities we worked with so closely. If TIL didn't perform or if our initiatives didn't have the desired outcomes, they wouldn't partner with us. That's why engaging those partners regularly and inviting constructive criticism paid off for TIL. (I'll go into more detail on how to create a culture of accountability in chapter 9.)

CONSISTENCY: Many commonly criticized Tulsa's civic organizations for lacking consistency in priorities and funding. Sudden changes in interests or funding priorities gives communities whiplash and causes confusion. TIL released our strategy with an action plan, and we stuck to it. We stayed focused on our mission and on executing our strategy; we didn't chase shiny objects or pursue the latest trend. People respected our follow-through and even the times we had to pass on a project because it didn't fit our strategy.

COMPETENCY: Fundamentally, trust comes when people see their leaders and civic institutions doing what they said they'd do. TIL earned the reputation of doing excellent work and getting results. As one CEO told me, "TIL's competence is a breath of fresh air." I found that a lot of interpersonal and political issues subsided when TIL started proving that we knew what we were doing.

Wherever you work, it's important for you to model these five elements—to be the partner you want others to be for you. This is how you build trust. And, I found out, you need trust to lead a community—or for a community to allow you to lead them. It's the only way to make impact together.

I took it as a personal mission to try and secure as broad and deep of an alignment as possible, starting with my peer LLCs. I wanted to inspire collective action, community-centeredness, civic virtue, and selflessness—not easy things to do. My inability to accomplish all of that humbled me, and in retrospect I had unrealistic expectations about the breadth and depth of alignment I could achieve with our tech niche strategy. The fiefdom mentality is strong in Tulsa. I discovered that there will always be people who simply want to do what they want to do, no matter the logic or power of your strategy or the pitch to put selfish interests aside for the greater good. Only through years of hard work and traction did the GKFF universe start coalescing around TIL's theory of change. But to ensure theory turns into outcomes, you'll need quantifiable goals and ways to measure them.

UNITE BEHIND GOALS

Growth for the sake of growth is a dead end. This type of expansion doesn't truly create opportunities for people and leads to rising inequality as experienced by San Francisco and Austin, where policies on transportation and housing, among others, didn't keep pace with growth. Many organizations aren't used to viewing growth through an inclusion and equity lens. Although these same groups likely virtue signal around DEI, they may not fully understand what inclusive growth is or how to achieve it—or they may content themselves with symbolic efforts. But what these groups do understand are metrics. Whether it's a fundraising or job creation target, or the more comprehensive set of metrics that follow, having quantifiable goals that require collective effort can inspire and challenge your partners to work together and hold them accountable.

THE ECONOMY FORWARD FRAMEWORK

I was well into my time at TIL when I first stopped to define, seriously, what inclusive growth meant. Starting to build out TIL's impact measurement system prompted me to do so. I wondered, beyond TIL initiatives' key performance indicators (KPIs), how I would know if TIL was moving the needle at the city level. I wanted to create a framework to help Tulsa monitor and track its progress toward inclusive growth, and I realized that I didn't have all the answers. I couldn't find outside models that fit a city Tulsa's size, and I figured that a lot of other Heartland cities had similar struggles.

To solve this problem and set TIL and Tulsa up for success, we partnered with Heartland Forward, a think-and-do tank promoting economic opportunity in the middle of the country (specifically Ross DeVol, their president and CEO, and Richard Florida, a senior fellow there), and the Aspen Institute (Cordell Carter) on **The Economy Forward Framework**—a first-of-its-kind model to help midsized cities measure their progress in building inclusive knowledge economies.

First, we defined inclusive growth, drawing on research from Brookings. Inclusive growth is "economic growth that 'translates into increased household consumption' whose 'gains are broadly distributed' across various demographics of the population."[8]

Then we identified nine metrics across three themes: industry, accessibility, and vibrancy. Midsized cities must develop targeted **industries**—also known as the tech clusters I've been going on about—and work to expand opportunities within them, ensuring jobs, capital, and education are **accessible**. This, along with place-making investments, such as walking trails, public transportation infrastructure, or community gardens, makes for a **vibrant** city.

Within each category, we identified the key drivers of inclusive growth—metrics that directly relate to investments in innovation ecosystems, reflect the impact of economic development investments, and are sensitive to changes over a five-year timeline. We then analyzed the trajectories of our peer cities. (In this case, we looked at thirty-eight cities with metropolitan statistical area populations between 750,000 and 1.5 million people.) For each metric, we established ambitious but reasonable goals for Tulsa based on the growth rate of its peers.[9]

INCLUSIVE-GROWTH METRICS

Metric	Description
Industry	
Share of Jobs in the "Knowledge Economy"	Many Heartland and industrial Midwest cities lag their peers in the share of jobs in knowledge-intensive industries, which are more resilient and better paying.
Young Firm Employment Ratio & Young Firm Knowledge Intensity	The share of employment at innovative firms less than six years old is an important measure of a region's ability to produce and retain potential high-growth companies.
Academic Research and Development Expenditures	R&D growth in noncoastal cities often lags the national average, leaving universities underutilized as anchors in local innovation economies.
Accessibility	
Labor Force Participation Rate by Race and Sex	Changes over time in the percentage of residents in the labor force can indicate whether vulnerable workers are being adequately prepared for the economic transition.
Diversity of Enrollment in STEM Programs	Diversity of enrollment in STEM fields is a nationwide challenge, especially among Black or African American, American Indian or Alaskan Native, and Hispanic populations.
Share of Minority- and Women-Owned Firms in Knowledge-Intensive Industries	Enabling entrepreneurs of all backgrounds to succeed in innovative industries is essential to ensuring equal opportunity in these industries and closing the wealth gap.

INCLUSIVE-GROWTH METRICS

Metric	Description
Vibrancy	
Public Investment in Quality of Place	Cultural and recreational amenities are increasingly important determinants of where knowledge-economy workers and the firms that employ them choose to locate.
Percentage of Residents with a Bachelor's Degree or Higher	While many tech jobs are available to individuals without bachelor's degrees, many of the key roles needed to commercialize innovations and grow start-ups require advanced education.
Retention of Graduates from Local Educational Institutions	In cities without large state or research universities, brain drain impedes efforts to cultivate the highly educated workforces needed to build and sustain an innovation economy.

TULSA'S GOALS

Metric	Tulsa in 2022	Five-Year Goal
Industry		
Share of Jobs in the "Knowledge Economy"	Knowledge-economy jobs make up a smaller share of total jobs in Tulsa (28.9 percent) than in its peer set (31.1 percent).	Tulsa increases the share of KE jobs to 30 percent of all jobs in the Tulsa MSA by 2026.
Young Firm Employment Ratio & Young Firm Knowledge Intensity	Tulsa's YFER is 0.9 percent lower and its YFKI is 1.8 percent lower than the average of its peers.	Tulsa cuts these gaps in half to 0.45 percent and 0.9 percent by 2026.

81

TULSA'S GOALS

Metric	Tulsa in 2022	Five-Year Goal
Academic Research and Development Expenditures	The Tulsa MSA has approximately 25 percent of Oklahoma's population but only 8 percent of the state's academic R&D expenditures.	Ten percent of R&D expenditures in Oklahoma are in Tulsa by 2026.
Accessibility		
Labor Force Participation Rate by Race and Sex	Tulsa's LFPR has generally been above the aggregate and median LFPRs of peer cities since 2010. (In 2019, 1.1 percent above aggregate and 0.4 percent above median.)	Tulsa's LFPR should remain 1 percent above aggregate LFPR of peer cities and retain consistency across racial groups.
Diversity of Enrollment in STEM Programs	STEM degree programs enroll far fewer Black (-51 percent), Native (-33 percent), and Hispanic or Latino (-31 percent) students than expected based on the state's population.	TIL-backed educational programs will strive for enrollment that is at least 8 percent Black, 7 percent Native, and 10 percent Hispanic or Latino, matching the MSA's demographics.
Share of Minority- and Women- Owned Firms in Knowledge- Intensive Industries	Although Tulsa performs well in comparison to cities with similar White/ non-White population breakdowns, only 0.93 percent of firms in key industries are owned by people of color.	Tulsa will double its share of minority-owned firms in these industries to 1.8 percent over the next five years.

TULSA'S GOALS

Metric	Tulsa in 2022	Five-Year Goal
Vibrancy		
Public Investment in Quality of Place	City appropriations for social and economic development and culture and recreation grew by 33 percent between 2011 and 2020, faster than the growth in overall city spending (24 percent).	By 2026, Tulsa's annual spending growth in public investment in quality of place should be 5 percent higher than annual spending growth in overall city budget.
Percentage of Residents with a Bachelor's Degree or Higher	The share of Tulsans with a bachelor's degree or higher (28.9 percent) is 3.8 percent lower than the aggregate of peer cities and the national average.	Tulsa's growth in this metric by 2026 should outpace peer cities, narrowing the gap to 2.5 percent.
Retention of Graduates from Local Educational Institutions	Controlling for students' home cities, OKC is 1.7 times more likely to retain a recent graduate of OU and 2.7 times more likely to retain a recent graduate of OSU.	Tulsa closes this gap by 10 percent by 2026.

Note: The tables above have been reproduced and only slightly edited from The Economy Forward Framework.

The analysis revealed strengths and weaknesses in Tulsa's economy. You can see from the table that Tulsa had mixed performance across the metrics, proving what most knew: Tulsa was behind the curve and needed to change direction. While the city performed well on average labor force participation rates, its low percentage of residents with a bachelor's degree or higher and low young firm knowledge intensity—how educated and specialized talent are at young firms—were signs of an immature innovation economy and placed it behind most of its peers. Tulsa's challenge was not so much increasing employment participation but rather upskilling preexisting talent, attracting educated workers, and fostering resilient knowledge-economy industries, especially through start-ups.

While we tailored our diagnoses and goals to Tulsa, any Heartland city can use the framework to chart a path forward for its economic development coalition. To fully operationalize the framework, you should consider creating an internal dashboard and data repository. Your coalition members can submit data to show how they're contributing to these ecosystem-wide metrics. You should also open source this data, where possible, and post the dashboard online for the public to see your progress. Finally, try and get corporate partners to sign on and contribute to the goals in their own ways. These ecosystem-wide metrics require collective action, and stacking hands as a community to accomplish them can spark increased civic engagement. Regardless of the particular metrics and mindful of not overpromising, the GKFF coalition would be wise to adopt macro-level KPIs, monitor and track them over time, and report on their progress to the community—this will earn the public's trust and confidence.

TIL needed to overcome a climate of mistrust and shape a growing and disjointed ecosystem, but we had an opportunity to inspire the community by pursuing economic development in a new way. I am proud that by creating more thoughtful, diverse, and impactful partnerships, TIL has earned respect and trust. In Tulsa today, individual efforts have been successful, but the city needs to continue focusing on ecosystem alignment with its tech niche. Of all the planks in my action plan, this is where Tulsa has the most potential. Indeed, Tulsa's economic development project represents an enormous chance to unleash a new generation of opportunity. But that takes the hard, unsexy work of coordination and implementation.

In this first section, we've covered the foundational elements of establishing a city's tech identity: the **industry cluster strategy** defines your city's tech niche and serves as the organizing principle for your entire economic development project; **leadership** encompasses the scrappy individuals and organizations cities need to implement their new strategy; and **ecosystem coordination** represents the ability of your city to align on a shared vision and make collective impact.

Now let's turn to how to transform your city into an innovation engine, the specific economic development investments that will drive inclusive growth. For most cities, the low-hanging fruit is the quickly expanding remote-worker population, so let's start there.

ACTION PLAN SUMMARY		
REINVENTION *What needs reinventing?*	**GROWTH** *How do you catalyze growth?*	**INCLUSION** *How do you advance inclusion?*
Civic leaders need to understand cities as ecosystems, not as a set of competing silos. Urban ecosystems are naturally disjointed, with organizations moving in disparate directions. Cities need to bust up silos, form partnerships, and inspire collective action.	Economic developers should assemble a coalition of partners because one leader or organization can't do it all. Key stakeholders should align on a shared vision, but this may require compromise to get partners on board. They'll then need to establish roles and responsibilities among the coalition, build trust, and work together toward quantifiable goals.	Coalitions must include organizations not traditionally considered part of economic development, such as universities and community-based groups. Cities must also set goals designed to measure inclusive growth, ensuring that the city's reinvention is benefiting a large swath of the population.

SECTION II

BUILDING
AN INNOVATION ENGINE

CHAPTER 4

ATTRACT REMOTE WORKERS

(TALENT ATTRACTION AND REMOTE WORK)

In April 2020, I made the trek from Tulsa back to New York. It had been a difficult time, locked down during the start of the pandemic. I was away from family and friends, unable to visit my then boyfriend (now husband), Chris, who had stayed in Manhattan. I wanted to surprise him, so I hadn't told him I was returning. Back then, there were no direct flights from Tulsa to New York—today, there are, another sign of progress. After eight hours of traveling, fully masked, I arrived at LaGuardia, got into a taxi, and headed toward America's COVID epicenter. Making our way through deserted streets toward the Upper East Side, we passed mobile morgues. The city looked nothing like the Big Apple I was used to. The eerie emptiness reminded me of the first time I returned to New Orleans after Katrina and the sad drive home through the hurricane's wake.

Chris's building was next to the New York Presbyterian/Weill Cornell Medical Center, where he was a general surgery resident.

I knocked on his apartment door; he cautiously opened it, a quizzical look on his face. Then he smirked, shut the door, and opened it again with a big smile. Although then performing cancer research for Memorial Sloan Kettering, he would soon redeploy to Weill Cornell to work in emergency-activated COVID intensive care units. There, he placed catheters in arteries and veins and managed patient ventilators. The mortality rates in New York were alarmingly high, and vaccines were several months away. The United States would soon enter another lockdown period, and I'd be trapped in his overpriced studio. But at least I'd be with Chris, and together we could watch *Tiger King*, the hit show about the big-cat breeder Joe Exotic—who, it so happened, ran for governor of Oklahoma.

Tulsa shut down like the rest of the country, and none of our local partners were taking in-person meetings, so working remotely from Manhattan was fine for the time being. Like a lot of people, though, I felt a little depressed. Time started to blur. I'd skip a shower, work in shorts, or stay in bed all day. I was in Manhattan working on strategies for Tulsa, but doing so entirely online left me feeling placeless. Life had migrated to Zoom and Slack and Outlook. As the days blended, I lost my geographic frame of reference, a sense of *where* I was. Ralph Ellison, who left his native Oklahoma for the Tuskegee Institute and then for Harlem, writes in *Invisible Man*, "Perhaps to lose a sense of where you are implies the danger of losing a sense of who you are."[1] For me, my identity had always intertwined with place. Not too surprising, I suppose, for an urbanist. But with no grounding in a place—whether it was Tulsa or New York—I wondered, *Who am I?* A strange feeling came over me, like I had been uploaded to the cloud, disembodied, and removed from any community whatsoever. It made me realize that the importance of place will only increase as our lives further digitize. But that doesn't mean we're ever going back to a time when everyone lives where they work and works where they live. The aim will be creating a sense of place *while at the same time* embracing the new remote work reality.

Two years earlier, in what now seems like a prescient move, the George Kaiser Family Foundation pioneered a remote work incentive program called Tulsa Remote. When I first heard about TR, I thought it sounded like a gimmick. *Should cities be incentivizing outsiders to move to their towns?* I wondered. *Is that the best use of funds? Would TR make a positive impact?* The answer turned out to be yes. Despite my initial misgivings, I've come to appreciate remote work as a critical lever for Heartland cities. And TR has turned Tulsa into a nationally recognized Zoom town. When done right, these incentives lead to fresh talent, increased entrepreneurship, greater commerce, and a more diverse community, all necessary elements in a burgeoning tech economy. TR anticipated the wave of remote work, which the pandemic accelerated. And many Heartland cities benefited from the exodus of talent from big cities during that period.

But just because remote work is the new normal doesn't mean juggernauts like New York are going away. Remote work being an advantage for Heartland cities and not their bigger counterparts is no longer a given. New collaborative research from Richard Florida and the Boston Consulting Group (BCG) reveals that remote work benefits coastal hubs too. It's not just that New York and San Francisco hold an enormous concentration of wealth and talent. These cities also form part of an exclusive global network of commerce that sustains itself in part through virtual networks and digital financial systems. Capital, talent, and opportunity flow between a digitally connected set of superstar cities, what Florida and BCG call the "Meta City": "a web of cities that operate as a distinct unit and are attached to a major—often global—economic hub. . . . The Meta City combines physical and virtual agglomeration, in seeming defiance of the laws of physics, making it possible to occupy more than one space at the same time."[2]

It's little wonder that all the US Meta Cities identified in the study have large populations—excluding one, Austin, which makes up for it with its concentration of tech talent. The US cities on the list are the "global superstar hub" of New York; the "global talent hub" of LA; the "significant hubs" of Chicago, Seattle, San Francisco, Austin, Boston, DC, Atlanta, and Miami; and the "regional hubs" of Houston and Dallas. In this elite club, there's little room for midsized members.

A city like Tulsa isn't just isolated geographically and through in-person human networks—as the Meta City suggests, it's also marginalized in the wealthy and gated parts of cyberspace in which deals and investments happen, demonstrating the structural challenges midsized cities face, as well as the power of agglomeration that helps sustain big, mostly coastal cities.

This research also makes clear that the much-discussed "doom loop" of big cities that were struggling post-pandemic now seems much ado about nothing.[3] While they still face rising inequality, these cities no longer lose people in droves, and what population losses they did suffer during the pandemic have been, to a certain degree, ephemeral. This shouldn't be surprising; coastal hubs are resilient. They became the powerhouses they are today because of a concentration of talent as well as an ability to constantly evolve. The lesson for Heartland cities is to invest in themselves regardless of how their coastal counterparts are doing—because, if they do so, they can still capture their fair share of remote workers.

Because of the pandemic, millions of people once attached to the coasts are suddenly free agents, empowered to live anywhere they want. Even if they haven't left yet, the important thing is that they *can*—whereas before the pandemic, this wasn't even a thought, much less a viable option. As much as medium-sized cities need to focus on homegrown opportunities, they also need new talent fast. People increasingly realize that the Heartland offers a lower cost of living and higher quality of life, and many millennials and Gen Zers have woken up to the fact that they no longer need to live in a place like New York, where the median rent is $3,460 per month.[4] Their professional appetites can be sated in many places outside the country's most expensive and crowded cities, in communities where they can buy a house and have children, mainstays of a lost American Dream. Big cities have simply not grown inclusively, and rising costs squeeze out even well-paid tech talent. The things that make Heartland cities like Tulsa appealing to remoters are the very ones that bigger cities exacerbate, namely cost of living and community.

To take advantage of this new work paradigm and to infuse your communities with the talent you need to innovate, Heartland cities should create an incentive program that attracts and retains remote workers in tech.

INCENTIVIZE A REMOTE WORK COMMUNITY

When Tulsa Innovation Labs returned to full-time, in-person work in the fall of 2020, I found that though our initiatives had progressed, our relationships with key stakeholders hadn't. TIL had become disconnected from our community and needed to reintegrate. It felt like a new world, especially following Trump's controversial campaign rally in Tulsa over the summer. The community felt on edge, tired of COVID and weary of politics. To help strengthen a sense of community within the GKFF universe, and to foster collaboration among our peer LLCs, in 2022 we began sharing an office in the Arts District with Tulsa Remote and inTulsa.

Next door to our shared office, which TIL still occupies today, is the Atlas School. Across the street is an old warehouse that will soon be the new home of Gradient. These organizations, clustered in one city block, constitute an emerging innovation district. In ironic contrast, this innovation district sits directly next to a rusting, yet highly active train track. Our building reverberated every time one of the robotically operated trains passed us. One recently caught fire, stoking fears of a Don DeLillo–like disaster, having occurred shortly after the train derailment in Palestine, Ohio, which released toxins into the community.

And in more troubling juxtaposition, an encampment of homeless people lies catty-corner to our office. Many homeless people struggle with addiction and mental health issues; fentanyl use, as in many cities, has spiked in Tulsa, and it's not uncommon to see hypodermic needles in the parking lot. In fact, my colleagues have witnessed drug use, vandalism, and arson and have been harassed walking to and from work—images that hark back to Larry Clark's disturbing 1971 book of photographs documenting Tulsa's drug scene. My own father got swept up in the cocaine epidemic of the '80s, but he had the good sense to take off and never come back, leaving me with a very real and felt understanding of the costs these drugs can have. Without economic opportunities and treatment, people turn to dangerous forms of self-medication from which they can't easily escape. A 2022 study showed that Tulsa's homeless population had increased 40 percent between 2021 and 2022[5] and an additional 6.6 percent between 2022 and 2023.[6]

This raises a big issue. On any given day, economic developers, entrepreneurs, and remoters walk past the homeless—a stark convergence of worlds that begs difficult but worthwhile questions about gentrification and civic priorities. To his credit, Mayor Bynum has announced a $500 million project to address Tulsa's affordable housing and homelessness challenges, and voters approved an initial $75 million ballot initiative, which kicks in in 2026. [7] But at times, it's hard to reconcile our work with the immediate struggles of such populations. A skeptic might ask, should we be devoting resources into drawing outsiders to Tulsa when its own residents need so much help?

My answer is yes. By improving the diversity and vibrancy of the city's economy, we can help effect broader change. Indeed, the twin investments of economic development and support for the homeless can work together. As economies flourish, job opportunities open up, tax revenues increase, resources for public support can increase, and as homeless populations decrease, cities have more funds to reinvest into the community, creating a better environment for everyone. While Heartland cities need to incentivize remote workers, they should do it in the context of the city's overall economic health—alongside support for the homeless. But before you can benefit from remote workers, you must first understand how to create an incentive program that gets them to town.

CASE STUDY: TULSA REMOTE

Tulsa Remote is America's best-known remote work incentive program and a true pioneer in the class. And medium-sized cities can easily replicate it. TR offers a $10,000 grant, a coworking space membership to Gradient, and resettlement assistance to remote workers to move to T-Town and live there for at least one year. The program looks to import talent diverse in age, race, and background and interested in contributing to the community.[8] As of December 2023, 2,819 remote workers have made the move to Green Country—and that number is only growing.[9] These aren't just transient interlopers either: it turns out that 88 percent stay longer than the required year.[10] While TIL works to develop the local workforce pipeline, TR attracts external talent. Together, the two approaches make for a winning equation helping solve the city's tech talent needs. With respect to local versus external talent, it's not either/or but both/and.

Tulsa Remote's focus on importing talent from a range of backgrounds starts during the selection process. To avoid implicit biases, they don't ask potential remoters about age, income, or ethnicity on their applications. Prospective remoters are, however, asked about why they're interested in leaving their current home and moving to Tulsa, how much they value community, and what their volunteer experience is.[11] All of these questions are meant to sift out candidates who may simply be interested in the cash and less likely to stay once their year is up.

The TR team then reviews the applications on their customer relationship management system before offering video interviews to those who score highly.[12] Those who advance to the next round get an opportunity, on TR's dime, to visit Tulsa for a weekend. TR treats applicants to happy hours, meetups with locals, and tours of the city.[13] If it's a good fit and the participant accepts the offer, then it's full steam ahead: members go through a background check and provide proof of residence and employment before then making the move to Tulsa.

For the program's first twenty-five slots, TR received a remarkable ten thousand applications,[14] and interest has remained high (twenty-two thousand people applied in 2022 for just more than a thousand slots).[15] This volume of applicants enables TR to choose the most qualified candidates who demonstrate serious interest in contributing to the community.

TR members work for a wide range of companies, from T-Mobile to IBM, Oracle to DoorDash, and Wells Fargo to Rosetta Stone.[16] Nearly 25 percent work in IT, another 21 percent in computer software, and more than 12 percent in financial services.[17] And according to TR's impact report published in 2023, 18 percent of remoters own their own business.[18]

Remoters also hail from forty-five states.[19] And, as shown on the next page, most come from bigger cities some would consider "more appealing" than Tulsa.

TOP FIFTEEN METRO AREAS OF PREVIOUS RESIDENCE[20]

Metro Area	Share of All Tulsa Remoters
New York–Newark–Jersey City, NY–NJ–PA	9.9%
Los Angeles–Long Beach–Anaheim, CA	9.6%
Dallas–Fort Worth–Arlington, TX	7.2%
San Francisco–Oakland–Hayward, CA	4.9%
Washington–Arlington–Alexandria, DC–MD–VA	4.9%
Denver–Aurora–Lakewood, CO	4.1%
Atlanta, Sandy Springs–Roswell, GA	2.9%
Austin–Round Rock, TX	2.9%
Houston–The Woodlands–Sugar Land, TX	2.7%
San Diego–Carlsbad, CA	2.6%
Chicago–Naperville–Elgin, IL–IN–WI	2.4%
Boston–Cambridge–Newton, MA–NH	2.1%
Kansas City, MO, KS	1.9%
Portland–Vancouver–Hillsboro, OR–WA	1.8%
Phoenix–Mesa–Scottsdale, AZ	1.3%

Tulsa Remote doesn't disappear from the remoters' lives once they move to Tulsa. TR provides an onboarding stipend, numerous check-ins, and meetup opportunities to get new residents involved with one another and the community at large. Justin Harlan, Tulsa Remote's managing director and the owner of a group fitness club in town, explains that TR's approach has more to do with connectedness than financials. "Tulsa is a big-small city where anyone can get involved and connected," he told me. "Our strategy to support members is built upon early touchpoints, typically within their first ninety days in Tulsa. Every member is assigned a member-integration specialist to help connect them with organizations, people, and opportunities that align with their passions, values, and beliefs. We also have many events for our members every month, ranging from social gatherings to volunteering to professional development. We consider it a success when members don't need Tulsa Remote to love life in Tulsa, which will also ultimately lead them to stay in the city long term."[21] Through curated programming that is conscious of building an inclusive and engaged culture, TR is creating a strong remote community. The culture- and community-building events help explain TR's high retention rates.

To make the program self-sustaining, ensuring a steady stream of talent for years to come, GKFF worked with the Oklahoma legislature to draw on state incentives. GKFF takes on the initial program costs, but were a remoter to stay, then the state would pay TR back through the Oklahoma Quality Jobs Incentive Program, which provides "companies creating at least $2.5 million worth of jobs . . . a quarterly payment of 5% of payroll for up to ten years."[22] This relationship is a great example of how the social sector can de-risk economic development and work with the public sector to sustain a mutually beneficial program.

And as you might have noticed, many of the remoters work in tech-related roles. When you're trying to build an inclusive innovation economy, it isn't easy to pull in highly skilled tech workers if you don't have the local corporations or start-ups to support them. Recruiting remote workers is the quickest and most efficient workaround for this, one that can provide a jump start for your tech ecosystem. In more mature tech hubs, workforce developers often try to skate to where the puck is going by producing talent to support *future* needs; but if that is slow to arrive, cities risk losing that talent for good. Remote work is an ideal way to keep talent "in reserve" in your community for when local opportunities do arise.

Member Profiles

I've encountered dozens of remoters throughout Tulsa, at restaurants and bars, business events, baseball games, or concerts—they're everywhere, particularly clustering downtown. Without fail, I am always impressed by the quality of members, each of whom seems to have a more interesting story than the next. Still, many will find it difficult to fathom who would pick up and move from Denver or San Diego to come to Tulsa—all for $10,000. But hearing from people directly about their experiences helped me understand essential elements of the American story. The recurring themes I hear from Tulsa Remoters for why they moved include cost of living, the ability to buy a home, the support to start a new business, and a stronger sense of community—all of which they see as important to their personal and professional lives and to their families' well-being. These themes illustrate people's changing needs and desires regarding where they live—needs and desires that, as these anecdotes and the success of TR demonstrate, are well met by Tulsa . . . and the other Heartland cities that follow suit. Here are a few of the remoters' stories:

Laura Landers (moved from Los Angeles, California). Landers found her mental health hitting rock bottom after the pandemic. She and her husband had lived in LA for a decade, but they spent an outrageous amount on their small apartment. "We knew it was time to move, and that's when I found #TulsaRemote through a Google search. Two months after we moved, my mental health drastically improved. I finally started building my streetwear fashion label, a dream I've had since I was twelve. It's been incredibly fulfilling to pour my creative energy into building my business, and I've connected with tons of other Tulsa creatives, which has made me feel connected to the city's creative heartbeat."[23]

J. Montana Cain (moved from Columbia, South Carolina). Cain believes her move to Tulsa was one of the best decisions she's ever made. "I've grown my personal and professional networks, and I genuinely feel like I have been able to find my people. The most powerful thing about moving to Tulsa is the opportunity I've had to be among many Black founders and business owners. The spirit of Black Wall Street is here and present. Since I moved in March 2021, I have pursued my dreams of entrepreneurship and founded JMC Consulting Firm. This would not have been possible had I not been in Tulsa because of the resources and support of organizations like Tulsa Remote, New U, Build in Tulsa, and 36 Degrees North [now Gradient]. I'm now part of Build in Tulsa's Launchpad program and am learning to build a strong foundation for my business alongside other founders."[24]

Lawrence MacAlpine (moved from Wells, Maine). Some remoters provide unique or unexpected value to the community. For example, MacAlpine moved to Tulsa with his wife, Breanna, as a cybersecurity engineering and compliance professional. But in 2021, they established Sourdough Tulsa. They now sell their bread by subscription at Gradient and other outlets. They also bake bread for a local nonprofit called the Common Good, which supports families in northwest Tulsa. MacAlpine explains, "We're all about community, and it's been incredible to see how baking sourdough has really provided an organic way for us to build that community in Tulsa around a shared love for bread."[25] He eventually left his job and now works as a cyber manager for the Tulsa-based Bank of Oklahoma.

As great as it is that Tulsa Remote makes a difference in individual lives, for it to be valuable as a program, it also must contribute to the city's economic and cultural growth. So does it? Answering this question takes us directly to the heart of why a remote work incentive can be a boon for Heartland cities.

Impact

Given the extraordinary interest, major media outlets including NPR, *Forbes*, the *Wall Street Journal*, *People* magazine, and CBS immediately hailed TR as a success. The *Economist*, for example, dubbed the city "a new honeypot for America's remote workers."[26] The Tulsa Remote story went viral, and for a time, the city became synonymous with remote work. This coverage helped put Tulsa on the map, bringing attention to the city's expanding innovation ecosystem. But TR wasn't just a PR coup—in its short life, the program has already contributed to the city's economy. The numbers show why.

Not only are remote workers contributing to the tax base, their presence also creates net new jobs. The Economic Innovation Group's (EIG) 2021 study of Tulsa Remote's impact found that the program's ideal candidate is highly educated, in their prime working years, and has skills for the city's in-demand industries. Remoters' average income is around $105,000 (almost double the average Tulsan's) and 88 percent have at least a bachelor's degree (double the percentage of Tulsans who do). According to EIG, "There is an estimated $13.77 boost in new local labor income for every dollar spent toward relocating a remote worker."[27] EIG found that every two remote workers relocating to Tulsa created one new job.[28] And in TR's 2023 impact study, it found that remoters have generated $560 million in direct employment income and $330 million in new labor income to the city.[29]

Another important, and often overlooked, benefit is that remote workers won't stay in their remote jobs forever, as Lawrence MacAlpine demonstrates with his move to Bank of Oklahoma. Millennials stay in their jobs an average 2.75 years,[30] while Gen Zers stay even less, at 2.25 years.[31] As people move on to new employment opportunities, they will hopefully stay in Tulsa and enter the local workforce. As TR's efforts show, it's important that remoters integrate into the ecosystem, become locals themselves, and aid in the cross-pollination of ideas and opportunities. Not only would they then become part of the city's fabric, but they would also provide cascading and enduring benefits to the ecosystem.

Political Challenges

Despite great success, Tulsa Remote still faces challenges—many of the same challenges facing the city and state in recruiting talent. For Oklahoma, the single biggest obstacle in attracting talent from outside has been its deeply conservative politics, made more challenging given the Supreme Court's 2022 ruling in *Dobbs v. Jackson Women's Health Organization*. That decision, which overturned *Roe v. Wade*, has allowed red states like Oklahoma to severely limit or eliminate access to abortion.[32] Tulsa is starting to have an even harder time recruiting women and pro-choice allies because of this and similarly controversial policies. During my time leading TIL, I met with one of Oklahoma governor Kevin Stitt's cabinet secretaries, who asked me what barriers to growth I saw for the state. I told the secretary that the state's hard-right politics turned off the coastal tech talent Tulsa was trying to recruit. The secretary grimaced and moved on to another line of conversation.

Though TR's recruiting and yield metrics remain strong, Oklahoma's political and cultural issues also turn off prospective members of color. TR wants to bring in diverse workers, but the Harvard Business School's case study of the program highlighted that many of those who turn down the offer are Black men.[33] It's hard not to attribute this to the city's past racial trauma, not to mention its present issues—like being ranked seventh-highest for rates of fatal police incidents per capita in 2020.[34] Oklahoma's record on Native American and Black civil rights is dreadful, so the concerns people of color may have about moving to the city are understandable—and TIL struggled recruiting Black candidates from outside the state as well.

TR was one of the earliest and most visible signs of change in Tulsa. Hundreds of outsiders, mostly from the coasts, regularly came to town; it was bound to cause tension. Tulsa has since found itself in a paradox: the city signals inclusivity and diversity to attract tech talent, but this virtue signaling—and real investments to back it up—can put it at odds with the Republican-led state government and the broader perception about Oklahoma's inclusiveness. One state legislator, for instance, reportedly accused TR of "importing liberals" through the program. While there is a certain amount of backlash, economic development tends to be bipartisan; hence the state's support for the program.

This dynamic is not uncommon; it reveals the urban–rural divide seen in red and blue states alike. But no matter Tulsans' personal views, building an innovation economy shouldn't be overtly or even particularly political. TR and TIL make a bipartisan case for inclusive growth while remaining true to and proud of our values, which inform the design of our programs.

I do worry that the state's politics will be its Achilles' heel, with self-inflicted legislative wounds turning off talent, in state and out. If the state of Oklahoma—and other Heartland states, for that matter—wants to support economic development, it should take mainstream positions on hot button political issues and recognize that decisions to placate their most fervent base sends chilling signals to the very talent they're trying to attract. Yet despite state politics, TR continues to be a success.

BECOME A STATUE OF LIBERTY CITY (FOR CODERS)

At the 2022 Bloomberg CityLab conference in Amsterdam, three Ukrainian mayors, Anatoliy Fedoruk of Bucha, Andriy Sadovyi of Lviv, and Vitali Klitschko of Kyiv, spoke about what it's like to lead cities in wartime. The complexity and scale of their challenges and their courage and determination in the face of the Russian assault deeply moved me. Democracy during the last several years has felt so fragile, and to have a land war in Europe in 2022 seemed like the undercurrent of authoritarianism had finally burst. It renewed my sense that we need to diligently protect American ideals at home and defend American interests abroad.

To do so, America must maximize its innovation potential, and Heartland cities need to attract all the tech talent they can. With the crisis in Ukraine and elsewhere, many talented workers need a safe and accommodating space. Supporting PhD and other STEM talent from vulnerable backgrounds, from anywhere around the globe, is a win-win: cities support a group in need and, in turn, benefit from their talent and labor. But the H1-B visa process is time-consuming, the odds are long, and immigrants often struggle to go through the process by themselves. For cities looking to bolster their tech talent, an additional solution is to attract, support, integrate, and retain immigrant STEM talent, most of whom can work remotely. Supporting immigrant talent can position cities as a Statue of Liberty for those who can speak the universal language of coding.

America was built by immigrants, including enslaved ones, and today, immigrants remain critical players in US tech and innovation. According to the George W. Bush Center, some of the cities that rank strongest in immigrant well-being are also major tech centers, including San Jose, San Francisco, Seattle, and DC.[35] In the United States, nearly 19 percent of the workforce are immigrants,[36] but they hold about 25 percent of all US patents and have founded about a quarter of all recent start-ups; they are also disproportionately likely to hold STEM degrees.[37] At the same time, foreign-born STEM PhDs are 56 percent less likely to be able to work for US start-ups despite applying for jobs with them at the same rates as domestic STEM PhDs.[38] Given language barriers and limited labor market opportunities, many immigrants start their own businesses.

CASE STUDY: INTULSA'S VISA NETWORK

Tulsa has been proactive in its outreach and support of immigrants, and, as it does with Tulsa Remote, it provides an example other Heartland cities could emulate. Much of the reason for this stems from George Kaiser's personal values and background and the sizable Jewish community in Tulsa. Kaiser comes from a Jewish family. His father lost his job because of his religion, and he and his wife and daughter escaped Nazi Germany in the late 1930s. After a brief stint in England, Kaiser's parents immigrated to the United States in 1940, settling in Oklahoma, where some of the senior Kaiser's family already lived. Shortly thereafter, the senior Kaiser and his family started the Kaiser-Francis Oil Company. And in 1942, George Kaiser was born in Tulsa; he would go on to take over the family business in 1969. This upbringing has helped shape the George Kaiser Family Foundation, which has long supported immigrant communities in northeast Oklahoma.

To attract immigrant STEM talent to Tulsa and provide direct assistance to those fleeing Ukraine, as well as to support them once they land there, the GKFF-supported talent-matching organization inTulsa created a visa network. The program offers free support in the visa process to immigrants looking to seek refuge in the US or become US citizens. Though started to support Ukrainians, it has since expanded and is now open to any qualified immigrant, prioritizing those with programming-language skills.

Successful candidates receive relocation support, such as transportation and temporary housing, and then, as in Tulsa Remote, get support with integrating into the community. According to a *Wall Street Journal* podcast, as of April 2023, fifteen individuals have gone through the inTulsa program, so it's still a small-scale effort in its early days.[39]

One of inTulsa's participants, Andrii Skorniakov, a data engineer and a Ukrainian citizen, fled Kyiv when Russia attacked, leaving behind a son, who enlisted in the military. Skorniakov explained to me how he ended up in Tulsa: "First we got to our relatives in France. They provided us with some temporary dwelling. . . . But then we decided that we have to move on to find something more reliable, more stable for us. Because children grow, they want something to do, they want new friends. . . . And then I came across this group of people on Facebook. They discussed this opportunity to find a sponsor and to go to the United States with this Uniting for Ukraine program [a refugee program of the US Citizenship and Immigration Services]. And I have posted a message in this group about our family, but nobody actually get in touch with us. But one woman, I don't remember her name, but she told me that you can go in other way. . . . She told me that there are a lot of programs in United States, but she actually suggested the inTulsa program to me. I just went to the [inTulsa] website and just filled the form."

InTulsa offered Skorniakov and his family assistance in finding a job as well as funding to live for the first three months. This included airline tickets for the whole family and rent. Skorniakov already had a job from his stint in France at an energy tech company called Oseberg and could work remotely. The original agreement with the Uniting for Ukraine program ends in December 2024, so Skorniakov is already working with inTulsa to try and secure a visa or temporary protection status that would allow him and his family to stay in America. inTulsa is guiding him through the process, and he's also applied for a green card through his employer.

So how does Skorniakov like living in Tulsa, a world away from his home country? "Here you have a lot of space around; it's not crowded," he said. "The traffic is very low. So I like it very much. I believe that it's safer. And people . . . always want to help you. If you ask for help, they always provide help for you. It's very good. I like it very much. And I believe that our neighborhood is very good for children. We can just walk around, we can go anywhere, and I can just let them go and walk around without fearing that they will get in trouble."[40]

Of course, it's one thing to attract immigrant STEM talent but another to connect them to local jobs. The power of visa support programs like Tulsa's isn't in getting needed STEM talent to the city but in connecting them to the community and supporting them in becoming active members of the ecosystem—that's how you can see catalytic benefits for the local economy. Skorniakov, for example, is on the Techlahoma Slack channel and is getting involved in local events. Visas are often temporary, so the federal government needs to do more to ensure that immigrants like Skorniakov can stay in Tulsa if they wish. Tulsa needs Skorniakov and other immigrant talent contributing to its economy but also working with start-ups, corporations, and investors to develop technological innovations. And America needs all the tech talent she can get to compete with China and Russia. For your city, a visa support service could complement a broader remote work incentive program. Such a remote work program will require you to understand and communicate your city's value proposition to outside tech talent.

DEFINE YOUR VALUE PROPOSITION

For Heartland cities looking to establish a remote work incentive program, you should consider building a package that articulates your community's value proposition. Tech talent with the flexibility to work anywhere are hot commodities, and it will take a compelling pitch to lure them to your city. Your value proposition must contain four elements:

Vision. Remote workers are looking for diverse and inclusive communities; they want to be part of something bigger than themselves. How you explain your city's vision—your tech identity and plan for fostering an inclusive innovation community—will be crucial. Tulsa's growing innovation economy, its investment in quality of place through amenities like the Gathering Place, and even the city's efforts at racial reconciliation help paint a picture of Tulsa's vision, one that people considering a move can easily grasp. While I didn't participate in TR, I knew I wanted to be part of the city the moment I visited because, collectively, big things were happening, and it was a chance to get involved and make an impact.

Cash Incentive. TR provides $10,000, but incentives vary by program. For example, a program in Vermont offers up to $7,500, while West Virginia provides $12,000, and Topeka, Kansas, and southwest Michigan offer $15,000. TR also offers to apply its cash incentive, which they pay out in installments, to a mortgage, helping members buy a home. In a survey by Bankrate, it found most Gen Zers and millennials saw homeownership as a milestone in achieving the American Dream, and three-quarters of Gen Z respondents and 69 percent of millennials said they would consider moving to a different state if they could purchase a home.[41] Don't sweat the amount too much: TR has found that minor increases in cash incentives don't lead to higher yield rates. If you provide a base level of financial support—based on cost of living and what you think it'll take to get people's attention—you'll be able to complement your other offerings.

Cost of Living Data. Your city's cost of living data is a key selling point for remote workers, as rising costs are a major driver for people looking to leave their current cities. Tulsa, for example, has a 40 percent lower cost of living than big cities like Boston across all areas, including food, housing, transportation, and health care. Average rent ($658 in Tulsa; $2,669 in Boston), median home price

($157,000 in Tulsa; $800,000 in Boston[42]), and average commute time (18 minutes in Tulsa; 32.6 minutes in Boston[43]) should be key planks in your messaging. While vision helps tell your city's story, quantitative data will make the business case for why a move to your city is in prospects' financial best interest.

Community-Building Events. One main reason people are interested in leaving big cities is a lack of community. The World Economic Forum found that "being in overcrowded environments increased loneliness by up to 38 percent."[44] There are several reasons why, including transience, technology, and work-life balance issues.[45] With increased mental illness and social isolation, young people in particular are searching for community. "What should young people do with their lives today?" writer Kurt Vonnegut asked. "Many things, obviously. But the most daring thing is to create stable communities in which the terrible disease of loneliness can be cured."[46] Remote work incentive programs should put a premium on community building. As Harlan explained, not only does TR offer members the chance to work in person together at Gradient, but it also holds a variety of meetups and outings, such as lunches, cultural excursions, and events like hiking, tubing, and camping. To forge synergies with your city's cluster strategy, remote work initiatives should consider developing special subgroups related to priority industries, such as one for cyber professionals, or for identity affiliations, which could create further community.

To maximize the value of a remote work community, cities should also pursue corporate attraction opportunities that build on or are adjacent to remote work.

MAXIMIZE RELATED OPPORTUNITIES

While remote work is getting easier thanks to new technologies, and Heartland cities should incentivize remote workers to move to their towns, they should not overlook other related opportunities for growth. Don't think about remote work as an isolated investment or economic development instrument. Cities can and should leverage a remote work incentive as part of their broader efforts to develop an innovation ecosystem, which includes recruiting remoters within your tech niche and leveraging the remote work incentive to attract corporations.

Cities should design their remote work incentive program to align with their tech niche's workforce needs, prioritizing the recruitment of talent essential to their clusters. For too long, Tulsa Remote and Tulsa Innovation Labs have operated without any strategic coordination. Despite some efforts, they need to do more. TIL and TR should launch a joint campaign, which could focus on recruiting cyber workers, for example. As one of Tulsa's "right to win" opportunities, cyber is a critical enabler of the city's virtual health, energy tech, and advanced air mobility ecosystems. By leveraging TR's recruitment channels and TIL's cyber initiatives, Tulsa could target cyber professionals who can work remotely. Focusing on select geographies and specific companies, the campaign could shine a light on Tulsa's growing cyber ecosystem. Although this approach wouldn't fill immediate job openings, it could grow the labor pool over time and source potential mentors, investors, and entrepreneurs who can contribute to the ecosystem's vitality. Tulsa should conduct similar campaigns for other high-demand occupations. TR and TIL have complementary missions and their respective work can and should be mutually beneficial.

Tulsa should also take steps to attract remote-first companies and companies that enable remote work or learning. Although such an effort hasn't taken hold in Tulsa yet, the possibilities are there. There's a growing list of new and established firms whose workforce is primarily remote. Established examples include Bandcamp, Invision, Automattic, and Stripe, but there are hundreds of growing start-ups that work remotely. And remote-enabling companies—those making the hardware, software, and infrastructure needed for communications and educational platforms—should also be targets. It might be a tough sell to attract Zoom, Microsoft Teams, Google Chats, or Slack, but countless start-ups are looking to be their competition—and those established companies have partners across the value chain that may be looking for a new home.

With COVID, not only did working shift online, but learning did, too, so don't overlook ed tech and future-of-work companies. There are also start-ups in the wider world of remote work, such as Pivt, a digital platform that helps workers relocate to a new community. Pivt recently expanded their offerings to economic development–related initiatives, including at Tulsa Remote, to help attract and guide remote workers to their new communities.[47] They function as a shared resource for Tulsa Remoters.

If you think of remote work as part of a broader strategy, adjacent opportunities like these will help your flywheel spin and civic reinvention happen. But as with most economic development investments, there can be unintended consequences. Remote work comes with its own set of hazards that you should not ignore. Anticipating these risks will help cities create impactful remote work incentives while mitigating negative downstream effects.

PROCEED WITH CAUTION

Although I have benefited personally and professionally from the flexibility remote work affords, I continue to have mixed feelings about it. As a team leader, I see the pros and cons of its effect on productivity. And, as an urbanist, I can't help but think about its impact on how communities form, downtowns thrive, and innovation happens. While it seems safe to say that remote work is now a cultural norm, be skeptical of anyone who claims to know how remote work policies will evolve in the coming decade, especially with AI just now entering businesses. Attracting remote workers, therefore, is a safe bet in the short to medium term, but you should be prepared to counter the following potential side effects as well.

Social Disruption. While on a team visit to Greenwood Rising, the museum commemorating the Tulsa Race Massacre, the question of reparations for victims' families came up. Our tour guide had no idea I was the founder of TIL or that we were funded by GKFF, which also supports Tulsa Remote. During the tour, she mentioned, offhandedly, that it was a shame Tulsa was willing to spend $10,000 on "outsiders from across the country" but that the city didn't want to offer reparations to victims of the massacre. The same could be said for getting the homeless off the streets with a home, cash, or treatment. The tension between local and external investment is real, and it's bound to arise as cities start to see change. Instead of giving $10,000 to someone to move to Tulsa, why not give $10,000 to Tulsans to upskill into tech jobs? Such debates are healthy, and I see where they're coming from. But attracting external talent doesn't need to come at the expense of investing locally, and you'll need to actively combat the perception that it does—and demonstrate that you're also making robust investments for existing residents.

Effects on Downtowns. With the rise of remote work, bustling city centers and the local businesses that make them a draw have felt the squeeze now that their employees don't commute like they used to. DC, LA, San Francisco, and New York were particularly hard hit during the pandemic. For example, in Washington, a large federal workforce as well as law, consulting, and lobbying firms have gone at least partially remote. This loss of activity has led to a decline in the value of office buildings, which will mean less tax revenue. DC mayor Muriel Bowser took the extraordinary step in her third inaugural address of calling for "decisive action" to bring "most federal workers back to the office most of the time."[48] The Urban Land Institute's *Emerging Trends* report for 2024, the survey of the real estate industry, ranked remote work as the third most important disruptor, above AI and natural disasters.[49] Any city's downtown could end up in trouble if they aren't careful to track how remote work affects commercial real estate and housing prices. In terms of real estate, clustering of people and companies is important to urban dynamism, and unused office space could make for great wet labs or start-up incubators.

Remote Innovation. With many more working from home, people and their teams are more likely to create silos. The question becomes, how do you innovate remotely? At the city and neighborhood scale, Jane Jacobs advocated for the cross-pollination of people and ideas, but the principle holds true in business too. This is a challenge for Big Tech and start-ups alike. Both need to recognize that their workforce wants flexibility and a higher quality of life even as innovation requires, I think, in-person collaboration. Plus, Big Tech's sprawling campuses are expensive and no longer sustainable and do not reflect the workforce's changing contours. Google and Meta, for instance, are shrinking their Silicon Valley presence. This trend should encourage Big Tech to establish smaller offices throughout the Heartland; another viable alternative would be to return to shared workspaces. Midsized cities like Tulsa can foster in-person innovation because their real estate is affordable, and it is easy to cluster start-ups and organizations into innovation districts.

Companies are still sorting out their remote work policies, with some returning to the office at least in part, but Heartland cities need to seize this opportunity and create a comprehensive strategy for attracting and retaining remote workers. As Tulsa Remote has shown, it is a real asset and one that is only growing in power: by 2025, TR is estimated to add $500 million in new earnings and support nearly five thousand jobs—including thousands of remote workers and at least fifteen hundred net new local jobs.[50] But attracting remote workers is no substitute for investing in local talent. A remote work incentive can accelerate the import of much needed tech talent—but once you put this in place, it's time to turn your attention to developing the bulk of your homegrown workforce.

ACTION PLAN SUMMARY		
REINVENTION *What needs reinventing?*	**GROWTH** *How do you catalyze growth?*	**INCLUSION** *How do you advance inclusion?*
The pandemic has changed how and where people work. Cities now need to rethink their talent-attraction efforts and create new tools to capture and retain the growing remote worker population.	Cities should build an incentive program to attract remote workers. To do so, they should define their value proposition, including their overall vision for the city, offer a cash payment, share cost of living data, and hold community-building events. They should also leverage their remote work community by pursuing adjacent opportunities, such as helping skilled immigrants secure their work visas and attracting remote work–related companies.	Not only should remote work incentive programs strive to create diverse cohorts, but they should also help remoters create affinity groups so people feel welcomed and can build community.

CHAPTER 5

UPSKILL AT MACH SPEED

(WORKFORCE DEVELOPMENT)

To better serve its growing East Coast market, in 2020, Tesla began searching for a site in the Heartland to build what founder Elon Musk called his biggest "Gigafactory" yet. This manufacturing plant would produce Tesla's new Cybertruck, an all-electric vehicle Musk colorfully coined the "North American ass-kicker."[1] The company's Fremont, California, and Reno, Nevada, plants employ ten thousand and sixty-five hundred workers, respectively, which meant that this new plant would bring several thousand highly skilled workers to wherever it ended up—making it a highly desirable prize for any city, but especially to one in the middle of the country.[2] Because of Musk's bizarre persona, the novelty of the Cybertruck, and its potential economic impact, the plant represented the highest-profile corporate attraction effort since Amazon's search for a second headquarters back in 2017–18.

I had been in New York during the Amazon HQ2 saga, however, and as Tulsa prepared to chase the Gigafactory, I knew that the process of pursuing corporations reveals a city's underlying strengths and weaknesses and tests the ecosystem's ability to coordinate.

Two Heartland contenders emerged, and in May 2020, Tesla announced the finalists: Austin and Tulsa—one a no-brainer and the other a surprising underdog. With twenty unicorns and counting, Austin was a veritable tech powerhouse.[3] Tulsa, on the other hand, was foreign to Tesla's board, and we were just beginning the long process of building the city's tech bona fides. But Tulsa could offer affordable land as well as energy and manufacturing assets that made it a viable candidate for the multimillion-square-foot plant. With Tesla announcing Tulsa a finalist in May and TIL launching our tech-niche strategy in June, the timing couldn't have been better: the Gigafactory would have been a major feather in our cap and a powerful catalyst for the tech transformation we hoped to achieve.

Tulsa marshaled its underdog spirit, formed a regional coalition, and launched a creative marketing campaign in the hopes of beating out Austin. Besides developing financial incentives, gathering requisite data, and documenting relevant assets, Tulsa stakeholders created the "Big Fucking Field" website to promote the prospective location of the plant (a nod to the "Big Fucking Rocket" Musk was building at SpaceX). The website showcased the field and gave it a character of its own, becoming something of a local legend. Tulsans held impromptu parades of Teslas around town, and they repainted the Golden Driller statue to be wearing a Tesla T-shirt.[4] The enthusiasm was contagious, and it was inspiring to see the city, chamber, GKFF, and others work together on such an ambitious pursuit.

Tesla ultimately selected Austin for their billion-dollar plant,[5] bringing some twenty thousand jobs to the city as of 2023.[6] But even though we didn't win, the competition gave Tulsa a national spotlight and the confidence it needed to continue its journey of reinvention—a belief that it could compete at the national level and be attractive to tech hardware companies, which are ideal for the Heartland, where land and labor are affordable. It was a major PR win, and it was a great exercise in cross-sector collaboration, demonstrating hustle, pride, and determination all over Tulsa. There's nothing like a big challenge to rally the community around, and the pursuit seemed to bring the ecosystem together.

My experience in New York during the Amazon drama was a different story. The New York City Economic Development Corporation was the lead agency for coordinating the New York region's bid, and my Cyber NYC team contributed subject matter expertise to the main task force. New York brought to bear unparalleled assets to successfully woo Amazon: a high concentration of diverse tech talent, waterfront property well suited for a potential corporate campus, and robust financial incentives. In November 2018, Amazon announced New York and Arlington, Virginia, the winners. But politics caused the win to unravel for New York, with intense backlash against the use of public incentives and hostility toward Amazon itself. The opposition fomented by Congresswoman Alexandria Ocasio-Cortez and the misinformation about the $3.5 billion incentive package (most of which was in tax credits based on job creation targets, not giveaways) helped scuttle the deal.[7] This is to say nothing of the rancorous bickering between local and state politicians or Amazon's reportedly "my way or the highway" attitude that left little room for negotiation or patience for politics. The company's fraught relationship with its Seattle home is well-documented, giving Amazon a reputation for not being friendly to local governments or communities.[8]

When New York fell through, Amazon doubled down on its second winner, Arlington, an urban suburb of DC. And with that, the New York region reportedly lost out on forty thousand jobs and some $27.5 billion in tax revenues.[9] Going from victor to vanquished was stunning. Neither Tulsa nor New York ended up winning their contests. But for Tulsa, it was a positive experience, while no matter which side you were on, it turned sour for New York—showing the wide range of how such stories can play out, and why you should always view such pursuits with some suspicion.

Attracting corporations holds a peculiar interest for cities. As with the Amazon case, these efforts have drawn criticism for the lengths that cities go to and the complicated, sometimes sweetheart financial deals offered to companies, which often include massive tax breaks. On the other hand, the allure of these projects is clear, especially for cities with vulnerable industrial economies—these corporations can bring with them instant jobs, tax revenue, and growth potential that would take considerably longer to generate from scratch. I can understand the thrill of the hunt for economic developers and civic leaders. But attracting corporations can sometimes feel like a game companies concoct to encourage suitors to beg for their attention, creating a frenzy that leads some cities to go to absurd lengths. (Chicago hired William Shatner for a promo video to charm *Star Trek* fan Jeff Bezos, for example.)[10] In these competitions, cities are pitted against each other to go lower and lower on taxes, creating a "race to the bottom" in which the companies come out on top.

Worse, attracting corporations can sometimes come at the expense of investing locally, as resources required to recruit external businesses can be diverted from investments in local infrastructure, public services, and educational programs—the very assets that draw new companies to town in the first place.

I also believe that, whenever you do try to attract corporations, it should typically be in service of your tech niche. Tulsa was a finalist for the Cybertruck plant because the plant aligned with Tulsa's existing assets as well as with TIL's future-oriented vision. But Tulsa's flirtation with Tesla taught me an even bigger lesson about what cities should prioritize.

Both the Amazon and Tesla cases offer the same powerful lesson for cities. Austin, New York, and Arlington won for the same reason: each had an evergreen source of engineering talent the companies needed, both quantity and quality. As the head of partnerships for NYCEDC at the time, Mark Anthony Thomas was one of the leads for the Amazon HQ2 bid. Now the president and CEO of the Greater Baltimore Committee, Thomas said that New York "offered an unprecedented talent pool to fuel [Amazon's] expansion." He noted that cities of all sizes should "define the assets that make them attractive to the tech companies' needs immediately *and* in the future."[11] Companies like Amazon and Tesla see such bids as long-term investments and will want to grow with their new community.

And if you've got the engineering talent, oftentimes companies will come anyway, even if you don't win the Bake-Off: that's the power of such an asset. Amazon, for example, has continued to grow in New York, even opening a new office in the old Lord & Taylor building in midtown[12] and expanding its partnership with the City University of New York (CUNY).[13]

Attracting corporations is rarely about money or the right PR campaign or who wants it the most. It's about another capital altogether: human capital. Kian Kamas led Tesla efforts for the city of Tulsa, and she recalls a question that a senior member of the Tesla team asked her: "*How can you assure me that the world's best engineers, not just great engineers but the world's best engineers, want to live in Tulsa?*" "And I think that's ultimately what it boils down to," she told me.[14] This was a harsh reality check: even if Tulsa did have the cash to throw at Big Tech companies to incentivize them to set up shop, it simply didn't yet have the talent they needed, and that was more important than money. The city also didn't have the reputation for being fun and cool like Austin does, a cache that helps attract and retain in-demand talent. But while this may have been the right question for Tesla to ask of Tulsa, it's not the right question for cities to ask of themselves.

I don't recommend tailoring your workforce development strategy to any one company, especially not one currently in your city; doing so may be counterproductive. Having the world's best engineers can't be the standard. Cybertruck plants are rare opportunities, and the winners will be cities like Austin with the engineering talent already available. Instead, when considering how to kick-start an innovation economy, ask yourself: How can you develop the talent you need to meet local needs, spur growth in your clusters, and become more attractive to external firms? And how can you do it within five years?

For your city, upskilling incumbent workers may be the path of least resistance to developing the talent you need for an innovation economy. Your city's role is to create upskilling programs that can scale as quickly as possible and help those workers pivot to opportunities aligned with your tech niche.

With that timeline in mind, I have three words for you: *forget the kids.* If you're looking to spark an innovation economy in the short term, the K–12 pipeline is simply too long. Instead, you need to focus on the immediate goals that are central to your strategy, developing the talent your industry clusters need to grow today.

TIL's workforce strategy, therefore, prioritized immediate needs over long-term investments and targeted interventions over ecosystem-wide efforts (an exception to my general rule). For Tulsa, the solution was to upskill its existing workforce. The incumbent workforce is a key asset; they outnumber individuals at or near college age and offer a huge source of potential tech talent. Many of these workers have bachelor's degrees and all of them have transferable skills that can be applied to tech-related jobs in your clusters.

Austin's success proves how transformative a high-quality and voluminous talent pool is to a city's economy and why other Heartland cities need to move with speed and scale to develop a skilled workforce. So, before diving into how to do that, let's learn more about why Tesla chose Austin over Tulsa.

CASE STUDY: AUSTIN'S TALENT ENGINE

The first time I visited Austin was to speak at South by Southwest EDU. It was 2022 and, appropriately enough, I was on a panel about building innovation hubs outside Silicon Valley. SXSW was every bit as exciting as I imagined. The conference has been an important contributor to the buzz Austin's earned over the past twenty years as it grew into a tech hub.

Today, Austin has expanded beyond its original focus on semiconductor chips, which gave rise to Motorola, Dell, and 3M in the city during the dot-com boom of the late '90s. Since then, Austin has developed a more diverse tech ecosystem and rapidly grown its population, nearly doubling the metropolitan statistical area from 2000 to 2020 to more than 2.2 million people.[15] A 2023 study by McKinsey found that from 2010 to 2022, the city outpaced its Texas sister cities as well as "high-growth peers," such as Nashville, Salt Lake City, and Raleigh on cumulative real GPD growth, cumulative population growth, cumulative productivity growth, GPD per worker, labor force participation rate, unemployment rate, and median household income—astounding findings.[16]

But despite its unprecedented growth, Austin is on a troubling trajectory, proving that tech-based economies can have unintended consequences. Rather than unicorns, start-up exits, or ground-breaking innovations, dominating recent press are structural inequality, rising rents, and traffic, creating a less positive brand. As gentrification and related issues continue to worsen, the city once known as an enclave of the "weird" is turning into a Lone Star retreat for the wealthy. A 2019 study, "The Racial Wealth Divide in Austin," revealed glaring disparities. For example, Black median income increased only $3,500 in thirty-six years, while Latino median income rose less than $2,000. Read that again—$3,500 and $2,000 in thirty-six years. Meanwhile, the city's overall median income rose more than $12,000.[17] Austin got wealthier and whiter as population increases for people of color slowed and their median income growth quickly tapered off. Like Pittsburgh, San Francisco, and New York, Austin's innovation economy is benefiting the same privileged class and embodying "dumb growth." To be fair to those New Yorkers who opposed Amazon HQ2, they didn't want Queens to turn into Austin, and with good reason.

So how do other midsized cities emulate the good parts of Austin's success while minimizing the bad? The answer is complicated, but it first requires identifying what it is that makes Austin exceptional. Although Austin has outgrown its initial semiconductor niche, it still maintains a strong tech brand. That's because Austin *does* have a tech identity; it just happens to be slightly different from the kind we've been discussing so far, and it adds another useful wrinkle to how your city might conceive its tech niche. If handled correctly, this element can provide the opportunity to build not just an innovation economy but an *inclusive* innovation economy.

Austin's tech identity? Engineering talent—the very thing that helped it beat out Tulsa for the Tesla factory. Now, engineering talent is less of a tech cluster and more of a horizontal enabler, but it still requires a concentration of assets, and it doesn't make it any less of a game changer. The University of Texas-Austin's Cockrell School of Engineering produces an enormous number of graduates each year, with nearly two thousand students completing degrees across disciplines and levels annually,[18] including 275 undergraduate computer engineers in 2021–22 alone. For perspective, the University of Tulsa's *total enrollment* was 3,769 in 2023.[19] UT-Austin's volume of engineering talent is staggering, but its quality is also impressive: nine undergraduate programs are ranked in the top twenty by *U.S. News & World Report,* while twelve graduate programs are ranked.[20] This is Austin's competitive advantage. Talent fuels (and attracts) nearly everything, and UT-Austin is an engine powering the city and luring companies like Tesla. To support more inclusive growth, Austin needs to triple down on building pathways to UT-Austin and other education and training programs specifically for people of color, while also addressing housing and transportation pressures.

John Berkowitz, the Austin-based founder and CEO of the real estate tech platform OJO, acknowledged UT-Austin as a critical asset to the ecosystem, but he also pointed to the company Trilogy as creating a "talent oasis that started the [Austin] flywheel," helping to form an ecosystem where his company could succeed.[21] As a new software company in the early 1990s, Trilogy recruited top-notch talent both from UT-Austin and from outside Texas, Berkowitz told me. Not only did Trilogy hire amazing young talent, but the company's intensive onboarding and talent development system, called Trilogy University, developed them once they got there. Inspired by the Marine Corps's basic training, the program was called a "best practice" with "phenomenal results" by *Harvard Business Review.*[22] As Trilogy's business excelled and staff turned over, many of its alumni stayed in Austin, going on to create start-ups of their own (they're called the "Trilogy Mafia").

As impressive as Austin's nurturing of engineering talent is, cities shouldn't be overwhelmed by it. Rather, when they look at Austin and Pittsburgh, other Heartland cities should fully commit to investing in local talent. That'll require expanding the capacity of your engineering school, if you have one, and most importantly, creating upskilling opportunities at Mach speed for your existing workforce. To do so, you'll need to prioritize the jobs you're trying to fill in your tech clusters.

DETERMINE PRIORITY OCCUPATIONS

Before you start upskilling as many people as you can, it's important to determine the most critical jobs in your clusters—those most in demand from existing employers and resilient to future disruptions. Your city's tech niche is based largely on future growth, which means that resilience to projected disruptions—especially automation—should have been factored in already. (Some databases even have an automation risk metric that allows you to toggle and see which roles are more prone to automation than others.)

Several elements should inform how you select your priority occupations, including current assets, local demand, and nuances within each cluster. Workforce development cannot be everything, everywhere, all at once. Heartland cities need to take the same targeted approach to workforce as they did with their industry cluster strategy.

One simple exercise you should conduct is to list the most in-demand occupations within each of your clusters. Doing so will allow you to see which occupations have the most crossover. For example, in Tulsa, a sizable lack of software engineers, as well as many local companies clamoring for help to fill those jobs, led GKFF to fund the Atlas School. Originally part of the Bay Area–based Holberton franchise, which teaches full stack development through a peer learning model, Atlas has graduated more than 120 students since its launch in 2020. The table that follows shows the most needed jobs within each of Tulsa's primary clusters from a national perspective (where possible, you'll also want to drill down to local needs to get more specific).

In Tulsa, I've noticed the impulse to create a new workforce program for each need or gap, but like economic development more broadly, you'll need to focus and prioritize. Select a handful of priority occupations and build out your city's production of them. Identifying common workforce needs will help you create efficient programs that benefit multiple clusters. To demonstrate, I've selected software engineer, data scientist, and cybersecurity analyst (highlighted below) as the priority occupations. You'll then want to break down each occupation by skills. Zooming in on these three roles will illustrate how to build the skills taxonomy, a list of necessary skills, needed to create training programs.

TOP OCCUPATIONS IN TULSA'S TECH CLUSTERS

Virtual Health[23]	Energy Tech[24]	Advanced Air Mobility[25]	Cyber[26]	Analytics[27]
Health Information Technologist	Data Analyst	Drone Pilot	*Cybersecurity Analyst*	Business Analyst
Medical and Health Services Manager	*Data Scientist*	Drone Technician	Network Engineer	Data Architect
Medical Scientist	Maintenance Technician	Electrical Engineer	Security Engineer	Data Engineer
Medical Technologist	Software Developer	Operations Coordinator	*Software Engineer*	*Data Scientist*
Virtual Health Care Advocate	*Software Engineer*	*Software Engineer*	Systems Engineer	Systems Analyst

Note: These are tech-focused jobs and exclude back office or support functions. The table is based on a composite of sources and has been adjusted by the author.

BUILD A SKILLS TAXONOMY

Creating a skills taxonomy for each occupation will help you understand how to train for select jobs. Job titles, roles, and particular business functions change more than the skills needed for those positions. For long-term job security, people need to focus on the skills they have today, anticipate the skills they'll need tomorrow, and pursue additional training to make themselves future ready.

Power skills are what I consider the most valuable and durable skills now and in the foreseeable future, and they include both technical and nontechnical skills. These are the "skills to pay the bills." They can transfer and be applied to different contexts, businesses, or applications—which means cities need to have a basic understanding of the technical skills important for each of their priority occupations and the nontechnical skills that cut across occupations. Doing so will allow them to build training programs on their own or vet educational providers (those that operate training programs) to do so on their behalf, ensuring curricula meet their needs.

Using software engineers, data scientists, and cybersecurity analysts as examples, on the next page is a breakdown of the core technical skills needed for each job, according to Coursera, a pioneer in online skills training that draws on a wealth of industry data to build its offerings. You'll notice several common skills, including programming language, coding, and cloud computing.

TOP TECHNICAL SKILLS BY SELECT OCCUPATION		
Software Engineer[28]	Data Scientist[29]	Cybersecurity Analyst[30]
Coding (Python, Java, C, C++, Scala)	Programming (Python, R, SAS, SQL)	Scripting (Python)
Object-Oriented Programming	Statistics and Probability	Controls and Frameworks
Database Architecture	Data Wrangling and Database	Intrusion Detection
Agile and Scrum	Management	Network Security
Project Management	Machine Learning and	Control
Operating Systems	Deep Learning	Operating Systems
Cloud Computing	Data Visualization	Incident Response
Version Control	Cloud Computing	Cloud
Design Testing and Debugging		DevOps
		Threat Knowledge
		Regulatory Guidelines

A prevalent misperception is that technical skills are sufficient in the training of tech talent. They absolutely aren't. Nontechnical skills are just as important, and I've found in my workforce initiatives that we often need to develop these abilities when upskilling workers, particularly those from underserved backgrounds. In truth, technical skills are often easier to train for than nontechnical skills. Do you remember when you started to think critically? Do you remember who taught you how to write an email? Or to prepare for an interview or how to work in a team? Without direct exposure or parental influence, some job seekers may need support. Among the most important nontechnical skills are grit, communication, teamwork, diligence, and problem-solving. Any upskilling program should include both technical and nontechnical skills and provide students opportunities to become "ready for work," a sometimes "hidden curriculum" that includes basic professional etiquette training.

Once you've built a skills taxonomy and know the skills you need to train for, you can then build a curriculum around them. You should also check with your educational providers to make sure they incorporate these skills into their boot camps. But before you design an initiative, you need to understand quantitatively what talent you have and what you need in your region regarding those priority occupations.

ANALYZE SUPPLY AND DEMAND

When TIL was conducting a tech-niche strategy meeting, one statistic blew my mind: in 2020, in Tulsa, there were eight hundred open cyber jobs. A hushed silence fell over the room after hearing this number. I knew that demand in New York for cyber talent was nearly unlimited, and Cybersecurity Ventures estimates that some 3.4 million cyber jobs are unfilled globally.[31] Like when we learned of the lack of software engineers, recognizing such cyber demand in Tulsa was a pivotal moment. It proved that we needed to create opportunities to quickly train folks for these unfulfilled jobs, and Heartland cities need to do so as well if America is to stay competitive globally. A STEM summer camp for sixth graders wasn't going to cut it.

Again, Tulsa isn't unique. This is a nationwide problem, and not just for cyber jobs but for a host of tech roles. "America's advanced industries have been struggling, both as a nationwide sector and as local clusters—and workforce issues are a core reason," a report from Brookings explains. "The U.S. faces an economy-wide shortage of skilled workers focused on two categories of skilled professionals: first, engineers and computer scientists with four-year and advanced degrees; and second, skilled technicians with two-year degrees or less and additional on-the-job or 'earn and learn' training."[32]

But you can't put workers in these jobs until you know that the need is there. A supply-and-demand analysis is a straightforward and necessary step to properly calibrate your workforce programming and fill what is likely a serious need in your city. The analysis hinges on two questions: Who is currently producing the talent you need, and who is hiring that talent? In your asset mapping exercise from chapter 1, you've already identified higher education institutions and other educational providers. Cross-checking that list with your priority occupations and gauging quantity will give you a sense of local supply. (The presence of a school doesn't necessarily mean graduates are gaining relevant skills, so you should also engage tools such as LinkedIn's Economic Graph to know how many graduates in your area list specific in-demand skills on their profiles.) You likely also have a list of top employers in your region. Cross-checking who is hiring software engineers, data scientists, and cybersecurity analysts and at what volume and pace will give you a rough sense of demand. Utilize multiple sources to get the snapshot you need to make informed decisions about the size and shape of your workforce programs. Looking at job openings based on title, which is data offered by the US Bureau of Labor Statistics, can give you some of the information you need and will likely be more current and specific than location quotients, another analytical statistic often used.

According to inTulsa, for example, the Tulsa region has seen a 128 percent surge in job opportunities for software developers since 2015. "Software engineering is the fourth most in-demand job in the metro area and the most in-demand position for national companies working in the city. And yet, nearly half of all software engineering roles went unfilled last year," Libby Ediger, the CEO of the Atlas School, told me in 2023.[33] Hence why Atlas was built. Ediger is an Oklahoma boomerang. She went to college in DC, joined a software start-up there, and then returned home to cultivate Heartland tech talent.

The table that follows is from the state of Oklahoma's Employment Security Commission, which has tallied current and projected jobs in the three target occupations in the Tulsa metro area.

TULSA MSA DEMAND FOR KEY OCCUPATIONS[34]

Job Title/Code	2020 Jobs	2030 Projected Jobs	Total Annual Openings
Software Developers and Software Quality Assurance Analysts and Testers	2,660	3,360	2,870
Information Security Analysts (Cyber Analysts)	310	430	380
Data Scientists and Mathematical Science Occupations, All Other	160	210	180

Once you've gathered this data for your city, the rest is simple arithmetic. Is supply greater or less than demand? Where are the gaps? What are the trends to be aware of? More than likely, your city isn't producing enough talent to meet local demand (either in the aggregate, in specific occupations, or at certain experience levels). In Tulsa, most cyber roles going unfilled were for midcareer professionals at the manager level, which is harder to fill than entry-level jobs. Cities must know the particular levels of experience they need to train for. Understanding your region's supply and demand will provide insight into what employers are looking for, who is hiring, who could be potential partners, and how to right-size your upskilling programs. While you'll want to retain as many graduates locally as possible, to establish yourself as a tech hub and attract new employers you'll need a surplus of talent. This means you may lose talent to other cities in the near term as you build up local need and better synchronize supply and demand.

Labor market tools can answer the questions above, monitor your workforce needs, and help you make savvy decisions. Economic development organizations and cities are starting to employ tech-based applications to monitor their labor force, such as those offered by Lightcast. As with defining your tech niche, having access to data leads to strong decisions and wise investments instead of untargeted, low-percentage approaches. To analyze their local labor markets, Heartland cities should consider upgrading their tools. You'll need access to quality, up-to-date data that's also user-friendly. Insight-generating dashboards and programs can help you identify needs and track fluctuations over time, enabling you to refine your strategy.

INDUSTRY COLLABORATION

As I said back in the first chapter, data without local context isn't insightful or actionable. Data from national systems is only going to get you so far in understanding local supply and demand. Industry insights, directly from your city's employers, must be woven into your entire workforce development strategy. And meaningful partnerships, with industry embedded throughout the life cycle of your workforce initiatives, are a must.

That starts with having a mechanism to get industry and workforce developers in the same room. Lauren Andersen is the associate provost for careers and industry partnerships at CUNY, the largest urban public university in the country, and the former executive director of Tech Talent Pipeline. "What you need are members of the local business community who can validate what you are seeing in the data and offer useful context," she said. "For example, in New York City, the mayor established an industry partnership called the NYC Tech Talent Pipeline that brought employers to the table to help define in-demand skills and quantify industry needs."[35] Building a means to engage industry is key to getting the data and intelligence you need to create workforce programs.

For TIL, we leveraged our advisory council and conducted extensive interviews with local employers to gut check and enrich our research findings. The GKFF coalition, however, has struggled to centralize its engagement with industry on talent issues, resulting in too many extraneous conversations and limited information sharing within the coalition. If possible, the organization taking the lead in your cluster strategy should streamline engagement with industry and serve as a data repository and labor market observatory, sharing information with the wider coalition. This helps coordinate outreach and reduce partner fatigue.

It's also important to align efforts by putting industry and educational providers in conversation with one another. Tejus Kothari, a trained urban planner turned strategy consultant at BCG, specializes in future-of-work and higher education challenges and has supported Tulsa-based projects. He said there's a disconnect between how educational institutions meet the needs of industry and how industry understands and communicates those needs. Rather than providing a list of assets or programs, he recommends that "industry and education create an integrated solution" to local workforce needs.[36] For a good example, Kothari pointed to a program of the Michigan Economic Development Corporation called the Talent Action Team.

Self-described as a "concierge-level service provided for key employers" in the state of Michigan, the Talent Action Team is a public–private coalition focused on building a tech talent pipeline from Michigan's K–12 and higher education systems to in-state employers. A fundamental part of the initiative is identifying the skills and experiences that key industries, like EV, mobility, and semiconductor producers, demand most and then incorporating appropriate curricula and workforce development programs into the educational system.

Notably, the Talent Action Team helped establish the Semiconductor Talent and Automotive Research initiative, a strategic collaboration between companies KLA, Imec, and General Motors and educators at the University of Michigan and Washtenaw Community College. They intend to develop "advanced semiconductor applications for electrification and autonomous mobility."[37] As of April 2024, the initiative has built relationships with multinational mobility players like Ford, Bosch, and Aisin. Through its work, the Talent Action Team serves Michigan students, workers, and companies by creating an environment ripe for effective job matchmaking.

You now have a clear sense of priorities. You know the skills you need to train for each occupation, and you have the data to understand supply and demand. Maybe you've even created a Tech Talent Pipeline or Talent Action Team of your own to engage and support industry. You're now ready to build upskilling opportunities that connect aspiring jobseekers to the training and education they need to pivot to tech.

CREATE UPSKILLING OPPORTUNITIES

Cleaning my high school bathrooms taught me everything I needed to know about the importance of skills. To make up for the part of my tuition that scholarships didn't cover, I did work-study over the summers, assisting the custodial staff with keeping the buildings and campus tidy. There were usually a half-dozen work-study students each summer, and I remember being so embarrassed that I had to work with the custodians. I felt both invisible and highly visible. I saw how easy it was to walk past someone taking out the trash, not to even notice them, and at the same time, I felt uncomfortably exposed. I'd hide when my classmates arrived for summer camp or sports training—I envied their ability to enjoy their summers while I had to work. My mom told me to do it with a "happy heart," that I was lucky to get a good education. I wish I had been proud of my work and grateful for the opportunity, but I was resentful.

Over time, however, I built relationships with the custodians. I was typically assigned to help Ms. J. She was wonderfully kind and generous to me, sparing me the messiest of tasks. On breaks, at the side entrance of the school, she would smoke a cigarette, and we'd talk about current events and our families. When school was in session, a mule-drawn carriage would sell Roman Candy (taffy) to students right across the street on St. Charles Avenue. Ms. J and I would talk about everything happening in the world, a greatest hits of the early 2000s—OutKast's latest album, the lingering effects of the O. J. Simpson trial and Clinton impeachment, weapons of mass destruction, Tarantino films, Britney Spears, and more.

From a socioeconomic perspective, I had a lot in common with my school's custodians, and we were doing the same job that summer. But there were a couple of major differences: While I was picking up trash, I was also getting A's in school and building the skills I would need to do something else for a living. And I am also a White male, a privileged position no matter the size of my family's bank account, while most of the custodians were people of color. Ms. J worked really hard—I remember how her face fell when campers left a huge mess in the cafeteria one day—and, like my mother, she showed that there is dignity in all work and that people's self-worth shouldn't be bound to their jobs. But she never received the training that would have given her the skills to seek a different career. Skills give people a better life, and everyone deserves the opportunity to secure a good job that will allow them to support themselves and their families.

Ms. J makes me think of all the people out there waiting to be upskilled. Another is an Uber driver I once talked to in Tulsa. It was a hot August day, and my driver told me that he was a farmer who lived and worked outside the city. He said it was too hot to work that day, so he decided to get in the car and drive for Uber. He said he wanted to "just drive around and see the city." There was a wistfulness in his voice, as though the city itself was both a respite from farming and an aspirational destination. As agricultural equipment is increasingly transformed into tech tools, many of which are automated, farmers need to be upskilled. At the same time, if Uber gets its way, there won't be human drivers—so that isn't the answer. Instead, workers in threatened roles need to be deliberately channeled into the jobs you've identified—jobs with a future and a greater role to play in your ecosystem.

To create the workforce you need in the short term, cities must create upskilling programs that produce quality and diverse tech talent out of their existing populations. In designing upskilling programs, there are a few key attributes to include:

Accelerated Pace. Programs need to quickly upskill people. Boot camps, while sometimes expensive, are good models. They range in duration, from three or six months to twenty months or even longer, depending on whether it's full-time or part-time. The Atlas School, for example, is twenty months. Upskilling programs should also build in the opportunity for students to earn microcredentials as they progress through the curriculum; this can motivate them through short-term wins that keep momentum going.

Experiential Learning. Opportunities to put lessons into practice should be embedded throughout the program, through such things as paid internships, apprenticeships, fellowships, in-person simulations, and paid try-outs during which students work with companies on a real business problem and get paid for it. Real-world, paid experience is a strong proof point for employers when evaluating candidates. But don't take my word for it. Hector Daniel Mujica sees experiential learning as essential and earn-while-you-learn models, in particular, as a valuable way of building "an inclusive AI-powered digital economy." Mujica leads Google.org's economic opportunity initiatives which are working "to encourage adoption of such practices" in cities throughout the country. As an example, he noted Google.org's support of an

Urban Institute effort to "pilot and scale apprenticeship programs in North and South Carolina.[38]

Inclusion. To attract, enroll, educate, graduate, and place students from diverse backgrounds, upskilling programs need to be intentional about inclusion throughout the program life cycle. Targeted marketing efforts, community-based partners, tailored admissions practices, diverse instructors, online and part-time options, wraparound services, and career advising all help to prepare students to succeed. It's important to think of inclusion as a value that permeates workforce programming in a comprehensive way, with tangible efforts, goals, and monitoring and tracking efforts.

Educational Pathways. Part of the current national conversation is the value of skills over credentials and formal education. To some, skills should trump all, but more and more people are getting their bachelor's degrees across all demographics.[39] I happen to think there will be a limit to the "skills revolution"—for most good jobs, the bachelor's degree will still hold sway, even if it's not a hard requirement. Corporate culture and middle-class traditions are too entrenched for the bachelor's to go anytime soon, and even while providing upskilling opportunities can help you fill a good many jobs, you'll need to provide pathways to higher education to maximize opportunities and achievement. Upskilling isn't right for every job, after all; many of the engineers needed to build companies require advanced education. Ideally, training programs should provide students with transfer credits to two- and four-year colleges so they can pursue degrees if they desire. The College Park initiative in Tulsa is a good example of how to build such pathways. In a single campus setting, students earn their associate degree at Tulsa Community College and then can complete their bachelor's degree at OSU-Tulsa, providing a seamless pathway to get the education they need.

Upskilling doesn't just benefit individuals looking to get ahead. It also benefits employers. The companies that adjust their culture, hiring practices, and internal structures to invest in people and prize skills will be the ones that are competitive in the twenty-first century. One of those companies is headquartered in Tulsa. QuikTrip is a national chain of convenience stores that include gas stations. The first store was opened in Tulsa in 1958, and it has since earned a reputation for being a pioneer in employee-centered management. MIT Sloan School of Management professor Zeynep Ton uses QuikTrip as a case study in her book *The Good Jobs Strategy*. Her research found that "QuikTrip's employees don't get treated well because its profits happen to be up. QuikTrip's profits are up because it puts its employees at the center of its business. They are the creators of that success—not its lucky or occasional beneficiaries—and they are treated accordingly."[40] This ethos imbues the company. Like Trilogy, QuikTrip is intentional about empowering its employees and prioritizing skills—both in its hiring process and in the professional development of its talent. The company offers opportunities to upskill throughout an employee's career, aiding retention. If employers find skills-based hiring difficult, they should consider skills-based promotions as an incremental step toward recalibrating how they hire, develop talent, and manage human resources.

CASE STUDY: THE CYBER SKILLS CENTER

Some QuikTrip employees have been students at the Cyber Skills Center (CSC) in Tulsa, a workforce training initiative Tulsa Innovation Labs launched in partnership with Tulsa Community College and the operator edX. Graduating about 120 students each year, CSC is a leading part of TIL's broader talent efforts, which all together are projected to grow the city's tech workforce by about 5 percent per year.[41] The center, which started in 2022, offers a rich example of an upskilling program, with many of the attributes identified previously.

The center offers twenty-four-week part-time learning programs online (with regular mandatory in-person events) on either the cyber or data science tracks. Thanks to support from the George Kaiser Family Foundation, tuition is free for Tulsa metro residents.

The center serves three demographics: (1) career changers who already have an associate or bachelor's degree but need specific technical training; (2) individuals already working in an entry-level or midlevel tech job who could benefit from additional skills in cyber or data analytics/science; and (3) individuals who are unemployed or underemployed and in need of technical skills to gain employment in the tech industry. There's a specific focus on training individuals from underrepresented communities, particularly people of color. In recruiting these populations, the center benefits from its affiliation with TCC, which has a diverse student population that skews toward people of color and lower socioeconomic backgrounds.

When embarking on an endeavor like starting a workforce training initiative, it's worth considering whether to invest in local institutions or hire outside service providers. There are some seventeen thousand workforce program providers in the United States.[42] TIL issued an RFP spelling out our needs and had several quality respondents. We selected edX due to their previous work in other areas of the country serving underrepresented communities through technical boot camps. Their approach stood out, as did their commitment to placing a student success manager in Tulsa. Also, there were no local institutions that would have provided comparable expertise and potential. While my instinct is always to build local capacity, workforce is a different animal. Local colleges can be slow to respond to industry changes and have rigid curricula or bureaucracies that make establishing a new internal program difficult. Cities will be confronted with the prospect of picking winners and losers, and difficult decisions need to be made. At TIL, we tried to split the difference by bringing on an outside operator and forging a partnership with our community college. I think augmenting Tulsa Community College's capacity through a national provider like edX was the right decision.

Once the boot camp operator was chosen, TCC and TIL began to identify other crucial stakeholders. We identified these people or organizations by category, including organizations serving minority and low-income populations, large employers, and chief information officers. Invitations were sent and meetings were scheduled for a one-week period during which TCC, TIL, and edX would meet with each group, share our plans, and get their input.

The initial admissions process featured an online interest form that individuals could fill out with basic information about themselves. From there, individuals would then receive an invitation to apply, during which they would be asked for more specific information to allow a panel of reviewers to get a better idea of their past and future plans—in particular, why they were interested in the boot camp. After completing the application process, candidates were given a free minicourse to take before the panel made final selections.

The curriculum for the two boot camp programs was already well constructed by edX, which had met with employers across the country to identify skills that would be required for security analysts and data analysts—saving TCC and TIL the burden of having to do this research ourselves. With TIL's local industry data, TCC's relationships, and joint interviews with employers, the curricula was adapted to Tulsa's needs. The industry-aligned curriculum and early employer participation helped build a strong foundation of engagement, which has resulted in the center attracting industry adjuncts and achieving high job placement rates.

Besides TCC and edX, it was also essential for us to partner with organizations that had credibility among previously overlooked communities, ensuring that diversity would be an input, not just a hopeful outcome. TIL worked with organizations in the Greenwood District that had long-standing relationships with the communities the center was designed to serve. By partnering with Black Tech Street, for example, TIL was able to source candidates directly from these communities.

Pete Selden is the vice president in charge of workforce development at TCC. In 2024, he was named workforce professional of the year by the National Association of Workforce Development Professionals. He and I bonded over a shared nostalgia for the Atlanta Braves of the '90s. Selden told me that outreach efforts resulted in more than three hundred applicants for an inaugural cohort of thirty-five cyber students. (The center aims to hold at least three cohorts each year across both tracks, depending on demand.) "Bringing community groups together in the beginning to understand what the project was aiming to do and how each organization could be involved and refer those they serve was a key momentum starter that allowed us to get the initial word out and have trusted partners,"[43] he said. This early momentum carried over into future cohorts, and there has been a surplus of applicants.

Preliminary data suggest the center is performing well. Initial cohorts had about a 90 percent graduation rate and an 85 percent net promoter score (a metric that speaks to how likely a participant is to recommend the program to others). Both metrics meet or exceed industry standards. Within six months of graduation, about 60 percent of graduates had a new job or promotion; more than 15 percent were continuing their education; and the rest already had a living wage and were not searching for a job.

The cohorts' demographic makeup demonstrates the center's intentionally inclusive design: about 30 percent self-identified as Black; about 25 percent identified as White; about 15 percent identified as multiracial; more than 10 percent identified as Asian; 10 percent identified as Hispanic or Latino; and a little more than

5 percent identified as American Indian. And over half self-identified as female, with 5 percent nonbinary. These cohorts are more diverse than Tulsa's demographics as a whole, with Black student representation double its representation in the city—and overall, it's dramatically more diverse than Tulsa's existing tech workforce.

The strong diversity outcomes are also due to the generous wraparound services the center offers in addition to free tuition, including access to childcare, transportation credits, career-readiness advising, and necessary technical equipment—reliable broadband and a laptop, which are both persistent challenges for Tulsa-area students. Also, the flexible schedule allows those currently working to participate, because the expectation is for nine hours per week of in-class learning and twenty hours or more a week of homework. Designing the center with inclusion at its core enables Tulsa to cultivate diverse tech talent and mitigate the side effects of a tech economy.

It's important to point out, however, that the center generally serves students with a hand already on the career ladder, not those who have yet to reach the first rung: it still requires a baseline level of education and skills. After all, graduates have to meet employer needs or the whole thing fails, which means a program like the Cyber Skills Center can't take applicants who lack minimum skills. The aim is rapid employability.

A few elements of the center didn't work out as planned. First, the original concept called for an apprenticeship, but we couldn't find an appropriate operator with experience in our student demographic. Second, we planned for the center to be an in-person learning environment, but we soon realized that the benefits of such an arrangement didn't justify the costs and other trade-offs. Instead, the program is primarily virtual, which provides even more flexibility. And third, the initial vision called for students to have the option to complete the program and go right into an associate or bachelor's degree program as part of the College Park initiative between TCC and OSU-Tulsa. Unfortunately, because of transfer credit rules and reimbursement issues, TCC hasn't been able to work through how to allow CSC students to qualify, but TIL is still committed to solving that problem.

Eunice Tarver, vice president of student success and equity at TCC, has some additional advice for building a diverse pool of tech talent. "Minoritized students and marginalized communities can't aspire to be what they can't see," she said. "There is a significant equity gap in the knowledge and awareness around technology careers and the degree and certificate pathways that align with those careers. . . . Marginalized communities need to hear from professionals who have had similar experiences navigating poverty and/or racism, and yet still have gained access to these transformational careers." In Oklahoma, where not many kids have parents in tech, tech jobs aren't just unknown—they can be daunting. Public awareness campaigns about opportunities in tech would help to mollify this intimidation factor. Tarver called on White males in particular to become "gateway champions and sponsors to students of color, sharing their knowledge, awareness, encouragement, and social capital" if we hope to truly develop inclusive pipelines at scale.[44]

There is a natural tendency to make every program sustainable. I share that goal. But during the early innings of a city's pivot to tech, the scale of workforce development must triumph over sustainability, if at all possible. This means big bets over incremental approaches. That's the way to reinvention. As much progress as Tulsa has made in recent years, it will take an order of magnitude more to catch up to Austin. Scale what works for your city but push it to the limits. With tech talent, there can't be a crawl, walk, run approach—Heartland cities need to come out of the gates fast and produce quality and diverse tech talent as quickly as possible. In Tulsa, this will require civic institutions to adjust their core principles and make even bigger bets. To help, the Cyber Skills

Center is experimenting with at-price and fully funded slots, to ensure philanthropic funding is going to those in need while those who can pay their way do so and thus help subsidize others. And TCC and TIL are open to leveraging the center's programmatic infrastructure to develop new curricula to meet Tulsa's workforce needs as they inevitably evolve.

AI AND THE NEED FOR AGILITY

Of course, an eight-hundred-pound gorilla lurks in every conversation about upskilling right now—and that's AI. In September 2023, I was in Manhattan to speak on a panel about rural vitality at the Fast Company Innovation Festival (ironic, I know). Down in the Financial District, I saw a billboard for Fiverr, a digital platform that connects freelancers to customers. The ad read, "AI TOOK MY JOB," and below it in smaller font size, "To the Next Level." Color me skeptical.

While AI and its adoption will be a cash cow to many, it will also accelerate automation across the board. Automation has loomed for years, but AI has struck new fear in workers, including those who thought they were immune from technological disruption. We've known that retail, service industry, and manufacturing jobs were highly susceptible to automation, but AI's reach has extended to other, more middle-class occupations, and we're already starting to see turmoil.

2023 was the year of the strike. The Writers Guild struck in Hollywood to guard against ChatGPT or other AI applications taking their jobs and to gain more in residuals from streaming services like Netflix. Can you imagine AI writing a TV series like *Veep* or *Broad City*? The Screen Actors Guild followed suit. They went on strike, in part, because AI could supplant performers, digitally putting their faces onto special effects bodies. Imagine if a "live" action movie's cast were played by avatars instead of real human actors. Or if Timothée Chalamet and Zendaya could star in unlimited *Dune* sequels long after they pass, as digitally resurrected performers. These ideas might sound like science fiction themselves, but Hollywood's most powerful unions are very worried about them.

Heartland cities aren't Los Angeles with its entertainment industry, but they all have creative, professional, and advanced manufacturing workers who will be affected by AI. In fact, the United Automobile Workers went on strike throughout the Midwest in 2023 because of the concern that electric vehicles would require fewer workers.[45] Stronger worker protections can mitigate the downsides of AI, but ultimately, power skills are what will be most valuable to both creatives and the professionals that build EVs—showcasing why workforce development is a national imperative. In the near term, one's ability to partner with AI, to use it as a tool, may well be a new power skill that everyone should have.

Jane Oates is the former president of WorkingNation, a multimedia platform that advocates for solutions related to the future of work, as well as the former assistant secretary of the US Department of Labor under President Barack Obama. She told me that AI is going to lead to a "white collar tsunami." "The people who will be impacted by AI are going to be very different," she told me. "They're not going to be blue collar. They're going to be entry-level writers, marketing departments, or junior associates coming out of law school." Hence why Hollywood shut down for several months as labor organizations and industry worked through the complicated and ever-changing implications of AI.

Oates pointed to the quick iterations of ChatGPT to impress upon cities the need for speed in workforce development. As of 2023, ChatGPT is on its fourth version in a year, and adoption and business integration will increase in the years ahead. "AI is going to throw the workforce system for a loop because if you take six months to get a credential, that credential possibly could be obsolete," Oates continued. "An employer knows what their needs are today, but they can't accurately predict what their needs are going to be in six months. So it means the system has to pivot."[46]

By helping your city's workforce ecosystem pivot, enabling it to quickly upskill talent for the most in-demand jobs, you'll be setting your fellow citizens, companies, and wider community up for success. Navigating the future-of-work period we're in as a society brings to mind a line from Frank Herbert's previously referenced sci-fi epic: "Survival is the ability to swim in strange water."[47] As AI and remote work mature, the years ahead for cities and their workforce development leaders may be tumultuous. But investing in the development of power skills is the best way to help workers be able to adapt, manage, and harness AI in the workplace. And to keep track of changing labor needs and their requisite skills, cities will need to monitor local, regional, and national data, taking action on those insights to try and stay ahead of industry demand. Agile programmatic infrastructure, like the Cyber Skills Center, or more targeted offerings like microcredentials, can allow cities to adjust curricula based on a changing world. As AI spreads and its disruption on the labor force becomes clearer, cities will also need to be even more conscious of creating accessible pathways to education and training.

Inclusion is the underlying principle in inclusive growth, so let's now engage more fully with what the Cyber Skills Center previewed: diversity, equity, and inclusion initiatives. They will be key to ensuring that populations historically shut out of tech can contribute to and benefit from the innovation economy.

ACTION PLAN SUMMARY

REINVENTION	GROWTH	INCLUSION
What needs reinventing?	*How do you catalyze growth?*	*How do you advance inclusion?*
A city's workforce development ecosystem needs to be recalibrated to train those in or near the labor force for the jobs most important to the development of its tech clusters.	To grow, cities need to expand their talent pipelines at speed and scale. They should prioritize the most in-demand and critical roles for their tech niche, understand the specific skills necessary for those roles, and analyze the supply and demand of jobs in the region. Working with industry throughout, they'll then need to create upskilling programs that transition adults to those roles.	Upskilling programs must be designed for inclusion at each stage in the process: recruitment efforts should leverage local partners to engage communities of color; the admissions process should reduce barriers to applying; the curricula needs to take into account cultural nuances, especially to ensure students are ready for work; and the program should offer scholarships and wraparound services to aid student success.

CHAPTER 6

LET "OTHERS" SHINE

(DIVERSITY, EQUITY, AND INCLUSION)

I came out via email the summer before my final year in college. It was less a moment of courage and more of exhaustion, built up over a decade of hiding who I was. As I passed by Lake Michigan on a brooding walk one night, I saw two men, cast in shadow, holding hands. It was a beautiful scene, but my heart sank, for it felt so far out of reach for me. I had had enough. I walked back to my apartment and impulsively emailed my mom saying that I was gay. I didn't want to talk about it or explain it. And over the next few weeks, I sent notes out to my family and friends as well, as if it were an update buried in the news ticker—a new data point about Nick for them to absorb and move on from. As I should have suspected, everyone was wonderfully supportive. My fear had always been internal, due, in part, to an external world that saw me as the "Other."

When fall quarter started, Northwestern had a campus drag show. It was the first queer event I'd attended since coming out, and I was still getting comfortable with my recently embraced identity and the new world it offered. As is customary, a queen served as master of ceremonies, propelling forward a series of performances by campus groups through caustic wit and musical numbers of her own. Her name was Vicious Crotch, and as part of her crowd work, whom do you think Vicious Crotch picked on? That's right—she asked me to stand. (Drag queens have a sixth sense about who to target in their audiences.) I rose from my chair, like someone learning to walk in heels. She asked me whether I was gay or straight. My voice trembling, I said, "I'm gay." My face turned red, and after a brief exchange, I sat back down. When the terror subsided, I felt proud of myself for coming out in front of my peers. And I've never forgotten how Vicious Crotch's question, which at the time felt so invasive, ended up being so liberating. I just needed a little nudge from a drag queen.

Since I came out at the tail end of the George W. Bush era, the United States has gone through a long stretch of civil rights wins for gays and lesbians, driven by landmark court cases and the lawyers and activists who helped build a national consensus on the issue in historically short order. I still remember walking to the White House, lit in rainbow lights, with a friend from the Urban Land Institute, Sara Hammerschmidt, on the night of June 26, 2015, the day the Supreme Court ruled gay marriage constitutional. (Seven years later, Sara would officiate my own wedding to Chris.) But progress isn't linear, and we've taken a few steps back in recent years, with controversies around drag queens and trans individuals weaponized to exploit divisions and feed the culture war.

Drag and minority rights more broadly continue to be misunderstood and attacked. Modern drag started with Dorsey Swann, one of the first drag queens. Born enslaved in America in 1858, Swann held drag balls in the 1880s in the Washington, DC, area, most of the other attendees also being formerly enslaved.[1] Drag balls continued to grow, especially lifted by the Black and Latino performers who were not allowed to win pageants held for White performers (many of these White performers wore blackface as a "yaller" gal—a man dressed to portray a light-skinned Black woman). Drag balls became more prominent in the late nineteenth century through the early 1920s, especially during the Harlem Renaissance.[2]

The relationship between Black and queer people in the United States evolved from cross-cultural exchange and artistic expression to the pursuit of civil rights. Drawing from the Black civil rights movement's nonviolent tactics, early gay rights activists in 1965 held a sit-in at Dewey's restaurant in Philadelphia, which gave rise to other demonstrations across the country.[3] Activism for gay rights intensified in 1969 when police raided the Stonewall Inn in New York. The six days of protests that followed were largely led by LGBTQ+ women of color, such as Marsha P. Johnson and Sylvia Rivera. (Rivera already had experience with the Black liberation movement.[4]) The Black and queer rights movements increasingly intersected from that point on. In 1970, the Black Panther Party wrote "A Letter from Huey to the Revolutionary Brothers and Sisters About the Women's Liberation and Gay Liberation Movements," which acknowledged the Gay Liberation Movement as legitimate in the eyes of the civil rights movement.[5]

While Blackness and queerness aren't equivalent, James Baldwin often examined the relationship between the two, saying, "The sexual question and the racial question have always been entwined. If Americans can mature on the level of racism, then they have to mature on the level of sexuality."[6] As Baldwin chronicled with such force, the feelings marginalized people face often span a spectrum: Black is beautiful or self-hatred, pride or the closet. For many, it can feel as though one is constantly traveling back and forth between happiness and despair—and every baffling emotion in between.

Despite the progress we've made, it remains true that the initial commonality between Black and queer populations is that they have unequal opportunities compared to their White, straight counterparts. And that is certainly true in the worlds of tech and innovation. But such inequality limits the potential of local economies and the country as a whole.

Cities should acknowledge that inequality exists—that people don't have equal opportunity—and then take responsibility to foster a more inclusive innovation ecosystem. To do so, they need to create DEI interventions that support people who have historically been shut out of tech.

Not doing so simply reinforces existing structures and prohibits inclusive growth. And for those who may be wary of identity politics, I say this: taking a race-, sex-, and class-conscious approach to economic development will help redress historical wrongs, but it will also help your city grow widely; incorporating cultural nuances into economic development can help create opportunities that will benefit all demographics.

Because of the 1921 massacre and present racial disparities, Tulsa is largely focusing its DEI efforts on supporting Black entrepreneurs. Through two targeted interventions, Build in Tulsa and Black Tech Street, the city is supporting underinvested segments of the innovation economy, working to level the playing field while creating opportunities that enrich the entire ecosystem.

This work is important and necessary, but in this chapter, I also want to illustrate how the interrelated experiences of different minoritized groups can bear great lessons about economic inclusion. If we consider the link between drag queens and Black entrepreneurs, we'll see that DEI interventions don't just address past wrongs—they make for thriving urban economies. To actualize this, cities will need to understand marginalized groups as vital economic actors, not fringe figures, and they should deploy DEI investments that go beyond symbolic efforts and support minorities to succeed in tech.

TIP YOUR DRAG QUEEN

Given the political climate, I understand why people wondered if I had trepidations about moving to Tulsa in 2019. A gay liberal moving to Trump country. What could go wrong? But being gay didn't factor into my decision. By that point in my life, I was comfortable with myself, confident in my ability to adapt to any environment, and ultimately trustful that Tulsans would treat me with respect and dignity. It was my geographic affiliation that caused controversy, as my signature black T-shirt and jeans, quick gait, and direct speaking style led folks, more than once, to whisper behind my back, either apologetically or accusatorily, "He's from New York." While non-White LGBTQ+ people may well have a different experience, I found a welcoming queer community in Tulsa. It's not Hell's Kitchen, but Tulsa's gay population was larger and more active than I expected.

Just as tech leaders may look down upon cities like Tulsa, many Heartland cities are perceived to be unwelcoming to gay people. Tulsa isn't perfect, but often local realities bely national perceptions or political prejudices. Louie Napoleone is a local civic leader and helped chair the 2024 Red Ribbon Gala, Tulsa's largest LGBTQ+ fundraiser. I attended the gala one year and saw corporate and elected leaders alike showing their support, including many that pleasantly surprised me. After completing his MBA at Columbia in 2020, Napoleone moved to Tulsa to be with his soon-to-be husband. Originally from Buffalo, New York—another scrappy middleweight—Napoleone worked at inTulsa, where he directed business development, before joining TIL after I left. He said,

"One of the benefits that buoys Tulsa is that it's full of intangible assets that need to be experienced firsthand to be understood. In my over four years in Tulsa, I've found a welcoming (and growing) queer community as well as acceptance by more heteronormative institutions. . . . This growth and evolution have helped attract new businesses to the city."[7]

Research speaks to the economic influence of queer people and the benefits of inclusive societies. UCLA's Williams Institute found in 2018 that, globally, legal protections and public acceptance of LGBTQ+ people are correlated with increased GDP per capita.[8] And in 2023, a study by Wells Fargo similarly found that US states with larger concentrations of LGBTQ+ people had higher rates of gross state products over the past decade.[9]

But despite this progress, there are still challenges. Nationwide, in the early 2020s, Republican-elected officials began a concerted effort to undermine LGBTQ+ rights by focusing their ire on drag queens, then trans individuals, and politicians in Oklahoma were among them. They openly took joy in ridiculing drag queens, seeing them as marginal figures or caricatures beyond their own creative personas. Attempts to suppress this community, though, are not only bigoted, but strategically misguided: drag queens are economic actors, and they create jobs. They are important symbols for LGBTQ+ communities, which, through their relative youth and higher education, have purchasing power (nearly $4 trillion in 2023).[10] And drag performances and queer cultural production more broadly generate valuable economic activity.

Attacking drag, however, isn't just an attack on individual performers or a segment of the LGBTQ+ demographic; it can do damage to a city's or state's relationship to a much broader group, the creative class, which Richard Florida has identified as important drivers of innovation and growth.

As on many issues, Florida was ahead of his time on the role gay and lesbian people play in local economies. In *The Rise of the Creative Class,* published in 2002, Florida presented his "Gay-Bohemian Index," which originated in a paper he cowrote with Gary Gates of the Williams Institute. The index measures the relationship between gay populations and local economic strength. Florida finds that the proportion of gay people in an area is positively correlated with economic vitality for two reasons: the aesthetic-amenity premium and the tolerance (or open culture) premium. The aesthetic-amenity premium is the concentration of cultural assets—from theaters to restaurants to clubs—which is higher in areas with large gay populations because creatives bring in amenities, making the area nicer and more desirable. Artistic and gay populations also orient toward creative occupations, tolerance, and self-expression, which is correlated with innovative and entrepreneurial endeavors. The tolerance or open culture premium speaks to the inclusiveness of a community; the more inclusive a place is, the higher demand is for housing since more people can feel accepted in those areas. Marginalized groups may also need to create new organizations, since they cannot easily access traditional ones. This pattern further contributes to the growth of local support organizations and overall development, which can increase cost of living in an area.[11]

Back in the early 2000s, public intellectuals and civil rights activists needed to make the case for why gays and lesbians were good for cities and economies. Today, the focus of social justice has shifted because many see trans people and drag queens through the lens of hate and discrimination and don't recognize their valuable role in local economies. But Florida's research and logic still hold true: he writes that a strong LGBTQ+ presence "signals that a location has the very characteristics that drive innovation and growth, driving further innovation and growth."[12] Sure enough, jurisdictions favorable to trans rights and gender-affirming health care are more likely to be welcoming and inclusive communities that attract and support creative-class workers. The same can be said for drag queens, who are the (fabulous) intersectional embodiment of the gay-bohemian demographic. It would behoove Heartland cities looking to build innovation economies to foster communities where drag queens and others like them feel safe to express themselves; this is important because of what it communicates to the broader creative class about their communities: that they are generally open, safe, and welcoming to all as well as full of the amenities that much of the creative class—gay or straight—are looking for.

THE DRAG QUEEN TEST

How cities treat drag queens speaks volumes about the inclusiveness of their communities and the vitality of their economies. To determine whether your city is inclusive in this undervalued aspect, you should take what I call the "Drag Queen Test," a shorthand for evaluating cities:

QUESTION 1: Does your city or state have laws restricting drag queens? (If no, plus 1 point): Efforts to restrict drag performers or drag readings at public libraries is the first red flag. Unfortunately, state legislatures often act against the economic best interests of their cities, and cities suffer as a result. Montana, Arkansas, and Tennessee have all passed prohibitive measures. State-imposed limitations on drag queens inhibit inclusive growth and send a powerful signal to tech talent: stay away.

QUESTION 2: Does your city have drag brunches occurring on any given weekend? (If yes, plus 1 point): Drag performances and the broader LGBTQ+ cultural expression create jobs and offer cities the amenities many knowledge-economy workers desire. Having drag brunches—the campy performance complemented with bottomless mimosas that have become a staple of the drag queen industry—suggests density, inclusion, and cultural vibrancy.

QUESTION 3: Does your city have multiple bars or performance centers dedicated to the LGBTQ+ community? (If yes, plus 1 point): Minoritized people need safe spaces where they can express themselves and build community. Spaces dedicated to LGBTQ+ people or heteronormative spaces that welcome drag queens are an asset to your city's economy. I saw Bianca Del Rio, one of the nation's leading drag queens, perform at Carnegie Hall in New York—hardly a fringe venue. Every Heartland city needs their own Carnegie Hall open to drag queens.

QUESTION 4: Has your city sent a contestant to *RuPaul's Drag Race*? (If yes, plus 1 point): Now hear me out! The pinnacle of drag performance is competing in and winning *RuPaul's Drag Race*. So, a city that nurtures drag talent who make it to the big leagues is like a university football program that sends athletes to the NFL. Having a hometown queen compete on *Drag Race* signals talent quality, density of population and amenities, and ecosystem support.

For a more comprehensive and scientific index of LGBTQ+ inclusion in cities, look at the Human Rights Campaign's Municipal Equality Index. The index has forty-nine criteria, including factors related to law enforcement, city leadership, municipal government employer policies, nondiscrimination laws, and LGBTQ+-related services and programs. The study found that city size does not predict score, meaning midsized cities can be and often are as inclusive as big cities, and some big cities aren't particularly inclusive (I'm looking at you, Houston, which scored a 73).[13] The score is out of 100. Here's just a sample of how Heartland cities scored: Cincinnati, Columbus, and Cleveland all scored 100; Indianapolis scored 80, with OKC and Tulsa scoring 78; while Memphis and Knoxville were near the bottom with 54.[14]

Despite Oklahoma currently trying to pass antidrag laws, Tulsa scored three points on my Drag Queen Test and a middling 78 on the Municipal Equality Index, driven almost entirely by the lack of nondiscrimination laws at the local, county, and state levels.[15] If your city scored less than three points on the Drag Queen Test or low on the index, then, in Ru's immortal words, "Sashay away." Or better yet, work harder to make your drag queens and LGBTQ+ community feel welcomed and valued. This could include public pride parades or elected officials visiting LGBTQ+ centers; or it could mean embracing artistic expression by staging the plays of queer writers; or perhaps it's supporting queer affinity groups, such as Out in Tech, oSTEM, StartOut, or Lesbians Who Tech & Allies, or offering more tangible things, such as scholarships for aspiring queer innovators and entrepreneurs. Targeted support and sustained engagement make a difference.

But I want to pivot from the value cities should place on drag queens to another minoritized group's experience in Tulsa. The city has concentrated its diversity, equity, and inclusion efforts on another underrepresented part of the innovation economy: Black entrepreneurs. Supporting this demographic through multiple initiatives has struck a chord with the community, particularly given Tulsa's history of racial injustice.

AFFIRM THAT "BLACK IS ENTREPRENEURIAL"

Two years before I came out, Hurricane Katrina struck my hometown of New Orleans. The storm awakened many Americans to the economic realities of race and crystallized the social forces I had experienced growing up. The hurricane turned my world upside down and left me disoriented and depressed for a long time. With my childhood home destroyed and family displaced, I shifted my undergraduate studies to concentrate on how literature explored racial politics in cities, ultimately writing my thesis on John Kennedy Toole's *A Confederacy of Dunces*. While traumatizing, the hurricane gave me a cause through which to channel my values and passions, and it set my career as an urbanist in motion.

I was guided by two fundamental questions regarding Katrina: How could this have happened, and how does New Orleans rebuild from it? I recognized that race and racial politics were the animating forces behind the disaster and its tragic aftermath. At its root, the effects of Katrina weren't about government neglect, incompetent local and federal responses, climate change, or faulty civil engineering; they were about systemic and structural racism. To get some answers, I decided to study post-Katrina New Orleans from an interdisciplinary perspective. And because I'm White, people are often surprised to hear that my master's degree is in African American studies, not urban planning, public policy, or business administration. I was lucky enough to earn a fellowship to Cornell, where I designed a course of study that blended urban planning, critical race studies, public policy, and cultural studies to understand New Orleans's recovery. I analyzed, in particular, how the city leveraged arts and cultural projects to interrogate racial politics and rebuild the city. Hence why my early experience at the Greenwood Cultural Center and the Tulsa Race Massacre arts project event left such a mark on me.

During my entire time at Cornell's Africana Studies and Research Center, the massacre didn't come up in any of my courses or research. What happened in 1921 wasn't in mainstream culture until the HBO series *Watchmen* came out in 2019. After the TV show and thanks to its centennial, the massacre has received renewed attention. In 2023, Oprah Winfrey's network aired a six-part series on the efforts to rebuild Black Wall Street. Understanding what happened in Tulsa in 1921 helps explain why the city is making such concerted efforts to support Black entrepreneurs and why inclusive growth is a powerful aspiration for many Tulsans.

THE TULSA RACE MASSACRE

Hannibal B. Johnson is Tulsa's resident historian. I've seen him speak around town a few times, including at the Greenwood Cultural Center, and he's as impassioned and knowledgeable as you get. Johnson has authored multiple books on the massacre, including *Black Wall Street 100*, which reflects upon the tragic event a hundred years after it happened. As Johnson explains, the massacre started by chance, though it was really fomented by generations of hatred: "On May 30, 1921, an elevator encounter between two teenagers, one Black, the other White, in downtown Tulsa, lit the fuse that set Tulsa's African American community, the Greenwood District, alight."[16]

Dick Rowland, a Black teenager, allegedly brushed up against Sarah Page, a White teenager, in an elevator. Like the Emmett Till murder in Mississippi in 1955, Page interpreted Rowland's action as an assault, and by 3:00 p.m. the next day, the *Tulsa Tribune* reported the incident with this headline: "Nab Negro for Attacking Girl in an Elevator." Notice how the paper uses the dehumanizing "Negro" opposite the innocent, youthful, and nonracialized "girl." By the time Rowland was arrested, a White mob had gathered at the courthouse, threatening to hang him.[17] The newspaper report worked Tulsa's White residents into a frenzy. Long resenting Greenwood's wealth, White residents channeled their grievances into the incident. The White mob at the courthouse was met by armed Blacks, and things quickly spiraled out of control. On June 1, widespread fires were started across Greenwood, and the governor ordered the mobilization of the National Guard.

One of the unbelievable, but sadly true, aspects of the massacre is the use of airplanes to bombard Greenwood from the sky. In *The Ground Breaking: The Tulsa Race Massacre and an American City's Search for Justice,* Scott Ellsworth describes the scene: "In the sky above the city, becoming more audible over the chaos on the streets below, comes the mechanical drone of airplanes. . . . They can be seen and heard over Greenwood from nearly the start of the invasion."[18] According to witness Mabel Little, these airplanes "dropped incendiary bombs" onto residents, leaving the Mount Zion Baptist Church, the Stradford Hotel, and numerous homes in flames."[19]

As the White mob enveloped Greenwood and went on their rampage, they attacked any Black person they came upon, including A. C. Jackson, a physician. Victor Luckerson reports in *Built from the Fire*, a history of Greenwood: "A teenager wearing a white shirt and cap fired two rounds of buckshot into Jackson. He fell on the second shot. Then his house, like all the rest on the black side of the street, was burned to the ground. He died later that day."[20] After dropping bombs from the sky and using torches on the ground, the White mob seized control of the district. Under gunpoint, more than two thousand Black residents "were paraded through the streets of downtown Tulsa to an internment camp that city officials had quickly set up at Convention Hall. . . . Blacks who resisted arrest risked immediate execution."[21] All of this, mind you, happened *after* the Civil War and more than twenty years after "Reconstruction."

During the massacre, Greenwood lost nearly fifteen hundred homes to burning or looting. A 2021 Harvard study estimated losses to be between $32.6 and $47.4 million in 2020 US dollars.[22] There has yet to be any restitution for the damages, from insurance companies or from the city, state, or federal governments, and discussions of reparations have long simmered. (A "Beyond Apology" movement has recently started in Tulsa to advocate for reparations.) The original Oklahoma Department of Health tallied thirty-six deaths, an intentionally low estimate that began a generations-long conspiracy to downplay, whitewash, ignore, and lie about the massacre by White leaders. This conspiracy worked, until new research and television shows brought the massacre into the zeitgeist, educating the nation and even many Tulsans who didn't know the truth about their city. The current consensus among historians is that Dick Rowland likely escaped Tulsa in the chaos but that at least three hundred Black Tulsans perished.

The destruction of Black Wall Street not only shapes generations of families but is reflected in Tulsa's present-day built environment. Sam Anderson notes in *Boom Town*—the title refers to Oklahoma City—that "the destruction of Greenwood had solved a long-standing problem for Tulsa's white city planners. After all the recent oil booms, downtown Tulsa wanted desperately to expand. But that expansion was blocked by Greenwood. The neighborhood could not have been easily cleared, as a slum might have been, in the name of civic improvement. Greenwood was affluent and solid. These were not tenants but homeowners. It was the American dream."[23] Some fifty years later, after rebuilding from the massacre, Greenwood would indeed be cut in half in the name of urban renewal with the construction of a new highway—once again destroying Black wealth and limiting the district's economic opportunity, while benefiting White Tulsans.

To this day, the legacy of 1921 remains omnipresent in Tulsa, as does the sacred importance of Greenwood as a historical and living neighborhood, and as a national symbol of hope and resilience in the face of racism and inequality. Rarely a day would go by when I didn't hear someone mention it—particularly because the centennial coincided with 2020 racial protests that fueled the Black Lives Matter movement. In my first two years, Tulsa was very much a charged environment, with tensions and emotions high because of the news and history converging to remind people of persistent racism.

The buildup to the centennial raised essential questions: How do communities reckon with history? How do you learn from the past without getting stuck in it? What does reconciliation even mean? I regularly heard from Black Tulsans that they didn't want to become synonymous with the massacre, that they want to harness Black Wall Street's memory to make Black Tulsa mean something new.

This ongoing conversation within Black communities is part of a broader national discourse on what Blackness means and to whom.

UNDERSTANDING BLACKNESS

In the 1960s, "Black Is Beautiful" became a cultural, political, and generational refrain, first through the photography of Kwame Brathwaite and then through music and literature. In 1969, Nina Simone released a song that would give voice to the movement, "To Be Young, Gifted and Black." Two years later, Aretha Franklin popularized Simone's anthem. Since as early as the nineteenth century, there has been an intentional and assertive effort by African American cultural producers to recast Blackness as a positive in a world bent on equating it with problems, inferiority, and subjectivity. Black is Beautiful is also a historical antecedent to the Black Lives Matter movement, which seeks to affirm Black dignity and self-determination in a world telling and showing Black people that they are expendable.

This approach can be applied on the civic level as well. When I was interning for New Orleans mayor Mitch Landrieu in 2012, his crime-prevention initiative conceived in partnership with filmmaker Spike Lee was called "Flip the Script" and was aimed at supporting young Black men who are particularly vulnerable to crime. It focused on investment and support rather than punitive measures, working to change how Black and White communities alike see young Black men. For another example, I think back to how the hoodie was reappropriated as a civil rights symbol in the wake of Trayvon Martin's murder in 2012. Or how, when I was in a predominantly Black middle school in the late '90s, our graduating year's theme was "diamonds in the rough"—I still remember how so many of the young Black girls in my class took to calling themselves diamonds.

We all want to feel important—to be seen and heard and valued. No matter your race, dignity and belonging are universal desires. Kids need to hear they have potential and a safe place in the world. Black kids, who studies have shown are overly disciplined and policed by both the public school and criminal justice systems, especially need to feel worthy of dignity.

There is a risk of equating Blackness with trauma alone, much like equating being gay with AIDS. Think back to the television coverage of Katrina, and how images of desperate Black families became a viewing spectacle. Yet you can avoid whitewashing issues, while also framing challenges in terms of opportunities and inspiring hope. Urban leaders should be cognizant of how they communicate about challenges, and they should recognize that if all Black kids hear is violence, poverty, and less than-ness, then that could sap their self-worth, erode their self-esteem, and stifle their dreams.

What if we were to challenge the White gaze and flip on its head the notion that Blackness means problems—to equate Blackness with excellence on a citywide level? Preeminent urban sociologist Mary Pattillo—who is also my former Northwestern professor, and whose course "Black Chicago" first taught me how to study cities—has developed a concept called the "Black Advantage Vision," which identifies and analyzes the myriad ways Blacks excel compared to their White counterparts.[24] This work seeks to counter the prevailing sentiment within her field of sociology that, through generations of scholarship, has institutionalized the White gaze and established a stigma against Black communities.

I wondered in writing this book what would happen if we took the Black Advantage Vision and applied it to Blacks in tech. Pattillo had pointed me to its urban planning cousin, asset-based community development (covered in chapter 1), and I realized that the concept animates much of TIL's work as well as efforts to support Greenwood. What if we focused on the entrepreneurial skills, grit, resilience, and strong social networks prevalent in many Black communities?

Hannibal Johnson told me that this is exactly what many Black Tulsans and Black businessmen and -women throughout the nation do; it's what he calls the "Black Wall Street Mindset." Johnson explained: "The moniker of Black Wall Street has become a brand and a rallying cry, [with Black Wall Street clubs throughout the nation]. . . . It is on that narrative that we have built, and other Black communities are building, a new narrative of succeeding against seemingly insurmountable odds." Johnson said the Black Wall Street Mindset is a "psychological dynamic that allows a person of color, specifically a Black person, to say to him- or herself, yes, there are systemic challenges that I face, I will challenge those systemic inequities, but at the same time I will be successful even in the face of them, and particularly successful in business."[25] Being conscious of both the challenges you face and the inner resilience you have is a powerful mental orientation.

To combat persistent narratives that lose the optimistic and solutions-oriented thread, urban leaders should consult, draw on, and help advance alternative, constructive narratives around Blackness, like the Black Advantage Vision and the Black Wall Street Mindset, or build a more hopeful and positive lexicon around asset-based community development practices.

Here's my proposal: as cities consider how best to support their Black populations in tech, nurturing the idea that "Black is entrepreneurial" better balances the narrative, highlights the positive attributes of Black communities, supports an entire population of talent who can contribute to the growth of your city, and inspires people to dream tall. "Black is entrepreneurial" also embodies the entrepreneurial legacy of Greenwood, which was built by dozens of talented and pioneering men and women. By reframing economic development interventions for Black people as building on community and cultural assets, not filling in holes, your city could support Black-founded start-ups and encourage investments by White allies.

But "Black is entrepreneurial" can't be a slogan. It needs to be a strategic goal, advanced by tangible investments. Initiatives like Black Tech Street and Build in Tulsa are aimed at doing just that and are supporting a new generation of Black entrepreneurs in Greenwood and throughout the city.

TULSA'S SUPPORT FOR BLACK ENTREPRENEURS

Encouraging Black entrepreneurship is important for reversing one of the most predominant imbalances in American society. According to the Opportunity and Inclusive Growth Institute at the Federal Reserve Bank of Minneapolis, the wealth gap between Black and White Americans is stark. The average per capita wealth of White Americans was $338,093 in 2019, but only $60,126 for Black Americans, and in 2020, Blacks were 12.4 percent of the US population but held only 2.5 percent of the country's wealth.[26] More broadly, as French economist Thomas Picketty found, the compound interest gained from capital grows faster than wages.[27] This helps explain, in part, the racial wealth gap. For generations, Blacks lacked the ability to earn or invest money.

We know that one of the best ways to achieve intergenerational wealth is through entrepreneurship.[28] Yet Blacks face disadvantages in accessing the venture capital investment necessary to grow their businesses. According to Crunchbase, Black-founded start-ups saw their market share drop from 1.5 percent in 2021 to 1.1 percent in 2022.[29] As Pattillo establishes in *Black Picket Fences: Privilege and Peril Among the Black Middle Class*, it's difficult to create a large Black middle class without this kind of transferable wealth. But such transferable wealth won't be achieved by happenstance: it requires intentional efforts. One example of such efforts is the GKFF-backed entrepreneurial support organization Build in Tulsa.

Ashli Sims, Build in Tulsa's managing director, told *Essence* that her mission is "to build the infrastructure needed to create multigenerational wealth for Black people."[30] To achieve this,

Build in Tulsa operates a series of start-up accelerators to support Black-founded companies at various stages of growth. The innovation organization Act House operates an accelerator for prerevenue companies; Lightship Capital, a VC firm, operates an accelerator for revenue-generating companies; and TechStars, the global accelerator chain, operates a program to launch and scale new firms. Build in Tulsa also runs a special accelerator for Black women, called W.E. Build, which is supported by Goldman Sachs's One Million Black Women Initiative. Importantly, in 2022, Build in Tulsa began hosting an annual summit in Tulsa of VCs dedicated to investing in start-ups founded by people of color.

Another example is the work of Tyrance Billingsley II, who is one of the leading Black visionaries in Tulsa for helping Black Wall Street live on in the twenty-first century. Billingsley founded the nonprofit Black Tech Street shortly before the centennial. His aim for the nonprofit is to revolutionize the Greenwood District and aid in Black wealth creation through tech, reimagining Black Wall Street as Black Tech Street. Billingsley has successfully harnessed the story of Black Wall Street into a positive, forward-looking vision for growth and opportunity.

Black Tech Street focuses on cultivating STEM and entrepreneurial talent in cyber as well as in business intelligence, analytics, and AI (areas that were chosen to align with Tulsa Innovation Labs). Black Tech Street is working to support the creation of a thousand Black cyber professionals in Tulsa by 2030. "I'm a born and raised Tulsan, and I'm a relative of survivors [of the massacre]. I asked myself the question, *What could Black Wall Street have been had it been supported and not destroyed?*" Billingsley explained. "When I thought about the level of tenacity that it took for those entrepreneurs to build such incredible businesses during Jim Crow, the smashing through walls and the out-of-the-box thinking reminded me of the tech industry. I had a three-pronged epiphany:

One, tech is one of the only industries you can build intergenerational wealth in seven to ten years via a successful company exit. Two, tech is the core medium through which all global innovation takes place. And three, by the year 2030, there are projected to be as many as 4.3 million high paying vacant tech jobs. When I put all three of these things together, I not only saw an incredible wealth-building opportunity for Black people, I saw the Black Wall Street vision pushed to a new horizon."[31]

Black Tech Street's mission is none other than the *rebirth* of Greenwood as the nation's premier Black innovation economy, to use Billingsley's word. In addition to supporting TIL in recruiting Black candidates for the Cyber Skills Center, Black Tech Street has also landed a major corporate partner, Microsoft, with assists from TIL and advisory council member Sean Alexander, a former Microsoft principal. Billingsley says the alliance with Microsoft has yielded student scholarships and investments in broadband for north Tulsa. They are also building a co-innovation lab around AI in which Microsoft staff can partner with local start-ups and nonprofits to develop AI solutions that enable them to scale their companies. The two are also actively experimenting to identify other catalytic investments that can aid Black talent development.

Plenty of other Black entrepreneurs are also extending Greenwood's legacy into the innovation age. Take two examples. Darrien Watson is the CEO of SquadTrip, a software as a service platform he says is "on a mission to foster community and connection through travel experiences by empowering trip organizers to plan and host trips, and to make it easy for people to find and attend trips that align with their interests."[32] Watson participated in an accelerator program, sponsored by Build in Tulsa. Another is Edna Martinson, cofounder of Boddle Learning, a "game-based learning platform that helps teachers deliver data-driven practice and assessments that boost engagement and motivation," particularly around K–6 math education.[33] Martinson has secured venture funding and been recognized as a Forbes 30 Under 30.

SIX WAYS TO ADVANCE DEI

Using Tulsa's efforts to support Black entrepreneurs to illustrate broader, transferable recommendations, here are a few ways cities can advance their DEI goals:

1. **Let the Community Shape DEI Initiatives.** I had a Black entrepreneur tell me about an initiative a Tulsa VC was pushing without including him, and he said, "Anything happening for me, without me, is happening to me." Especially in crafting DEI initiatives and engaging minoritized communities, economic developers need to defer to local leaders of those communities. The communities you're trying to support will know what they need better than you will. Local stakeholders can help identify the right problem, craft a solution, and help you implement it. TIL has found that engaging specific communities on the front end helps drive outcomes because we've built buy-in throughout the economic development process.

2. **Ensure Existing Programming Is Inclusive.** Existing initiatives to foster entrepreneurship may be inclusive in spirit but not in practice. It's worth assessing your ecosystem's incubators, accelerators, mentorship programs, and incentives to evaluate how diverse participants are and whether community voices are fully involved in those programs. Oftentimes, certain community groups—especially those that are marginalized—may not be tuned in to the specific channels of outreach or promotion that existing initiatives utilize. Certain programs may require

thresholds of experience that act as arbitrary barriers for entrepreneurs from marginalized backgrounds, whose upbringings may have precluded them from attaining these credentials—like a skills certification—or gaining access to VCs. Such initiatives need a thorough review through a DEI lens; even minor tweaks can open more doors for people. This should also include a review of DEI goals and how they're tracked.

3. **Make Big Bets That Are Industry Agonistic.** If you're going to support Black entrepreneurs or any other specific demographic, then you should craft bold initiatives that move the needle. Such an initiative is likely going to be industry agnostic, meaning it may not perfectly align with your industry cluster strategy. A program like Build in Tulsa needs to be industry agnostic because there simply aren't enough Black-founded start-ups in a particular cluster or even set of clusters to make a viable and scalable business model in Tulsa. My advice would be to open your support to any Black entrepreneur working in tech, which will benefit your ecosystem immediately and your clusters over time.

4. **Design Discrete Efforts That Align with Your Tech Niche.** In addition to big industry-agonistic initiatives, you should also create more discrete efforts and embed them throughout your core programming. TIL, for example, has been able to align efforts with Black Tech Street around cultivating cyber talent. You should identify other synergies. Perhaps it's a special cohort of entrepreneurs-in-residence for Black founders working in your select cluster or scholarships for students of color in your workforce initiative. As you look across your projects,

figure out how to create plug-in opportunities that develop your clusters while advancing DEI.

5. **Build a Dedicated Space.** In New York, a community college professor told me about a class trip she took her students on to Google's Lower Manhattan offices. Google's security is robust, and several of her students of color felt terribly uncomfortable because of the uniformed security guards. While minoritized people should feel safe in the offices of Google, they also need spaces of their own. I regularly heard from stakeholders that Tulsa needed a dedicated hub for Black entrepreneurs, where they could build community together. Build in Tulsa fully operates one of Gradient's buildings, creating that center of gravity for Tulsa's Black tech world.

6. **Provide Access to Capital.** As earlier stats attest, access to capital for Black founders is abysmal, and bias against Black founders is prevalent in tech and the VC world. If traditional sources of capital aren't providing the cash start-ups need to grow, then your city should raise a special fund for Black founders or partner with accelerators with a proven track record of supporting founders of color. Like Build in Tulsa is doing, cities also need to participate in the growing national network of VCs dedicated to women, people of color, and other minoritized founders.

A note of caution. While some DEI interventions may not directly align with your cluster strategy—particularly interventions that focus on a specific demographic—programs targeting Black founders (or any other group) will need to be fully integrated into the city's tech ecosystem. Black founders may need a space of their own or a dedicated fund, but they'll also need clients and investors (read: White clients and investors). You should consider how to facilitate introductions, relationships, and partnerships between Black founders and White stakeholders. You should also work to deconflict existing programming with those dedicated to minority-founded start-ups, ensuring you're not creating a separate but equal world of entrepreneurial support. (For example, should a Black founder in energy tech go to EIC Rose Rock, TIL's energy tech–specialized accelerator, or to Build in Tulsa?) Coordinating between organizations and aligning offerings will help you communicate coherent pathways to the start-ups you're looking to support.

Chicago: "The Promised Land"

Tulsa and other Heartland cities could take further lessons in how to advance DEI from Chicago. As the largest tech hub in the Heartland, Chicago is leading the way in creating an inclusive ecosystem that supports founders of color. In 2023, Tulsa tried to do just that when the Coretz Family Foundation convened a fireside chat in Greenwood with Aspen Institute president Dan Porterfield and John W. Rogers, founder of Chicago-based Ariel Investments and one of America's most famous Black investors. I attended the event, where Rogers spoke about the importance of Black wealth creation and his and Chicago's efforts to support founders of color.

Here's how one entrepreneur describes Chicago: In 2021, Kathryn Finney, a Black founder of the preseed venture fund Greenhouse Fund, moved operations from Atlanta to Chicago, which she perceived as the "Promised Land," a city rife with opportunity and support for Black innovation.[34] Although Chicago lags coastal peers (third most populous US city, but ranked tenth for start-ups),[35] it's distinguishing itself with respect to supporting Black founders. According to Crunchbase, 5.4 percent of Chicago's seed and preseed funding went to Black and brown founders, while this share was only 3.5 percent in leading tech cities like New York, San Francisco, and Los Angeles.[36] A marginal but significant difference.

What could account for this? Part of the equation is how dynamic local initiatives like TechRise and BLKTech have created pathways for Chicago's Black entrepreneurs to capitalize on their ideas. TechRise, an early-stage incubator run by the inclusive growth nonprofit P33, provides funding, knowledge, and connections to underrepresented founders. Since launching in 2021, TechRise has given more than $2.5 million in grants to 110 founders, 68 percent of whom identify as Black and 24 percent as Latino.[37] Additionally, BLKTech is an accelerator equipping Black-led start-ups with mentorship, workshops, and the chance to secure VC funding at the end of the program.[38] It's also worth mentioning that a report from JPMorgan Chase and Nasdaq attributes progress to state policy, particularly initiatives of the Illinois Department of Commerce, which, they find, are "breaking down systemic barriers faced by minority and women entrepreneurs through specialized business collectives and access to venture capital."[39]

Local initiatives that work to bridge the racial-funding gap have been vital to making Chicago into the aforementioned (and obviously aspirational) "Promised Land" for founders of color, and these initiatives have contributed to growing the city's historically strong Black middle class and community of professionals—demographics Tulsa is still working on.

While Tulsa has made laudable efforts at supporting Black entrepreneurs, the wider environment for DEI poses serious challenges. As Black Tech Street and Build in Tulsa were doing their important work, in December 2023, Governor Stitt signed an executive order banning publicly funded DEI programs, including at Oklahoma's state universities.[40] Stitt's action occurred in the national context of setbacks to affirmative action and backlash against DEI more broadly, which has distorted the intent of DEI initiatives and stoked racist tropes among White people. For a state like Oklahoma, with a poor track record on minority inclusion, economic developers must tread state politics carefully. You may find that your city doesn't value DEI as much as you do or specific organizations are turned off by the rhetoric. Through relationships and intel gathering, you can figure out how to tailor your messaging to best connect with potential partners. Ultimately, most people want to support tech talent and entrepreneurs—regardless of color or sex. So, there may be times in which DEI is your stealth objective.

THE CENTENNIAL AND BEYOND

The day of the centennial commemoration, June 2, 2021, was unlike anything I'd ever experienced. It started with the opening of the Greenwood Rising Museum, an interactive exhibit showcasing the horrors of 1921, complete with artifacts and multimedia displays. Then, the community gathered at the John Hope Franklin Reconciliation Park, named after the preeminent Black historian and Oklahoma native who wrote *From Slavery to Freedom*. At the park, under a still blue sky, survivors sat in wheelchairs, surrounded by their families, as we listened to dignitaries speak. The daylong ceremony had the gravity of a funeral, with a palpable sense of community-wide mourning.

As I sat in the park, I thought back to my first visit to Greenwood in 2019 and how I had only scratched the surface of what a vibrant and promising community this was. In two years, I had gone from an observant outsider to a local integrated into the community, enriched by personal knowledge of and relations in Greenwood. I don't know if the district felt or experienced reconciliation—the centennial's central aim—but I did notice a collective sense of catharsis. You could almost hear people exhale when the event was over; a pall had been lifted even as social justice and equity efforts continued. The two years leading up to the centennial, with Black Lives Matter, the fight for reparations, incendiary national politics, and a global pandemic, had left many in the community drained. This day was the culmination of years of emotional energy, and a much longer effort to bring 1921 into full light.

I asked Hannibal Johnson, the historian, what reconciliation means to him, and what it looks like in practice. "Reconciliation is not something to be achieved because it is purely aspirational," he told me. "Reconciliation is a continuous journey . . . [and there are] three critical components to it: acknowledgment, apology, and atonement."[41] For Johnson, cities need to acknowledge the unvarnished truth of past wrongs; communicate empathy for misdeeds through the act of apology; and through atonement, make amends and repair the damage to the extent possible. Johnson said that reparations are just one way to atone for the massacre. Investing in the future is even more powerful: investing in education, cultural assets, and entrepreneurial training are all ways to honor Black Wall Street. For Tulsa, I think, reconciliation is necessary for community-wide reinvention.

After the ceremonies, the centennial events turned toward a more festive vibe. I walked with some of my TIL teammates through Greenwood and saw the public arts project funded by Bloomberg Philanthropies. Leading the project was Rick Lowe, a Black artist and MacArthur Fellow. Lowe guided the community through a project he calls "social sculpture," where he worked with residents to engage all aspects of their neighborhood and tapped their creativity to produce a work of art. Similar to his New Orleans project after Hurricane Katrina, the exercise was aimed at helping Greenwood residents process their thoughts on the massacre while envisioning a brighter future for the district.[42] Lowe's art took the form of large, colorful murals vividly depicting those terrible events a hundred years ago.

Playing throughout the day were various musical groups, including Fire in Little Africa, a musical and multimedia collective formed for the centennial.[43] Dozens of Tulsa-based artists came together to record an album and are producing a documentary as well. Their signature song, "Shining," expresses the feeling of Greenwood, the hope and resilience many Black Tulsans feel. Greenwood was built by and for Black Tulsans, the song says, and it argues that reinvention can occur when Black communities stand together and support one another—while maintaining a healthy skepticism of outside investors. I was most struck by the recurring use of "shine" or "shinin'" in the song, which evokes the pride Greenwood residents have for their community and the beauty, promise, and excellence Blackness can represent. On a personal note, it harkened to my middle school's "diamonds in the rough" theme, and it called to mind a song we all know and that speaks to America's aspiration of unity, "America the Beautiful": "America! America! / God shed his grace on thee / And crown thy good with brotherhood / From sea to shining sea!" When President Ronald Reagan drew on a similar motif to describe America as a "shining city on a hill," many were quick to point out that America doesn't shine for everyone equally. Greenwood knows this better than most.

It's easy to idealize Black Wall Street or to imagine Black Tech Street, the vision, as a mythological Black utopia—like Harlem of the '20s; Howard University in DC, which Ta-Nehisi Coates calls his "Mecca"; or Wakanda in a futuristic imagination.[44] But America needs vibrant Black communities, and there's a generational opportunity to harness the legacy of Black Wall Street to help Greenwood thrive in the digital age. Investing in Black entrepreneurs and supporting drag queens and gay-bohemian communities can help citywide systems become more inclusive. Through dedicated and meaningful investments, cities need to create tech ecosystems that enable Others to shine.

ACTION PLAN SUMMARY

REINVENTION	GROWTH	INCLUSION
What needs reinventing?	*How do you catalyze growth?*	*How do you advance inclusion?*
To expand opportunities in the innovation economy to those historically shut out, civic organizations will need to create DEI interventions that support specific populations. This will require that cities understand marginalized people as valuable economic actors and create investments that go beyond symbolic efforts and provide tangible support.	Cities can advance growth through DEI investments. To do so, DEI initiatives should be informed by significant community engagement. Civic institutions should ensure that existing programming is inclusive, including by tracking goals. And for new programming, cities should make big bets that are industry agnostic and discrete bets that are tied to their industry cluster strategy.	DEI initiatives support populations typically shut out of tech, but they can also increase broader awareness of cultural nuances and community needs. As a result, DEI programs can lead to more thoughtful, responsive, and inclusive economic development initiatives and challenge private companies to improve their own practices.

CHAPTER 7

SHAKE UP HIGHER ED

(ACADEMIC INNOVATION)

Spring semester 2019 was coming to a close when the University of Tulsa underwent one of the most dramatic restructurings in its history. The Henry Kendall College of Arts and Sciences shrunk from fifteen departments and sixty-eight degree programs to three divisions with thirty-six degree programs. Gone were religion, philosophy, musical theater, and scores of other programs. The liberal arts bore the brunt of the cuts, but the college of business and law school were also reduced. Spared were engineering and health sciences.[1] The turmoil was the talk of the town when I first started advising the George Kaiser Family Foundation. The reorganization left TU administrators, faculty, and students reeling and the Tulsa community concerned about the university's future.

What could justify such a radical plan? For starters, the University of Tulsa, a small private school, had a $6.8 million operating loss in 2018,[2] and enrollment had been declining for years (down 38 percent between 2018 and 2021).[3] You could feel it on campus. Even during the day, TU often felt deserted, its land-scaped lawns untrafficked. With an unsustainable fiscal trajectory crashing into broader changes in academia, the university needed to take decisive action—and most of this happened *before* COVID threw higher ed into further disarray. But painful as they were, the cuts weren't reactive—there was a method behind them. They were designed to better align TU's academic offerings with student needs, bolster graduation rates, and stabilize the university's financial standing.

Then provost Janet Levit led TU's historic pivot. She would go on to serve as interim president when Gerard Clancy resigned the post less than a year later. "For too long, we have tried to be everything to everyone," Levit said of the cuts. "We have been spread too thin and, in many cases, have not been able to achieve excellence as a result."[4]

TU's cuts reflect broader challenges within higher ed, and other universities have had to make similar decisions. The University of Central Missouri,[5] West Virginia University,[6] and the University of Nebraska have all recently made steep cuts to their liberal arts programming.[7] Studies show that completing a four-year degree increases lifetime wages, and more students are earning bachelor's degrees than ever—yet the continuing rise of tuition and consequential increase of student debt, along with opportunities in the gig economy, remote learning, and training boot camps, are leading many to conclude that the bachelor's is no longer the necessity it had been seen as—especially in liberal arts degrees not directly tied to a job.[8]

Despite this shifting landscape, universities are and will continue to be a foundational element of the Innovation Flywheel. The university can and should be a powerful source of technical innovation and talent if its core business is sound, programs are aligned to a city's economic development strategy, and if it has the resources to invest in applied R&D. The challenge is to update the university for our current moment, when old truisms about education should no longer be taken for granted and everything is up for reimagining.

In that spirit, Heartland cities need to ask whether the liberal arts, as traditionally configured, are best suited to meet the needs of our contemporary world. A core curriculum in the liberal arts is increasingly vital as AI and fake news risk destroying a shared set of facts humanity needs to exist. The liberal arts should be about skills, though, not costly programs. Universities should help students build these skills—among them critical thinking, reading, and writing—and develop a code of ethics. But many small Heartland universities—public and private alike—need to provide a liberal arts education without multiple departments and unnecessary overhead. This is coming from a college English major, but by modernizing and rightsizing the liberal arts, universities can free up cash to invest in STEM, making the university more competitive while contributing more talent, innovation, and growth to their regions, creating a virtuous cycle in the process.

Higher ed needs a shake-up, not just in Tulsa but all over the country, and Heartland cities in particular must reorient their universities to work in concert with their economic development strategy. Universities as ivory silos, disconnected from their local tech ecosystems, are no longer sustainable for either the school or the community. Every US tech hub has an anchor university or two driving applied R&D and producing STEM talent. And many of the Heartland cities that have successfully navigated volatile economic transitions—as we saw with Pittsburgh in chapter 1 and Austin in chapter 5—have counted on strong universities to provide innovation and talent. But while most Heartland cities have universities, few are geared toward contributing to their region's innovation economy.

Despite the initial anxiety it caused, TU was right to make the changes that it did. TU's bold action has stabilized the university, and its new strategic plan has allowed it to invest in applied R&D programs critical to the future. According to Boston Consulting Group, which supported TU's transformation plan, in the two years following the reorganization, TU "boosted first-time-student enrollment by 33% . . . all while increasing access and diversity on campus and taking better care of its faculty and staff."[9] (TU saw a 12 percent increase in students receiving Pell grants and a 6 percent increase in racial diversity.)[10]

In 2021, the university hired a new president, Brad Carson. Regularly clad in three-piece suits and cuff links, Carson had a CV tailor made for the job: he was a Rhodes Scholar, the former Democratic congressman for Oklahoma's 2nd district, and the former undersecretary of the Army. Carson reminded me of the Blue Dog Democratic senators I had growing up in Louisiana, John Breaux and Mary Landrieu. Echoing his predecessor's sentiment, Carson said that TU should "be best in class in a couple of things while being good enough in others—because you cannot be best in class in everything."[11] I found this sentiment strikingly similar to the approach that I had followed with determining Tulsa's tech niche—universities need to identify and invest in their strongest opportunities.

What I concluded during my time in Tulsa was that the city's success is dependent upon TU's success. Their fates are linked. Someone once asked me what I would do if I had a billion dollars to spend on the city. My answer was to pump that money into the University of Tulsa. I see TU as a mission-critical asset for the city's talent and innovation production. Without a successful university, the flywheel simply can't spin. And I am bullish on TU's potential to grow into a more active player in Tulsa's tech ecosystem. I believe the same is true for currently underachieving universities across the Heartland.

These universities function on an outdated operating system; they're not built for twenty-first-century challenges, despite holding spectacular promise to address them. Universities face a multitude of sometimes competing priorities: they must balance education, basic research, and tech and innovation, all of which can be either a burden or an opportunity. When the balance is struck well, universities are a perfect place for the talent- and tech-hungry private sector to partner with and leverage public sector investments. This also means that there can be funding from across sectors all channeled into a single institution, which is why universities must play a leading role in a city's innovation economy. And it's why TU's turnaround has been a key factor in Tulsa's recent resurgence.

Times of crisis like the one TU faced can often reveal what you need to do to survive—as the Great Plains novelist Willa Cather writes, "There are some things you learn best in calm, and some in storm."[12] Becoming a pared-down and more focused university has enabled TU to better meet Tulsa's needs and position itself for the future.

Civic ecosystems, and economic developers in particular, need to help reorient their universities as anchors in the innovation economy—enabling them to more intentionally produce talent and technologies that help grow regional clusters.

To modernize the university in this way, cities must include higher ed as they form economic development strategies and work to align on regional strengths and needs. When universities are active members of the tech ecosystem and leading contributors to a city's economic development coalition, they can be more than just places of learning—they can become engines for reinvention, aiding both regional growth and national competitiveness.

EMBRACE THE FULL CYCLE OF INNOVATION

Universities traditionally conduct foundational or basic research, but Heartland universities need to generate knowledge with an expressed practical, market purpose. In the words of Erwin Gianchandani, who leads the National Science Foundation's (NSF) technology, innovation, and partnerships directorate, universities need to embrace the "full cycle of discovery and innovation."[13] This means translational or applied research—the kind that will make universities vehicles for economic growth.

The process of commercialization (otherwise known as **tech transfer**) requires taking research and translating it into market-ready services or products. Here's how it works: Universities conduct research and development, which leads to an invention; that invention is evaluated for the potential industry uses of its intellectual property. The IP is then protected by the university through copyrights or patents. Next, the IP is marketed to potential licensees in industry. If there's interest, then the IP gets licensed to that third party. It's not uncommon for the initial inventors to found an independent start-up and license the IP they created for the university. Those licensees can then develop a marketable product, sometimes with outside consultation by the researchers. That's when the product enters the public domain and becomes a commodity, contributing to economic growth. This process captures the fullness of the innovation cycle, which many universities don't adequately achieve because of differing institutional priorities and lack of infrastructure. Yet once universities can birth a new company, they face even more challenges.

Once an academic-based start-up is conceived, they often suffer the same risks as start-ups originating in the private sector, but they face an even steeper hill to climb. These start-ups need to survive what is commonly called the "valley of death": the time when basic research funding has expired but before industry and most VCs are willing to invest. If companies cannot rise out of the trench, they're in danger of depleting their initial capital and failing. As we'll see later, that's why ecosystem partners are so critical. When universities do late-stage innovation well and have strong relationships with industry, VCs, and federal agencies, they can become a start-up factory, as Stanford, MIT, and Columbia are for their respective regions.

Academic innovation drives competitiveness at all levels—cities, regions, and countries. Orin Herskowitz is the executive director of Columbia Technology Ventures (CTV), the tech transfer office of Columbia University. While most universities aren't good at tech transfer and commercialization, Columbia is an exception thanks to its endowment, concentration of talent, legacy of excellence, and its New York City home. Every year, CTV manages an average of four hundred invention disclosures, one hundred licenses, and the creation of twenty to thirty new start-ups, which constantly feeds New York's dynamic start-up scene. "The reality is that many of the most transformative deeptech innovations of the past thirty years have emerged from America's research labs, and of those, most from university science labs," Herskowitz explained. "From Google to mRNA vaccines to climate tech, US university research labs are saving and improving lives around the world [and they are] spinning out over a thousand start-ups per year . . . up nearly threefold from twenty years ago."[14] These start-ups create thousands of jobs. By not capitalizing on their innovation potential, universities are leaving value on the table and inhibiting their ecosystem's development.

PICK A WINNER

Most universities aren't Columbia, though. I often hear Heartland leaders bemoan the state of their region's higher education, with some pining to build new universities that, they presumably think, will magically solve their problems. Even worse, some cities try to recruit external, brand-name universities to set up satellite campuses, further underinvesting in their homegrown schools. As I've espoused throughout this book, the key to success is investing in, connecting, and leveraging your local assets—and universities could not be more important.

The answer isn't to give up on your local university just because it's underresourced. The answer is to pick a winner to double down on. For smaller schools like the University of Tulsa, you might have to choose just a few STEM-related fields to prioritize, and that means aligning them with your city's tech niche. Picking a star department or two will help you beef up your R&D in this area and make the best use of limited resources.

For TU, this was cyber. In 2021, the program was ranked among the top twenty-five cyber programs by *U.S. News & World Report*, with no other aspects of the university—except for petroleum engineering—coming close in terms of prestige or success. The university's reputation in cyber was largely a result of Cyber Corps, an under-the-radar program with national clout.

Cyber Corps focuses on producing talent for cyber warfare and national security careers, training what TU faculty call "MacGyvers," after the jack-of-all-trades secret agent from the '80s TV show. The selective program offers free tuition, a stipend, and a summer internship in Washington. With a decades-long relationship with the National Security Agency, more than 350 students have enrolled since 2001, and 70 percent of its graduates have gone on to work for the NSA, the Central Intelligence Agency, US Departments of Homeland Security or Defense, the Federal

Bureau of Investigation, or the National Aeronautics and Space Administration. TU is also consistently designated an NSA Center of Excellence in Cyber Operations, and students work directly with government personnel as part of the program. Students also receive assistance in acquiring security clearances that make them competitive for federal jobs.

TU's partnership with the NSA has birthed new talent and innovations that protect America's cyberspace, testifying to the quality of both TU faculty and students and proving that a little university in Green Country could punch above its weight and contribute to national security. The program is one of the largest of its kind in the country and has received millions of dollars in funding from the NSF,[15] but opportunities were being missed. After interning with federal agencies, graduates returned to the DC metro to start their careers. While this gave students invaluable opportunities, because Tulsa wasn't able to retain the talent, it limited the program's impact on the local ecosystem. (Recall that retention of graduates from local schools is a key metric in The Economy Forward Framework from chapter 3.)

I remember when I first met the founder and director of Cyber Corps, Sujeet Shenoi, a computer scientist and chemical engineer. I had begun my advisory work with GKFF and was conducting a landscape assessment of TU's cyber offerings. Shenoi walked me through the history of the program. I was told I couldn't take notes, making me feel as if I were in a SCIF, a sensitive compartmented information facility used by the government. In my conversation with him, Shenoi explained that the program's singular focus was producing talent and innovations for US national security, not market-ready innovations. The unintended consequence was that Cyber Corps was exporting talent and innovation rather than creating benefits within the community.

This is indicative of higher ed more broadly: there tends to be strong foundational research but little interest in or capacity to translate this into real-world products and services. Take Oklahoma's universities. None fare poorly in terms of federal R&D funding, which is the critical mana that underwrites academic discovery. According to the 2022 NSF Higher Ed R&D Survey, OU, OSU, and TU each ranked well above the national average for R&D expenditures. Where these universities fall behind is in the commercialization of that R&D, as evidenced by a Milken Institute study. See the tables that follow.

2022 NATIONAL SCIENCE FOUNDATION HIGHER ED R&D SURVEY (OKLAHOMA UNIVERSITIES)[16]			
	Rank (out of 1,042 universities)	Percentile	R&D Expenditures (in thousands)
U. Oklahoma, Norman, and Health Science Center	72	91.9	408,656
Oklahoma State U., Stillwater	137	84.6	195,041
U. Tulsa	306	65.7	17,416
U. Oklahoma, The, Tulsa	374	58.0	7,945
U. Central Oklahoma	385	56.8	7,070
Southwestern Oklahoma State U.	766	14.0	531

MILKEN INSTITUTE TECHNOLOGY TRANSFER AND COMMERCIALIZATION INDEX, 2017: UNIVERSITIES & RESEARCH INSTITUTIONS[17] (SCORED OUT OF 100)						
Rank (out of 225 universities)	Institution	Patent Issued Score	Licensing Issued Score	Licensing Income Score	Start-Up Score	Index Score
121	Oklahoma State University	59.97	58.44	84.28	56.46	72.51
132	University of Oklahoma All Campuses	65.07	57.24	83.14	50.76	70.55

Note: The University of Tulsa was not ranked.

All of this meant that the challenge for TU was to take its star department and turn it into something that could benefit the city and its tech niche. So, TU crafted its strategic plan to build on its strengths in computer science and engineering and make its cyber program best in class. "We want to create a Michael Porter-esque cluster around cyber," Brad Carson told me. "TU will likely be the apex of a [local] economic chain (with our PhD programs) that includes workforce development (community colleges) and basic IT training (other universities)."[18] Meanwhile, TIL will work to develop the ecosystem in tandem with these priorities, creating job opportunities that will be worthy of the high-quality talent TU is producing and keep them in Tulsa after they graduate.

Of course, one great program won't solve all your problems; this is just the beginning. After you've shifted your mindset to prioritize innovation and after you've picked your winner, you'll need to identify the institutional and cultural barriers to innovation.

IDENTIFY BARRIERS TO INNOVATION

University professors are scholars in their fields, trained to research, analyze, and publish. They did not enter the academy to commercialize research, develop technological innovations, or found start-ups—nor have they been trained to do any of these things. Some faculty may even see commercialization as capitalism seeping into the sanctity of knowledge creation and education. It's little wonder, then, that most professors with whom I engaged shared an ambivalence for translational research and market-ready innovations. If I had any hope of leveraging TU's cyber program for the success of Tulsa's economy, I needed to better understand the barriers to innovation that TU and other regional universities faced.

Having worked as a strategic partner with every major university in New York as well as in the state of Oklahoma, I can say with confidence (and respect) that university bureaucracy is designed to stifle technological innovation—no matter whether they're in the Heartland or on the coasts. University systems were never meant to facilitate technological innovation, and many of their business processes are intended to reduce risk, not encourage entrepreneurial endeavors. As a result, universities are often the most difficult of economic development partners—but it's well worth the effort to bring them into the fold.

With little institutional knowledge or historical precedent for technological innovation, universities themselves are often their own biggest enemy when it comes to tech transfer. There are a host of barriers embedded in universities that reinforce institutional norms and stifle innovation, prohibiting evolution of the school and cutting off the support academic-based firms need to bridge the valley of death.

No one knows these challenges better than Tom Wavering, who served as the executive director of the Tom Love Innovation Hub at the University of Oklahoma. In 2024, he became the chief university strategy and innovation officer of Texas Christian University in Fort Worth. The Hub he led supports emerging companies at all stages within the OU system by connecting them with various resources.

Universities are good at innovation within their traditional academic activities, such as teaching and foundational research, but "they often lack a holistic translation of these activities into their ecosystem," Wavering told me. As a result, universities can find themselves out of sync with their local innovation ecosystem and unable to speak the same language as technologists. While universities generally take pride in themselves as steady institutions, start-ups and innovation teams are moving fast, breaking things, and just trying to survive. "So, what prevents universities from translating research into products and start-ups? The university itself," Wavering said. "This is why universities must look beyond themselves and become part of the broader ecosystem."[19]

But change must start from within. Intermediary organizations like Tulsa Innovation Labs can help universities expand their perspective and identify barriers to growth, then design solutions. These pain points include:

MISALIGNED INCENTIVES: Faculty have been trained to publish or perish, not to innovate tech, so within the tenure track process, there aren't incentives to encourage professors to think beyond a paper or a book.

POOR INSTITUTIONAL SUPPORT: Most universities have underfunded tech transfer offices and other shoddy mechanisms to translate research. As Wavering suggested, faculty are often left on their own.

LACK OF ENTREPRENEURIAL KNOWLEDGE: Academics aren't trained to be entrepreneurs, and it's unfair of anyone to expect otherwise. Basic understanding of company building and innovation aren't taught in PhD programs. Scholars do what they know and often don't take the next step in their research because of simple lack of familiarity.

LOW VOLUME OF IP: Many smaller universities don't have enough IP that can be commercialized to merit internal support structures, much less robust ones.

UNIVERSITY SILOS: Like many of the civic organizations in Tulsa, university departments often function as silos, undermining partnerships. This limits interdisciplinary research and faculty collaboration, isolating IP with potential from other faculty, researchers, or support that could take it to the next level.

MINIMAL INDUSTRY INVOLVEMENT: Many academics scoff at the idea of partnering with industry, concerned that it would interfere with their research. As a result, universities often don't know how to make these partnerships work, perpetuating the academy's insularity and inhibiting the full cycle of discovery.

SCARCE FUNDING: If academics do get to a point where they're interested in translational research, there's typically a dearth of funding to support the earliest-stage start-ups (the proverbial valley of death). With scarce resources to begin with, universities aren't likely to fuel the development of new companies.

LIMITED ACCESS TO FACILITIES: Inventors need space. Just like the garage of yore, academics require research labs and facilities that enable their research and the commercialization process, but Heartland cities often lack science-enabled real estate.

OVERSTRETCHED FACULTY: Professors have teaching, research, and administrative duties, not to mention personal and family lives. Many are contingent, not tenure track, which further limits their ability to innovate.

WEAK INNOVATION NETWORKS: Academics hoping to successfully launch companies lack the necessary connections to support them, such as technical and business hires and mentors and advisers—as well as large-dollar VC funding. They're not going to find these people on the traditional academic-conference circuit.

Identifying these barriers is the first step in creating solutions that foster systems-wide change. These challenges are doubly true in midsized cities, smaller institutions, and places without an existing innovation ecosystem. To pivot to more translational research and help start-ups survive, universities need to reach beyond their walls and work better with federal agencies, industry, VCs, and economic development organizations, and they'll need to build internal support systems to create a culture of innovation.

BUILD A SUPPORT SYSTEM

A stakeholder once asked me a fair question: "How do you expect universities to successfully manage innovation programs when many are struggling to keep the lights on?" My response was that you may need to start small, manage expectations, and anticipate investment over the long term—something funders may not want to hear. Like cities, universities won't change in a blink, so urban leaders will need to work with their universities to build systems-wide solutions over time.

This effort was of such importance that I devoted an entire person to it. To help drive change at TU, I relied on TIL's director of cyber, Conor Godfrey. Conor had a background in national security and diplomacy related to cybersecurity from the US State Department, so he was well equipped to tackle this big, hairy problem.

To recalibrate your university, civic leaders and economic development organizations will need to work with higher ed partners to build internal systems that address structural barriers to innovation and inspire cultural and behavioral change. This will be a frustrating and long-term process that's going to take a lot of patience. Here are seven recommendations, all of which address the problem points mentioned previously:

1. **Make Innovation an Institutional Priority:** Innovation needs to be a top-down priority, communicated directly and regularly from the university president and reinforced by deans and department chairs. The university's board should also set metrics and hold university leadership accountable to achieving them.

2. **Provide Entrepreneurial Training to Faculty:** Similar to what TIL did with our local corporations (covered in the next chapter), universities should work with ecosystem partners and create an Entrepreneurship 101 Program for Academics that gives scholars a road map for translating their research into products that can be commercialized.

3. **Offer Tangible Incentives:** Universities should amend their performance evaluation, promotion, and tenure criteria—including recognizing patents, licenses, and start-ups as wins. They should also offer cash bonuses and faculty buyback time to celebrate achievements and allow for additional innovation sabbaticals.

4. **Hire Innovators:** I've seen a single faculty member veto good ideas and stand in the way of progress. If all else

fails, universities need to retire hidebound faculty and bring on new, more diverse, and entrepreneurial-minded scholars. The war on talent is immense, but you really need only one or two great professors with big dreams to create an impactful lab. Within the university, individuals drive innovation, so invest in a rock star or two.

5. **Establish a Tech Transfer Office:** Universities should consider creating a tech transfer office to convert research into commercializable products, manage the IP, and connect it to industry and investor partners. Such an office is warranted if sufficient research occurs across the university. The goal is to provide clear rules of the road, a standard menu of options for licensing IP. Universities are typically set up to squeeze all of the revenue possible out of successful inventions and rely on case-by-case negotiations. But that makes the process long and frustrating and clouds the ROI for would-be industry partners. By ceding ground on an individual invention and developing a reputation for being easy to work with ("industry friendly"), you can grow the whole pie of sponsored research.

6. **Create an Office of the Vice President for Research and Economic Development:** This office works to move the university beyond its traditional role and expand its impact through research. TU created such a role as part of its investment in the university's research enterprise. The VP collaborates across disciplines and engages with stakeholders such as economists, entrepreneurs, economic developers, and policymakers to come up with research solutions for contemporary and practical issues. Part of this work includes IP development and commercialization of research findings for use with private sector partners.

7. **Build Industry Partnerships:** In *National Innovation Systems*, evolutionary economist Richard R. Nelson writes that in successful innovation systems around the world, the relationship between universities and industry goes beyond "simply doing research of relevance to the industry in question."[20] Rather, he explained, "The connections were much broader and closer than that, involving information dissemination and problem solving. They were co-partners in a technological community."[21] While Nelson published this extensive study in 1993, the tech revolution that was taking off around that time has since proved that insight to be even more true. Industry-led research labs, embedded within universities, can help foster that type of collaboration.

This support system can be best activated when it's focused on a university's star department. By prioritizing a handful of departments that play to a university's strengths and that align with the city's tech niche, the university can feel confident going all in on those research fields and creating a support system around them.

EXAMPLES FROM THE HEARTLAND

We touched on Carnegie Mellon and its work on robotics earlier in the book, but let's explore a few other examples of academic R&D programs outside the coasts to see how they do it.

Purdue University's Office of Technology Commercialization is among the national leaders in tech transfer. Located in West Lafayette, Indiana (more than an hour outside Indianapolis), the university attributes its success to its high-powered research and expert commercialization pipeline, made possible by investing in most of the recommendations mentioned previously.[22] The office currently stewards the IP of more than four hundred university innovations. In 2017, a report by Ross DeVol, then at the Milken Institute, ranked Purdue twelfth in the country on its technology transfer and commercialization index, jumping twenty-seven spots since the institute last conducted the study back in 2006.[23] And in 2023, university researchers led Purdue to rank fifth in most US patents created.[24] The university has built a robust internal system for tech transfer, with many technologies birthed at the Purdue Innovates Incubator, which helps students and faculty create companies, commercialize IP, and attain venture capital. Another asset is Purdue's Discovery Park District, a four-hundred-acre campus innovation ecosystem where "businesses of all sizes can access a business-minded University, global talent pipelines, and advanced R&D activities."[25] The university's technology license menu skews heavily toward engineering and manufacturing technology,[26] a trend that folds into the Indianapolis-Carmel region's broader strategy for economic development. In 2024, Purdue leveraged its manufacturing expertise as part of a consortium of regional stakeholders and landed an EDA Tech Hubs grant for biotechnology manufacturing.[27] (More on why that's a BFD in chapter 10.)

The **University of Cincinnati** (UC), meanwhile, demonstrates how state governmental support can be instrumental in fostering academic innovation as well. In consultation with the Intra-University Council of Ohio, the state of Ohio championed the "Ohio IP Promise." The IP Promise establishes uniform principles so that researchers know how to make their research available for public use. All fourteen of Ohio's state universities have agreed to the IP Promise, and they are required to provide a step-by-step process for commercialization and provide standard option/license agreement templates to inform both faculty and students about the terms of commercialization.[28] UC has seen success since the IP Promise was implemented—comparing fiscal years 2013–17 to fiscal years 2018–22, invention disclosures rose by 51 percent, filed patents rose by 62 percent, deals with faculty rose 109 percent, and the number of start-ups through the UC Venture Lab rose from one to two per year to an average of fourteen per year.[29] UC's available technologies are mostly in the life sciences, with a focus on diseases and disorders, biomedical uses, and diagnostics.[30] UC's technology both responds to and feeds the regional economy; from 2017 to 2021, Cincinnati's life sciences sector witnessed a 25.5 percent increase in jobs and accounted for almost $5 billion in gross regional product in 2023.[31]

Like TU, **Wichita State University** (WSU) in Kansas demonstrates the power of picking a winning department and investing in it. WSU's Office of Tech Transfer and Commercialization supports some of the most dynamic university research commercialization in the Heartland, particularly in aviation and military technology. The university inspired TIL in its development of its advanced air mobility initiatives. Wichita is known as the "Air Capital of the World" thanks to its long-standing relationship with the aviation industry, and this legacy continues to shape the university's innovation activity today. The NSF has consistently ranked WSU number one of US universities for industry-funded aerospace R&D, and in 2024, the NSF ranked WSU number two for industry-funded engineering R&D.[32] In January 2024, WSU's National Institute for Aviation Research inked a massive deal with the US Air Force, increasing its funding ceiling to $200 million on a project to improve the capabilities of the Air Force's B-1 bomber fleet.[33] Beyond just aerospace, the university's tech transfer office recently introduced a general matchmaking program, designed to connect industry innovators with commercialized technology developed at WSU.[34] And, by April 2024, WSU's ten-year-old Apex Accelerator had guided its start-up and small business clients to more than $1 billion in government contracts, showing how the university has helped grow the region's innovation economy.

Purdue's robust internal support system, the University of Cincinnati's state-sponsored IP commercialization initiative, and

Wichita State's industry and military contracts illustrate that supporting start-ups and new technology may take different forms depending on institutional dynamics and nuances with technologies. Regardless of the particulars of a university's support system, it will need to bring resources to bear on its star department and invest in high-impact initiatives that maximize the opportunity its research affords.

INVEST IN A GAME CHANGER

As TU president Carson said, universities should challenge themselves to become best in class in just a couple of areas. For midsized cities looking to grow a tech economy, local universities need to go big in a STEM field or two at most. Instead of spreading resources across a number of small efforts, TU has invested in three signature cyber initiatives that reinforce one another. Investing in a game changer doesn't require a $100 million up-front investment. It can start small and build over time, such as an executive-in-residence or doctoral fellowship program. But regardless of what form it takes, it should be focused on your university's strengths and synchronized with your city's tech niche strategy.

Today, TU is doing the right thing: specializing in cyber and building out. One good program, such as Cyber Corps, has ripple effects: it can increase funding, faculty, and enrollment, which helps lift all departments. In recent years, TU has become a key player in the world of cyber innovation. In addition to Cyber Corps, three new investments together represent a significant step forward for the university: the School of Cyber Studies and two innovation initiatives, which TIL codesigned with TU, the Cyber Fellows and the Oklahoma Cyber Innovation Institute.

School of Cyber Studies. Established in 2021, the school expanded and organized all of TU's cyber curricula under one umbrella. It includes the newly created bachelor's degree in cyber, a master's in cyber security (with in-person and online options), and an interdisciplinary PhD in cyber studies. The school also offers new scholarships to support these students. The cyber talent that TU will produce in the coming years will be a tremendous asset to Tulsa's innovation ecosystem, feeding the city's virtual health, energy tech, and advanced air mobility verticals. TU's graduates will go on to fill local jobs, grow existing businesses, and create start-ups, providing a pipeline of talent that's hard to overvalue.

Cyber Fellows. This doctoral fellowship was designed in 2019 as a cousin to Cyber Corps but dedicated to keeping talent and innovation in Tulsa. Originally including Team8, a cyber venture firm out of Tel Aviv, but expanding to other industry partners, Cyber Fellows nurtures scholar-entrepreneurs and helps bring their innovations to market. Doctoral students work with TU faculty and industry scientists. The program provides full funding to about ten PhD students each year to support their pursuit of cyber-related research as well as a retention bonus upon graduation, with the hopes of keeping graduates in Tulsa to register for patents, commercialize research, and establish new companies.

Oklahoma Cyber Innovation Institute. I told my TIL teammates that the institute was my white whale because it took nearly five years and overcoming every obstacle you could imagine getting it over the finish line. Finally launched in 2023 with an initial $75 million, this institute turbocharges TU's cyber R&D capability. Through expanded research and commercialization support, including new faculty, staff, and industry research labs, the institute is pursuing three goals: (1) build TU into a worldwide leader in cyber research, which includes critical infrastructure, smart installations, network security, robotics, and autonomous systems;

(2) develop top-tier cyber talent to meet the needs of business, science, and engineering on regional, national, and global scales; and (3) drive commercialization, with a particular emphasis on use-inspired problem-solving, experimentation and analysis, and producing novel hardware and software.

One of the stubborn challenges TIL encountered in its academic innovation programming is how difficult it is to achieve our DEI goals through doctoral and applied R&D initiatives. STEM fields are notoriously male, and cyber in particular is a predominantly White field. Unfortunately, the Cyber Fellows program reflects these industry demographics. In addition to expanding efforts to identify, recruit, and support women and people of color in the program, TIL and TU also need to work with the university's undergraduate programs to better cultivate an earlier and more diverse talent pipeline.

Through investments in cyber, TU hopes to secure the coveted designation of an R-1 research university, which will bring TU into a new echelon of universities, making it more competitive for grants, faculty, and students. And, over time, the Oklahoma Cyber Innovation Institute could apply for long-term, sustained designations, such as the Federally Funded Research and Development Center (FFRDC), NSF Engineering Research Center, or a corporate innovation campus. FFRDCs, in particular, operate as strategic partners for the benefit of the public and help their sponsoring federal agencies conduct research with integrity and technical excellence. While not focused on commercialization, such a prestigious designation brings with it a robust pipeline for federal research dollars to the FFRDC, typically housed within universities or a consortium of universities.

TU's three new cyber initiatives, along with Cyber Corps, have established TU as a holistic leader in cyber through talent development, applied research, translational research, and commercialization. The comprehensiveness of TU's suite of cyber assets is awesome, and if integrated into Tulsa's innovation ecosystem, it could be a game changer for the university and the city, while also contributing to national security.

OPPORTUNITIES IN NATIONAL SECURITY

TU's cyber assets and the talent and innovation that will emerge from them puts the university and Tulsa in a strong position to take advantage of any remilitarization America will undergo in the future. The peace dividend the world has benefited from since the end of the Cold War is disappearing, and the United States needs Heartland cities to once again contribute to national innovation and security, while working to retain talent and IP locally.

Global competition is mounting. A 2023 US State Department–funded study found that China leads all nations on "37 of 44 critical and emerging technologies," such as electric batteries, 5G, and nano manufacturing.[35] China's aggressive stance against Taiwan, the hub of semiconductors; Russia's invasion of Ukraine, which is now suddenly investing in defense technologies, particularly drones; and Hamas's assault on Israel, one of the world's leading innovators—all foreshadow disruption and danger to come. Already the US Defense Department budget increased 10 percent between fiscal years 2022–23.[36]

This is an important economic opportunity for Heartland cities and their universities. Bruce Katz, Milena Dovali, and Victoria Orozco argue that the increase in federal funding going to national security should cause cities to anticipate a "defense dividend." They recommend that beyond pursuing defense contracts, cities should leverage those opportunities to create catalytic opportunities for growth. In other words, think about the defense dividend in cluster terms: cities should connect defense opportunities to local emerging tech investments that may benefit from one another.

Katz and partners offer a five-point typology that shows how the Department of Defense organizes itself to help cities anticipate future opportunities. The five points are: (1) military bases, (2) command centers, (3) production hubs, (4) innovation hubs, and (5) distributed R&D. "Realizing a defense dividend," they write, "requires local and state leaders to understand their special role and function within the nation's sprawling defense establishment and work to leverage its impact to the maximum extent possible."[37]

To benefit from this defense dividend, cities should consider pivoting universities to be drivers of tech and talent to meet both military and regional economic needs. Imagine a Venn diagram, where one circle is your city's tech niche, and the other circle is US defense needs. How do universities pursue opportunities in the middle? How might you create adjacencies and synergies between your tech clusters and the government's needs?

The Israeli Model

An example worth emulating in how to best connect universities to the military, industry, and regional economies can be found in Israel. One of TU's early industry partners—brokered by GKFF—was Team8, which builds and invests in new tech companies. The firm's cofounder and managing partner, Nadav Zafrir, is a pioneer in the field of cybersecurity and was also a partner of mine at Cyber NYC. Zafrir commanded Israel's military technology unit, 8200, and established the Israeli Defense Forces' Cyber Command. Israel's academy-industry partnerships are best in class and can be informative for cities looking to forge similar connections.

Many Israelis enter university after their military service, bringing with them hands-on technical and problem-solving skills that can enrich the research environment and catalyze new technologies. This mutually beneficial relationship partly explains why tech firms started in Israeli research institutions grew to 13 percent of all

Israeli start-ups in 2020, up from 3.2 percent in 2016.[38] Universities work with industry, while the military serves as a fertile training ground for future innovators—an arrangement that has made Israel "the start-up nation."[39]

This model, as well as the near unlimited need for tech talent—cyber especially—should inspire Heartland cities to partner with industry and double down on academic innovation and talent. "Historically, the largest companies in the largest cities (like Tel Aviv and New York) have been able to attract the majority of cyber talent," Zafrir told me. "However, as the cyber industry matures, cyber talent will become critical to companies and cities of all sizes and geographies, and we will need an 'all-hands-on deck' approach. As a result, I believe cyber workforces will develop in unexpected places, particularly in small and midsized cities with university cyber education programs to train the next generation of cyber professionals. An excellent example of this is the Be'er Sheva cyber hub developing around Ben Gurion University in Israel."[40] I've visited Be'er Sheva, well more than an hour south of Tel Aviv, in the Negev Desert. If Israel can turn Be'er Sheva into a cyber hub through partnerships between the government, Ben Gurion University, Jerusalem Venture Partners, a billionaire-dollar VC, and start-ups, then so can Tulsa reinvent itself into a cyber leader.

Israel serves as an interesting counter example to TU's Cyber Corps and the US national security world writ large. Israelis have a culture of rotating through the academy and military service en route to industry. In the United States, once you've joined the NSA, you're probably staying there for twenty years, which is why the Cyber Corps program has had limited economic value to Tulsa but why it has contributed to US national security.

TU shows that even small universities in Heartland cities can be important contributors to US innovation and defense. Researchers there have built groundbreaking encryption and malware protections for the US intelligence community, and their cyber program provides a national asset that helps to deter dangerous and costly cyberattacks.

For Tulsa and your city, the objective should be to leverage academic assets, retain talent, and translate university research into new start-ups. Academic innovation, however, takes years to generate new companies. In parallel, cities must also work to attract and support promising start-ups and plug them into their local industries.

ACTION PLAN SUMMARY		
REINVENTION *What needs reinventing?*	**GROWTH** *How do you catalyze growth?*	**INCLUSION** *How do you advance inclusion?*
Operating on an outdated system, universities are an underutilized asset in cities across the country. To better contribute to economic development and the local tech ecosystem, universities must embrace the full cycle of innovation and commit to tech transfer.	Universities can catalyze growth if they identify and invest in their strongest department's talent production and commercialization capacity. Cities will need to help universities identify barriers to innovation, build a support system for tech transfer, and create new programs that turbocharge innovation in their star departments.	Advancing DEI in higher ed STEM programs is challenging. Cities and universities need to work together to diversify early-stage talent pipelines, encouraging women and people of color to pursue graduate degrees. And scholarships and fellowships should be offered to recruit and support women and people of color in those programs.

CHAPTER 8

CONNECT THE NEW FIRM WITH THE OLD FIRM

(START-UPS AND CORPORATE INNOVATION)

When Martin Scorsese filmed *Killers of the Flower Moon* in and around Tulsa, he brought history into the present. Shot at many of the real places where historical events took place—some as close as a few blocks from my apartment—the film exposed me to a book I hadn't read and, more importantly, to a period in American history I didn't know much about. One breathtaking scene in the movie struck me because of how it depicted an event that changed the world: when the Osage Nation struck oil. In slow motion, as if time itself were marking the moment, we see several members of the Osage dance bare chested in an oil geyser, their bodies drenched in the black gold that would give their tribe wealth beyond measure.

That the oil industry was built in Tulsa—and that oil money built the city itself—underscores the need to transition the city's economy to a new tech-forward age. And I realized that to put TIL's tech niche strategy into operation and make this transition, we'd need to partner Tulsa's gas companies with relevant energy-tech start-ups.

> To catalyze the transition to tech in your city, you'll need to connect start-ups to your local legacy companies. Attracting start-ups that meet corporate innovation priorities can enable those start-ups to thrive immediately, creating durable jobs and fostering a culture of innovation across the ecosystem in the process.

TULSA'S OIL LEGACY

Forced migration brought the Osage from Kansas to Indian Territory, in what is now Oklahoma. The state of Oklahoma lies within the Mid-Continent Region, which encompasses Kansas, Texas, Arkansas, Louisiana, and New Mexico. Settlers observed oil seeping through the rocks there as early as the 1850s—before the settlers' arrival, Native Americans used it as medicine for humans and animals. But the first major oil well was discovered in 1897 near Bartlesville, Oklahoma, and it kicked off massive growth. Between 1900 and 1935, Oklahoma was the top producer of oil in the Mid-Continent Region for twenty-two of those years, producing more than nine hundred million gallons of oil worth more than $5 billion.[1]

The industry started taking off in the Tulsa metro in 1905, when the Glenn family found an oil well south of Tulsa (now the suburb of Glenpool). The Glenpool oil was particularly light and sweet, making it well suited to refine into gasoline and kerosene. This oil boom led to rapid development and established Tulsa as the "Oil Capital of the World." Pipelines were built to the Texaco and Gulf refineries to get access to the high-quality crude. Tulsa's population skyrocketed from 1,390 people in 1900 to 18,182 in ten years,[2] and it continued to grow steadily for the next seven decades. One of the reasons for Oklahoma's staying power as an energy hub is that it had every kind of oil and gas, even as extraction techniques changed and certain sources were depleted.

Native Americans got in on the riches early. According to the Oklahoma Historical Society, in 1896, businessman Henry Foster leased mineral rights to the Osage for ten years. After Henry's death, his brother Edwin B. Foster organized the Phoenix Oil Company for Osage Interests, eventually creating the Indian Territory Illuminating Oil Company (ITIO) in 1901. Henry's son Henry Vernon Foster became president of ITIO, and he subdivided its lease into 348 lots, in which more than 350 oil pools were found on Osage land. In 1906, land was allotted among the 2,229 tribal members, each receiving one headright—an equal share of the oil and natural gas royalty.[3] The windfall was so great that, according to historian Kenny Franks, one Osage woman spent more than $40,000 in a single day in 1927—the equivalent of more than $700,000 in 2024 dollars[4]—on an assortment of clothing, automobiles, and transportation costs.[5]

The massive wealth among Osage members precipitated the Osage Reign of Terror, popularized by David Grann's book *Killers of the Flower Moon* and the eponymous Scorsese adaptation. From 1918 to 1931, the Osage headright holders were often swindled and murdered by resentful Whites for their inheritance, with about sixty members killed in total.[6] The Osage Reign of Terror and the 1921 Tulsa Race Massacre are Tulsa's own terrible contributions to the unholy American tradition of taking what you want from someone who has it, epitomized by the usurpation of Indigenous land and the transatlantic slave trade. As reported by Grann, however, an Osage chief in 1928 offered a prophecy: "Someday this oil will go and there will be no more fat checks every few months from the Great White Father. . . . There'll be no fine motorcars and new clothes. Then I know my people will be happier."[7]

While early oil extraction and field discovery were formed on "creekology," the practice of observing nearby creeks for signs of oil, there came an increasing focus on science and geology. This shift propped up universities in the region. In 1901, the University of Oklahoma began offering courses in geology, and in 1928, the University of Tulsa opened its School of Petroleum Geology.[8] (Today, TU's north campus is dedicated to oil and gas research.) During the Great Depression, the price of crude oil dropped considerably. Yet the industry remained steady until the onset of World War II spurred additional drilling, which led to the discovery of forty-one new fields all over Oklahoma. Incidentally, the war was triggered in part by an oil embargo that the United States put in place against the Empire of Japan after it invaded French Indochina in 1941, to which the Japanese later responded by attacking Pearl Harbor. World War II was also a time when the aviation industry started building in Tulsa, and later, those defense plants would convert into peacetime industries.[9]

The oil industry would not thrive forever, though. Through the 1950s, oil field depletion exceeded discoveries, marking the start of a downward trend. Despite a short oil boom in the '80s, production dropped throughout the late twentieth century as overseas oil production edged out domestic supply. In fact, Oklahoma's oil production in 1999 was only 40 percent of its 1986 production level.[10] Still, the legacy of black gold manifests throughout Tulsa today. Grand Art Deco buildings, erected in the early days of the oil boom, anchor downtown,[11] and philanthropies built on successful oil and gas companies, like the George Kaiser Family Foundation and the Schusterman Family Foundation, continue to shape the city's cultural and civic life.

Oil, however, isn't just another business, with ebbs and flows. It's a mythic force, playing a major role not just in Tulsa but in our country and in our global society. Oil has fueled America and the world for nearly two centuries, and still today it holds a firm grip on us all. Yet the Osage chief's wisdom rings truer than ever, and we now need to look to a world without oil. In *The Prize: The Epic Quest for Oil, Money & Power,* Daniel Yergin writes, "Oil, which is so central a feature of the world as we know it, is now accused of fueling environmental degradation; and the oil industry, proud of its technological prowess and its contribution to shaping the modern world, finds itself on the defensive, charged with being a threat to present and future generations. This has put a new imperative on technological innovations to mitigate the environmental challenges."[12]

Today, it's no longer an accusation but an empirically proven fact that the atmospheric carbon dioxide emissions created by converting fossilized carbon into energy pose an existential risk to the biosphere. Absent dramatic changes in public behavior and lifestyle, the energy industry finds itself between a rock and a hard place, called on to produce more energy but with fewer emissions. The industry laments the difficulty in addressing the "energy trilemma": balancing energy production that is at once sustainable, reliable, and affordable. Fossil fuels are proving an increasingly problematic way to achieve that goal. Oil might have shaped our world, but it's looking increasingly likely that its days are numbered—or numbering ours.

While oil and gas are leading contributors to climate change, the energy industry and the private sector broadly have a business opportunity if it confronts inconvenient truths and mitigates climate change through the development and adoption of new technologies. The most innovative industries are often those facing serious disruptions. They innovate out of necessity. While climate tech and clean energy are emerging in places like Knoxville, Salt Lake City, and Columbus,[13] the established oil and gas industry in Tulsa has catching up to do. The large corporations in the region, such as Williams, Devon, ONEOK (which recently merged with another company, Magellan), ONEGAS, and Helmerich and Payne, don't have a long history of working with start-ups, and they are still relatively new to sustainability initiatives. There's a dearth of energy-tech start-ups in Tulsa despite this strong corporate base, which is why Tulsa's economic future has been in such a precarious state. While oil may be with us for another few decades, it won't be forever. And if Tulsa doesn't transition to energy-tech and cleaner sources and methods, such as hydrogen, carbon capture, decarbonization, renewables, grid modernization, and sustainability, northeast Oklahoma will be hollowed out like Pittsburgh was when steel imploded.

Just as the globe needs to transition to renewable forms of energy, so, too, do the communities that oil built need to transition to a more resilient economy. Tulsa's industrial base in energy offers the opportunity to connect this old industry with new, forward-thinking firms. The critical infrastructure built by Tulsa's energy sector, such as oil and gas pipelines, also offers opportunities to test new digital and cyber technologies to analyze data and protect infrastructure from cyberattacks. Tulsa's energy corporations need to innovate and transition faster or other, more tech-based and cleaner companies will eventually put them out of business.

Even progressive urban thinkers like Jane Jacobs would concur that sustainable development aspirations are futile without balancing desirable and undesirable sources of growth. Jacobs said that she hoped oil for fuel would end, yet she also knew that for communities to grow they needed to build on what they had, no matter the industry. "There is no new world that you make without the old world," she said.[14]

Heartland cities looking to transition to a sustainable tech-led economy should take a page out of Jacobs's book and start with what they have—and that's unlikely to be growth-stage start-ups, even if conventional wisdom says that for cities to become tech hubs, they should attract new start-ups and support local entrepreneurs. While I agree that new firms are mission critical to innovation economies, I have a different take on how cities can grow them. Instead of focusing on the start-up (or even the individual entrepreneur), I recommend beginning with the local customers that hire, partner, and invest in start-ups: your corporations.

Urban innovators need to connect the right start-ups with their local corporations, associating the new with the old, the small with the big. For Cincinnati, as an example, it's fintech start-ups collaborating with its five Fortune 500s, two of which are in banking and finance (Western & Southern Financial Group and Fifth Third Bank), or life science start-ups working with health care–related Procter & Gamble. For Tulsa, partnering energy-tech start-ups with the oil and gas industry was the way to go.

START WITH CORPORATIONS

Heartland cities typically struggle with new firm recruitment and development but often have at least a handful of established companies that can serve as anchor partners for new start-ups. David Hall knows this well. He is the managing partner of the Rise of the Rest Seed Fund, the seed investment vehicle at Revolution, a DC-based firm launched by Steve Case, the cofounder of AOL. The fund invests in companies raising seed or early-stage venture capital. What differentiates Rise from other funds, Hall says, is that they "see the world primarily through the lens of place." Rise invests only in start-ups outside of New York, Boston, and Silicon Valley to "level the venture capital playing field alongside strong returns." Hall sees corporations as critical partners for midsized cities looking to grow their start-up scene. "The most successful corporate executives recognize that disruption is coming and look beyond their industry for partnerships with start-ups that are upending age-old ways of doing things," he says. "They embrace new ideas and brands that help them remain at the cutting edge."

But why should corporations work with start-ups, and why should cities concentrate on growing new firms? New firms are the lifeblood of urban economies, and they can often only grow by partnering with existing, larger companies. Hall explained, "Macroeconomic data suggests that all net new job growth comes from start-ups, so supporting their creation and success is critically important to a city's economy." He points to the new talent and ideas that start-ups bring that enrich the ecosystem. "It's worth noting," Hall adds, "that the majority of Fortune 500 companies are located in the nation's Heartland, making it compelling for start-ups to set up shop there and benefit from corporate partners." For corporations themselves, Hall says, they often "underestimate the impact of nascent technology, believing that disruption is further off than they realize."[15]

At the same time that start-ups are key to the future, local corporations are critical assets in the present that often have major influence in midsized cities (think FedEx in Memphis or Eli Lilly in Indianapolis). Ensuring that they remain innovative and globally competitive is existential for the future of the city—otherwise, they might end up like Detroit when the automotive industry collapsed. (To invest in Detroit's future, in 2023, Ford funded Michigan Central, an accelerator operated by Newlab and focused on advanced mobility technologies.)[16] By focusing on a corporation's innovation needs and connecting these established companies to new firms, cities are able to play defense and offense simultaneously—protecting the value of existing companies while attracting and growing start-ups. If it's seen as investing in local businesses that already employ a lot of people rather than speculatively chasing new firms, this approach may also make it easier to secure local support and funding for economic development initiatives.

But let's consider the opposite approach: What if cities began with the start-ups or the entrepreneurs rather than their corporations? A lot of cities start with a generic entrepreneurial support organization that offers basic services to any aspiring entrepreneur, regardless of whether they're building a software company or a bakery—and these organizations can often have dubious impact. Without strategic focus, these types of organizations reflect a traditional economic development mindset. While it's important to instill an entrepreneurial culture in your city, entrepreneurial support organizations that aren't focused on priority clusters take a long time to yield results, if they produce a winner at all, so I recommend deprioritizing them. Similarly, what if you reach out to any and all start-ups and try to coax them to your city? Spray and pray rarely works. Even if you're able to attract start-ups aligned with your tech niche, your ecosystem is likely too immature to support a start-up on their own—you may not have the customers ready to sustain the new firm.

Now, if your corporations are already innovative, or conversely, if they're opposed to innovation programs, then you may need to take a start-up-first approach. But that scenario is unlikely. So, instead, you should begin with corporations and target new firms that can serve their needs immediately. That way, you'll be able to identify specific types of companies that can quickly plug into the ecosystem and thrive from the get-go because they have a ready, willing, and able partner to fund them or buy their services. But corporations in midsized cities—even Fortune 500s—may need some guidance in all of this.

TEACH CORPORATIONS INNOVATION 101

Just as academics aren't natural entrepreneurs, many established corporations, especially in midsized cities without a strong tech ecosystem, may not know how to innovate, at least from a technological perspective. What I learned in Tulsa was that our energy corporations had little precedent working with start-ups. For most of their history, they didn't need to. By and large, their business model was stable, and they had everything they needed to make massive profits—they'd extract oil and gas, refine it, distribute it, and then sell it. And because the energy industry is so cyclical, there is high mergers and acquisitions activity, with wild swings in the workforce. The industry is designed to expand massively in the boom times and then cut to the bone when the market drops. This makes investing in R&D more difficult or uncommon in energy. As a result, Tulsa had very few energy-related tech start-ups because its corporations weren't drawing them to the region. At Tulsa Innovation Labs, an early step in our process was to educate our corporations on how to work with start-ups, what I called **Innovation 101**.

But first, we needed to understand a bit more about why they didn't work with start-ups to begin with. I discovered several reasons, which apply to many corporations across industries.

RISK AVERSION: "Risk isn't in our DNA," one Tulsa energy leader told me. To Tulsa's generations-old energy companies, start-ups seemed dangerous. In oil and gas, operational failures can lead to physical harm or death, so there isn't an incentive to take risks on start-ups or their technologies. As one energy insider told me, "Corporations and executives can say they want to be innovative, but in reality, the safest path forward is to use the same process as everyone else: the industry standard."

UNCERTAIN RETURNS: A local corporate leader told me that "investors have certain expectations," and that doesn't typically involve taking "speculative risk on new markets or technologies." The returns of working with start-ups—financial and otherwise—are difficult to understand, much less quantify, for many corporations. The trouble is that many companies, especially in energy, create business goals at an annual (or, at best, quarterly) cadence, so they can lack patience and an ability to invest over the cycle time needed to get innovation fully baked into their culture or for partnerships with start-ups to pay dividends.

ACCESS TO TALENT: Many corporations in legacy industries like oil and gas can lack the technologists needed to champion and work with new firms. Corporations may just not have the in-house know-how to innovate. In Tulsa, what I heard regularly was that in addition to technical talent—data analysts and scientists, in particular—the city lacked middle managers and executives who can run start-ups or corporate innovation programs, a problem that could be solved only by a strong executive-in-residence program and MBA pipeline. To create a more dynamic talent pipeline that infuses corporations with folks other than petroleum engineers, Tulsa's energy companies need to form stronger and more diverse partnerships with local universities.

NO CORPORATE VENTURE CAPITAL (CVC) TEAM: Most of the energy corporations in Tulsa didn't have CVC teams before TIL got to work, meaning there wasn't an approved mechanism to engage or invest in new firms—much less a budget for doing so. This lack of CVC capacity is no doubt linked to the same risk aversion of corporate business models, which favor reinvestment into existing products and processes over an unproven team. CVC, however, can provide corporations with clearer insight into potential market-disrupting firms and technologies.[17] Also, a dedicated CVC team making the right bets can expand the corporation's revenue and footprint in the given industry without changing product or process focus internally.

NONEXISTENT CULTURE: Without precedent, there's no internal culture of working with start-ups. The lack of technological innovation and start-up partnerships was a feature of the industry standard and became an unfortunate cultural trait. Like universities, corporations can become too insular and disconnected from the innovation ecosystem and stuck in their ways.

These blockers to innovation generally fall into two buckets: mindset (risk version, uncertain returns, hubris) and internal capabilities (teams that work with start-ups, talent to work on these teams, a CVC arm). Changing your mindset likely requires a burning platform (you are losing market share), education (here's how innovation will help your business), and time (this is a process of changing culture and attitudes). Changing internal capabilities likely requires training and programs (either consultants or organizations like TIL and its initiatives), and new partnerships to build this out at an industry versus company level.

Economic development organizations can help de-risk innovation even for successful corporations, which is why TIL and GKFF's strategic guidance and financial support were helpful in getting Tulsa corporations on board with new programs and willing to tackle long-standing internal barriers. With that context, you'll want to find or build a program to guide your corporations through the innovation process. Think of EDOs as innovation Sherpas for local corporates. This is as much about change-management as it is technological innovation. Consider this five-step synopsis of my Innovation 101 course:

Step 1: Commit to Innovation. Like everything else, if you're not committed, you're not going to succeed. Half-hearted efforts, symbolic investments, or ambivalent gestures are a waste of time and money. For a corporation looking to start an innovation practice for the first time or work more closely with city partners on tech-led economic development, you'll need the CEO's buy-in to set innovation as a company priority, approve budgets, and appoint an executive champion who can devote bandwidth to driving the effort internally. For TIL, we engaged directly with Williams CEO Alan Armstrong and Devon CEO Rick Muncrief—Muncrief even sat on TIL's advisory council—and both empowered deputies to drive action on their end. To get CEOs on board, it was good that I had George Kaiser in my camp—which meant access to a network of corporations he partners with as well as start-ups and firms he invests in, including a respected VC, Energy Innovation Capital (EIC), that would be TIL's future operator for our energy-tech initiative. You'll also need local champions who can sway CEOs. We had GKFF's CIO, Robert Thomas, personally engaged and advocating for the program.

Step 2: Understand Needs. Corporations need an internal mechanism to review and analyze their innovation requirements and to prioritize them. Outside partners can help with this process. In assessing innovation needs, corporations must ask themselves a couple of basic questions: First, how do we continue to improve what we do every day (aka innovation in the core business)? And second, how do we continue to evolve and strengthen as a company (aka innovation in new business areas)?

Step 3: Define Success. More times than not, the relationship between start-ups and corporations doesn't work out as either party planned. McKinsey finds that "the majority of CVCs stop investing after two to three years, and . . . only 28 percent [of start-ups] said they were satisfied with their corporate partnerships."[18] Having a clear set of strategic goals, complete with key performance indicators, will be important in guiding your investments and partnerships. As I witnessed, stakeholders can often leap too soon, excited by a technology or a founder without doing the due diligence or defining goals for the relationship. If you're looking to enter a new technology, create a new business line, or just find a solution to meet a discrete need, each of these goals requires different investments, partners, and KPIs.

Step 4: Explore Solutions. A BCG study finds that corporations use a multitude of ways to drive internal innovation: "At the end of 2018, 19% of corporations were using at least one innovation lab or digital lab, 17% were using one or more accelerators, 17% were using one or more CVC units, 13% were using one or more partnership units, and 6% were using one or more incubators."[19] A few notable examples: Starbucks launched a twenty-thousand-square-foot incubator space; Barclays partnered with TechStars on a fintech accelerator; and others have created internal investment groups, like Intel Capital or Google Ventures. Each model has pros and cons, and corporations should work to find the right method to achieve their goals. Internal organizations, for example, can be challenging because successful CVC requires expertise, expensive labor, and clear alignment with the core business.[20] If these internal options are difficult to implement, external sourcing is a fair option. VC-as-a-service models involve partnering with a proven VC firm to invest in start-ups, but corporations don't have to own new companies or necessarily operate innovation programs themselves. Becoming a start-up's customer is also a great way to dip toes in the water; it immediately adds value to the local ecosystem and could infuse some creative thinking into the corporation.

Step 5: Plan to Integrate. Executive commitment is particularly important when it comes to integration and adoption of new technologies, as "only 14 percent of incumbents that invest in young companies have adopted the practices necessary to sustainably generate value from such relationships."[21] Committing to innovation means more than pilots and testing: it means partnering with start-ups, adopting new technologies, and integrating them into the existing business in a way that generates new, scalable opportunities. To do so, corporations should plan to identify gaps in culture and methodologies so they go into relationships with eyes wide open for potential hiccups and brainstorm, on the front end, ways to mitigate them. A common obstacle is misalignment on timelines—as one investor told me, a "six-month delay at Shell is no big deal, but six months might be all the cash runway a start-up has before bankruptcy." Corporations will need to be clear on the timeline they can move on and communicate that to start-ups.

You've now graduated Innovation 101 and are ready to design and launch a corporate innovation initiative.

SUPPORT START-UPS THAT MEET LOCAL NEEDS

After you've engaged your local corporations, understanding their innovation needs and giving them a framework to partner with new firms, you're now ready to build an initiative to attract start-ups that can plug into your ecosystem and succeed. You should tailor-make an initiative that fosters an innovative culture at your corporations, sources high-potential start-ups that are suited for them, and generates job growth in your ecosystem.

CASE STUDY: EIC ROSE ROCK

Tulsa Innovation Labs did something most Tulsans thought impossible. For the first time, TIL brought the city's leading energy companies together for a major economic development initiative. EIC Rose Rock launched in September 2022 as the Tulsa division of Energy Innovation Capital, an energy-tech VC firm originally from Houston with a preexisting relationship with GKFF. EIC now has a presence in Houston, San Francisco, New York, Boston, and Tulsa, with more than $275 million under management and twenty-seven start-ups in its portfolio.

The EIC Rose Rock partnership was sponsored by the Tulsa region's largest energy corporations, including ONEOK, Williams, Helmerich & Payne, and Devon (which has since merged with WPX). They each contributed about $7.5 million, along with a $20.5 million contribution from GKFF, with the goal of raising $100 million through new partnerships.

David Clouse leads the ongoing implementation of this effort as EIC Rose Rock's managing director. He previously spent more than fifteen years with British Petroleum as a principal on their new ventures team in Houston. Clouse remarked that Tulsa is in its "infancy" compared to Houston's energy-tech scene. Yet he believes Tulsa has the opportunity to be more innovative than Houston because of its supportive ecosystem. "In Tulsa, you can get everyone you need into a room within a week to make a decision and go test something," he explained. "The companies are more agile; they understand they aren't global goliaths and need to remain innovative to stay alive."[22]

EIC Rose Rock is a suite of corporate innovation programs: EIC Fusion, Rose Rock Bridge, and the EIC Fund. They are designed to work together across the innovation pipeline: understanding corporate innovation needs, recruiting start-ups that meet those needs, and providing those as well as other start-ups the capital they need to grow.

EIC Fusion is a proprietary corporate program likened to an innovation consulting club. Participating corporations regularly meet with the EIC team to discuss innovation pain points, shape a strategic vision, and learn about start-ups with whom they could potentially partner (the Tel Aviv–based consultancy SOSA played a similar role for Cyber NYC). On average, EIC meets with more than a thousand new start-ups each year to establish deal flow that can solve its corporate clients' challenges. Each Fusion member selects an area of interest into which EIC will conduct a technical deep dive. During this process, EIC builds a market landscape of relevant technologies and identifies start-ups with whom they can partner. EIC also convenes its Fusion partners from across its full portfolio—not just Tulsa partners—to share perspectives and source solutions.

Rose Rock Bridge is the nonprofit accelerator arm of the initiative. Bridge provides the programmatic infrastructure to incubate early-stage technologies that are of interest to the corporate partners. Inspired by the Arch Grants program in Saint Louis, Bridge provides $100,000 in nondilutive grant funding to the start-up, along with ancillary business support services such as coworking space at Gradient, legal, marketing, and financial guidance as well as help in pursuing federal grants. Bridge's goal is to turn an initial idea into a business that can deploy a pilot with one of the corporate partners within twelve months.

The **EIC Fund** is the venture fund component investing in seed and early-stage companies that meet the needs of participating corporations and that generate a return on investment. Fusion identifies start-ups that offer relevant technology, and the EIC Fund can move forward with an equity investment. The fund provides the capital to the start-up, while the corporation brings industry expertise. Together, the corporation becomes an early, paying customer of that start-up, and the start-up grows. The fund prioritizes investing in start-ups that have or will have some presence in Tulsa.

While the founder is essential to any start-up, EIC assesses both the founding team and the business idea. For early-stage programming that aims to grow the entrepreneurial pipeline, an approach that focuses on the individual may be sound—after all, investing in people is a better bet, over the long term, than a single company idea. But for a start-up program tied to an ecosystem-wide strategy that's aimed at catalyzing growth, the founder isn't sufficient; they'll need a strong business idea with demonstrable market potential to enter the EIC Rose Rock initiative. The relationship between participating start-ups and the corporations is also key. The corporations can either serve as the first customer for the start-up, or they could simply function as a strategic partner. There's an investment committee and advisory board to ensure companies and investments meet funder expectations and to pinpoint ways to improve work processes.

Finally, TIL's DEI priority cuts across the three prongs, with each having their own DEI goals. Because the energy sector is so male dominated, extra efforts are being made to recruit and support women leaders and founders, including exploring university partnerships to inspire and support young, diverse talent—the start-up founder or corporate executive of the future.

To better understand how corporations and start-ups should work together, I interviewed two partners participating in the EIC Rose Rock initiative—one a corporate innovation strategist and the other a start-up founder.

Finding Your Fairway (The Corporation's Perspective)

Brian Hlavinka is a vice president at Williams's headquarters in Tulsa, where he leads digital transformation. He previously led new energy ventures and corporate strategic development. An early champion of the EIC Rose Rock initiative, his portfolio focused on decarbonization business development, which means commercializing projects that lower Williams's emissions footprint. Hlavinka was born and raised in Texas and studied chemical engineering in college and then global energy in business school. He is also the founding vice chair of the industry group Clean Hydrogen Future Coalition. His expertise in clean energy innovation led him to testify before the US Senate Committee on Energy and Natural Resources in 2022.

Hlavinka said that Williams chose to participate in the initiative because of its commitments to Tulsa and innovation. "We have been here for over a hundred years and plan to be here for the next hundred years," he said. "We are committed to making clean energy happen. We want to continue to find ways to improve our business and invest in the technologies of the future. Rose Rock gave us an avenue to make investments that we traditionally would not have pursued on our own. Through our investment, we hope to gain a better understanding of technologies that can help us improve our offering to customers, build new products, and best leverage the incredible asset base that we have. We believe our ability to partner with start-ups by deploying our capital and utilizing our assets differentiates us from traditional investors, creating a symbiotic relationship and fostering growth for both sides of a deal."

For corporations, it's important to be crystal clear in your priorities and your goals for engaging start-ups. "Be willing to get out of your traditional comfort zone and engage with nontraditional partners," Hlavinka said. "But also set boundaries for a reasonable fairway of opportunities—there is an abundance of cool 'stuff' that sound interesting but can easily distract from the core goals you are trying to achieve. Set those goals, set your fairway, and don't be afraid to fail."[23]

Hlavinka makes a good point about defining a particular "fairway." What cities and their economic development organizations need to do is to work with corporations on understanding what that fairway is and then creating an initiative to find start-ups that land in the right zone. Bringing in start-ups that fit ecosystem needs and can serve corporations helps create a cluster of activity that generates growth.

Remembering You're Nimble (The Start-Up's Perspective)

Garrison Haning is the cofounder and CEO of Safety Radar, a "system that ingests information digitally and uses artificial intelligence to assess risk level" for energy and other industrial companies. "We pull that information into Safety Radar's risk visualization tools to make it easy for safety professionals to intervene and take action," he explains. Haning previously worked for Magellan in Tulsa. Originally from New York, he graduated from West Point. The military first brought him to Oklahoma and then deployed him to Iraq. Once his active-duty tour was complete, Haning earned an MBA from Wharton, assuming he'd stay in the Northeast. But he and his wife decided to return to Oklahoma. If you have a good idea in a place like Tulsa, Haning says, "people will move mountains to help you accomplish it." Tulsa helped him raise his first round of investment: "Now, we are in the middle of our seed fundraising round, and EIC Rose Rock has helped us get to a point where we have a product, customers, and a company worth investing in!"

Haning explained the relationship his start-up has with corporations. "These are businesses that have already established their success in the marketplace, and so often we find that they are looking for small and nimble partners who can help bring innovation to the table," he said. "Especially because we are a safety company and larger entities tend to prioritize safety, our value proposition resonates with them. They make commitments around ESG [environmental, social, and governance], and so often they include safety metrics in their corporate culture and incentives programs."

For start-ups, corporations are not merely customers or clients: they're partners. Start-ups bring something corporations need—it's often both a product or service as well as a perspective and cultural style. "My advice is to remain flexible," Haning offered. "Corporations have a way of doing things that has served them well, and your job as a start-up is to figure out how to leverage their strengths and your strengths to add value to their organization. Be ready to learn from them because they are going to teach you a lot! But remember, too, that you are nimble. That is such an asset. It allows you to iterate quickly and let your first customers lead you down the path of product market fit. For large companies looking to work with small ones, the best advice that I can give is to just start. The sooner you start getting reps in, the better. This type of collaboration is iterative, and it gets better and better with practice."[24]

Such partnerships will create friction as the start-up works to integrate into the corporate's existing structure while bringing new ideas. Thinking about the start-up's role as partnering with the corporations can lead to mutual benefits. Like most relationships, open communication and feedback are important to ensuring satisfaction all around. My former TIL colleague Kastle Jones, who joined EIC Rose Rock when it launched, sums up successful start-up–corporate partnerships this way: "Innovative corporations put in effort to provide valuable feedback [to start-ups], and successful start-ups stand ready to pivot and implement. As the relationship strengthens, the cycle repeats at scale: better knowledge of the problem, improved feedback loops, and optimized paths to implementation."[25]

BOTTOM-LINE WAYS TO SUPPORT START-UPS

Cities should be aware that when you are specific from the start—when your fairway is narrow—you will shrink the top of the funnel. Rather than casting a wide net, you're more targeted in your outreach to start-ups you're looking to attract. This is a good thing because you're following your tech niche strategy and giving yourself higher chances of landing start-ups that can succeed in your city. But you'll need to be ready with specific offerings to land prospective start-ups and support their growth. As EIC Rose Rock does for energy-tech start-ups looking to come to Tulsa, cities should offer the following to their target start-ups:

NONDILUTIVE GRANTS to incentivize start-ups and make the transition to your city easier

ACCESS TO FOLLOW-ON CAPITAL to provide a runway for continued growth

ESTABLISHED CORPORATE PARTNERS to solidify the value proposition over the long term

COMMUNITY-BUILDING EVENTS to grow their networks and foster a vibrant ecosystem

Of course, creating an innovation economy is one thing. Energy corporations and start-ups will need to take their partnerships to a whole new level if they're going to work together—and with government—to transition the United States to more sustainable forms of energy and combat climate change.

THE RESILIENCE OPPORTUNITY

Octavia E. Butler writes in her dystopian climate change novel, *Parable of the Sower,* "All that you touch / You Change. All that you Change / Changes you."[26] Despite the ambivalence seen throughout the American public as well as with our impotent political system, we must always remember that our actions affect the planet and that we have the ability within our societies to act more responsibly, developing faster and bolder ways to mitigate and adapt to climate change.

But at the same time, if we want our communities to come on board for this fight—and we need that to happen to win it—we must also acknowledge that climate change measures will affect cities and their economies. Global efforts to curb the use of fossil fuels pose an existential threat to oil- and gas-dominated cities like Tulsa, and the shift to a more tech-based and sustainable economy won't happen overnight. Tulsa and its peers need to move in earnest, but methodically, toward (clean) tech. The key to convincing cities to fall in line is to stress that this isn't solely climate alarmism—it's also an opportunity to reinvent their economy.

The transition to clean energy offers Heartland cities a plethora of opportunities. Michael Berkowitz is the former president of 100 Resilient Cities, the global network of cities launched by the Rockefeller Foundation to strengthen urban resilience to climate change. He is now the founding executive director of the Resilience Academy at the University of Miami. Berkowitz sees the opportunity for oil and gas towns to create more diverse economies with multiple resilient benefits.

"The landscape is littered with cities overexposed to a single industry, whether that's Detroit and cars—you could argue in some ways New Orleans and oil and gas is another—and there's this opportunity to really set yourself up for the next century," Berkowitz tells me. "There's a lot of energy. We're still going to need energy. There's a lot of energy expertise in Tulsa. We need those minds, people who have years of experience in the energy sector, to help think about what that transition looks like. And that is where Tulsa could go from a legacy city to a vibrant, growing one."

One of the leading fears of the energy transition is the loss of jobs. While job displacements are inevitable as companies evolve and markets shift, eventually, new jobs will be created, both in new firms and in old firms that have adapted to the twenty-first century. It's also why TIL is investing in the innovation economy and creating new opportunities. Already, 20 percent of energy jobs globally are in renewables,[27] and research from the World Resources Institute finds that "additional federal policies that bring US emissions down to net-zero by 2050 can create an extra 2.3 million net jobs by 2035."[28] Many of the workers in legacy energy can be upskilled to these new roles.

Oklahoma is taking an all-of-the-above approach to energy and making some laudable efforts toward sustainability. The state is trying to diversify how it gets energy: 44 percent of Oklahoma is fueled by wind energy, and 43 percent is fueled by natural gas.[29] But recent efforts at other sustainable forms have also picked up speed. In Tulsa, Enel, the Italian multinational electricity and gas manufacturer and distributor, is building a billion-dollar solar-panel plant, for instance.[30] While new clean energy companies will be essential, the key to the transition will be legacy corporations' willingness to evolve, innovate, and build new partnerships.

What's the message to energy companies? "Part of it's going to be about finding ways to get out of the quarter-by-quarter evaluation that oil and gas companies find themselves in," Berkowitz said. "You have two or three bad quarters, and your CEO could be on rocky ground with their board. . . . That puts the incentives to short-term action and maximizing profits now, but it's not a sustainable business strategy." And Berkowitz thinks it's not just oil and gas companies but the ancillary businesses—the full supply chain—that have a role to play in innovating and moving toward sustainability: "I think we've found over and over working in cities that the path to innovation and to long-term shared prosperity is paved through sustained partnerships over time. And so, to the extent that oil and gas as they transition can create those partnerships, that can help spread both the risk and the reward. It can bring new constituencies to the table that might be helpful."[31]

Part of this supply chain includes and is formed by start-ups—which is why EIC Rose Rock isn't content with internal corporate innovation but is focused on finding and pairing relevant start-ups to corporations and bringing them to Tulsa. Laura Fox is the cofounder and managing partner of Streetlife Ventures, a VC specializing in the urban climate sector. Fox explained why start-ups are so important to the energy transition and urban resilience efforts: "Developing and utilizing new technologies are crucial to addressing these gaps, and we can't accomplish them otherwise. For example, we need energy storage and production solutions, a wide range of software technologies to manage and optimize loads, hardware solutions to make grid infrastructure more resilient and make buildings more energy efficient, and more." This technological innovation, its adoption, and its benefits to society will create jobs in places like Tulsa, Fox says. "By 2030, clean energy projects alone are expected to produce 10.3 million jobs globally, a net jobs increase of nearly 3X from the related fossil fuels jobs. If we manage this transition right, we'll have more jobs, more resources, a strong economy, and a healthier planet."[32]

Heartland cities with oil or gas legacies are primed to be leaders in the energy transition if they work with their corporations and build a base of new firms around them that provide disruptive technologies. These cities can innovate because of, not despite, their geography and legacy industries. Rise of the Rest's David Hall sums up the opportunity well: "As we seek to disrupt major real-world sectors—agriculture, health care, finance, energy—we must leverage the sector expertise that exists all over the country. It is hard to understand farming culture from Palo Alto or New York City. We predict that this will result in more and more founders recognizing the knowledge-based benefits of being in cities with legacy industries."[33]

Midsized cities should tout their assets, prioritize understanding their corporations' needs, and create an initiative that helps them innovate, attracts new firms, and gives those start-ups the support system they need to grow. New firms alone won't cut it; cities need to connect the new with the old and to chart a path into the future that emerges out of their valued and unique past. As the wisdom from the Osage chief suggests, there is opportunity and benefit in imagining and anticipating the future.

In this second section, we've explored the five different ways to transform your city into an innovation engine: **talent attraction** and **remote work** offers incentives to remote workers who can enrich your tech ecosystem; **workforce development** calls for training boot camps that rapidly upskill incumbent workers, giving your clusters the talent they need to grow and the skills that talent need to get good jobs; **diversity, equity, and inclusion** initiatives support populations historically underserved to participate in this new economy; **academic innovation** requires universities to become engines of talent and technology; and **start-ups** and **corporate innovation** programs help connect existing companies with start-ups to create a culture of innovation that benefits new and old firms alike.

Each of these efforts, however, will require financing, so, in the final section, let's turn to how to raise the money you need to fuel the future. And just as TIL did, let's begin with the social sector.

ACTION PLAN SUMMARY

REINVENTION *What needs reinventing?*	GROWTH *How do you catalyze growth?*	INCLUSION *How do you advance inclusion?*
To increase the presence of start-ups, rather than chasing random new firms, cities need to work with their existing corporations to attract and support start-ups that meet corporate needs. This approach will help ensure start-ups can succeed with readymade clients and investors while also supporting corporate competitiveness and fostering a broader culture of innovation.	Many corporations don't have a history of working with start-ups. Civic organizations will need to guide corporations through the process of partnering with start-ups. Cities will then need to work with corporations to codesign programming that attracts, supports, and invests in start-ups that meet corporate innovation needs.	Cities looking to advance inclusion through start-up and corporate innovation initiatives must set DEI-related goals and work intentionally to achieve them. University partnerships can help by developing young, diverse talent.

SECTION III

FUELING THE FUTURE

CHAPTER 9

PARTNER WITH PHILANTHROPY

(SOCIAL SECTOR ENGAGEMENT)

In the fall of 2022, Tulsa Innovation Labs convened its advisory council for its first in-person event, a milestone long delayed because of COVID. TIL's council comprises many of the major figures in Tulsa's business, civic, and academic worlds as well as industry-leading experts from across the country. It's an impressive bunch. Each of them generously gave of their time to support TIL, and we wanted to thank them for their service by hosting them in Tulsa for an educational and fun summit.

The highlight of the two-day event was the cocktail reception at the Gathering Place, Tulsa's sixty-seven-acre park along the Arkansas River. George Kaiser himself and his philanthropy's leadership team were there alongside TIL to welcome our guests. The privately run park was a personal dream of Kaiser's, and the George Kaiser Family Foundation led funding for it. The Gathering Place is also the most visible example of Tulsa's ascent—proof that place making not only brings communities together but also attracts new talent, investment, and visitors (over ten million since its opening in 2018).[1] The park was the perfect venue to celebrate TIL's work and the people who support it.

Kaiser's remarks at the reception gave the council an overview of how he approaches his philanthropy. He explained the science behind why a child's earliest years are so formative and outlined GKFF's birth-through-eight initiatives. He described the Gathering Place as an asset that could help attract new businesses. And he addressed Tulsa's need to pivot to a tech-based economy as well as the city's particular challenge of not having a major research university. In an impromptu Q&A, Kaiser demonstrated both an eagerness to chat and gratitude for the council coming together, reflecting a humble Tulsa sensibility toward anyone who makes the effort to visit.

Following drinks, Jamey Jacob, an OSU professor and aerospace engineer on the council, set up a drone flying station on the park's main lawn. Under his supervision, we flew advanced drones through an azure sky, swerving them in and out of late afternoon clouds. Life really doesn't get much better than flying drones at the Gathering Place. Amid all this activity, Kaiser gave council members a tour of the park, which you could tell from his buoyant demeanor was his pride and joy. This was one of those postcard memories I'll cherish from my time in Tulsa. The scene reminded me of my first presentation to GKFF in 2019, in which I said that I wanted Tulsa to become a "gathering place for innovation." Here we were, just a few years later, in this majestic park, and that vision was becoming real.

The Gathering Place is a town square for Tulsa—a place anyone and everyone can come to and be together. In its short life, the park has become Tulsa's heart and city center. For Tulsa to become an inclusive tech hub, TIL and others would need to bring the community together in a similar way. A gathering place for innovation means the city itself becomes a supportive ecosystem, imbuing Tulsans with a spirit of entrepreneurship and innovation—and giving them the tools and opportunities they need to benefit from it.

GKFF made this vision possible. The common denominator between the Gathering Place and Tulsa Innovation Labs is philanthropy. While many important players have contributed to Tulsa's reinvention—and I hope this book gives you a glimpse of many of them—Kaiser's philanthropy has underwritten TIL and much of the city's economic development investments. That it was TIL that took GKFF's economic development work to the next level, however, also points toward an important truth: philanthropy needs new and experienced perspectives to help steer its giving. If philanthropy invests in the seeds of a city's regeneration, then think of these other perspectives as helping build the garden and cultivate the plants.

For many cities, the social sector will be a central part of your economic development coalition as philanthropy can serve a powerful role in driving inclusive tech-led growth. Understanding how to raise money from philanthropy is paramount to the success of many related projects and can help fuel your reinvention.

At the same time, cities must also delicately balance philanthropy's wealth with the need for communities to have a say in how it's deployed. For growth to be inclusive, economic development cannot be exclusive. A multitude of local voices—not merely economic developers, the experts that guide them, or the wealthy donors that fund the work—must be engaged throughout a democratic process of economic development. A city must enlist engaged citizens, not just elites, when building its future.

UNDERSTAND PHILANTHROPY'S ROLE

Philanthropies can be extremely valuable partners to cities trying to solve any type of complex social challenge. They can often deploy capital in more creative and expeditious ways than government and, as a more neutral party, can help forge alliances between the public and private sectors, activating far-reaching networks to raise funds and collaborate on solutions. Philanthropy inhabits five main roles, often simultaneously, regardless of the particulars of their grant making:

CONVENER: bringing leaders and organizations together from across sectors to foster collaboration on social challenges

CAPACITY BUILDER: investing in local organizations through grant making designed to strengthen those organizations' ability to perform their mission

ECOSYSTEM BUILDER: filling in critical gaps within various ecosystems and facilitating coordination between stakeholders—all to strengthen interconnected support networks

CAPITAL MOBILIZER: deploying grants and leveraging philanthropic capital to unlock funds from other partners

INCLUSION CHAMPION: advocating for equity, advancing DEI goals, and lobbying those in power to better support inclusion efforts

When philanthropies fulfill these roles with a particular geographic focus, they can be especially well suited to contribute to urban place making and economic development. As the George Kaiser Family Foundation demonstrates, many philanthropies are enmeshed in urban ecosystems, functioning as power players in regional politics and civil society, giving them a unique ability to influence a city's housing, education, public health, arts and culture, and economic development all at once. As GKFF's executive director Ken Levit described, "The return on investment [is high] for a philanthropy in a community where they live, where they know the partners, where they're dealing with big problems. . . . And as sizable as a foundation is with, say, $5 billion of assets, when you're working in a community of a million people on problems that are as hard as homelessness or food insecurity or mental health, it's [good] to focus that philanthropy as close to that community as possible."[2] That GKFF is a valuable anchor partner for Tulsa is an understatement; its $5 billion endowment is a critical regional asset with the ability to stimulate the entire Innovation Flywheel. (GKFF's endowment is likely to triple in size upon Kaiser's passing.) But GKFF isn't as unusual an asset as you may think.

Almost all midsized cities have philanthropies, and many, like GKFF, take a special geographic interest. Community foundations, in particular, serve as backbone institutions throughout the Heartland. Dedicated to serving the people of a particular city or region, community foundations typically get their funding from a cross section of donors with ties to the area—they often manage what are called donor-advised funds, which are individual accounts created by donors for the foundation to dispense. As a result, community foundations typically don't have a cause mandate but rather a place mandate. For example, GKFF itself is nested under the Tulsa Community Foundation. Although grounded in a particular place, community foundations often give to a range of causes, while family foundations and other models can more easily prioritize and focus their giving. (GKFF blends both models to stay rooted in Tulsa but with maximum flexibility for how it makes grants.) Many private foundations, usually founded by an individual or a family, focus on a city or region, such as the Gilbert Family Foundation and the Kresge Foundation in Detroit, the Heinz Endowments in southwestern Pennsylvania, and the Ewing Marion Kauffman Foundation in Kansas City, Missouri. And Warren Buffett, who spreads his giving across multiple institutions, especially the Gates Foundation, maintains a strong affinity for his hometown of Omaha.

Foundations dedicated to an urban community deploy their capital in a variety of ways, many aimed at supporting entrepreneurship, tech talent, and innovation. Consider the **Cleveland Foundation**, a pioneer in community-based philanthropy. The foundation emerged in 1914 with an adaptable style of philanthropy when traditional philanthropies were bogged down by the "dead hand" of long-deceased grantors' wills.[3] The foundation was established to be able to make grants in response to Cleveland's changing needs. With an endowment of nearly $3 billion,[4] the foundation made $122 million in grants in 2022, and its original model shines through in its economic development work.[5]

Instead of seeking to restore Cleveland's twentieth-century manufacturing heyday, the foundation strives to leverage the city's industrial past to forge an equitable and tech-led twenty-first-century economy. Since 2020, the foundation has partnered with four other Cleveland-based organizations—Fund for Our Economic Future, Greater Cleveland Partnership, JumpStart, and TeamNEO—on an economic growth initiative called the Cleveland Innovation Project (CIP). With more than $800 million invested as of 2022,[6] CIP unites academic institutions, companies, and the public sector to grow Cleveland's leadership in three clusters: smart manufacturing, health innovation, and water technology.[7] The foundation and its partners are also intentional about using CIP to rectify racial and gender disparities. The project aims to fund a pool of new tech talent, STEM graduates, and corporate offices that are 25 percent Black or Latinx, and 50 percent female.[8]

One of the largest private foundations in the United States also serves a geographic region. Located in Bentonville, Arkansas, the **Walton Family Foundation** boasts an endowment slightly larger than GKFF's, at nearly $6 billion.[9] (The Waltons famously made their fortune through Walmart, the national retail behemoth, and channel their giving through the foundation and other entities.) The foundation made $566 million in total grants in 2022 alone. In addition to the environment and education, the foundation focuses on its home region of Northwest Arkansas (NWA) and the Mississippi River Delta. As GKFF does in Tulsa, in recent years the Walton Family Foundation has contributed to home region projects that support entrepreneurs. This is a rural part of the country, and the foundation sees entrepreneurs as key to creating an ecosystem of start-ups to attract talent and build density there. Examples of initiatives include the Arkansas Small Business and Technology Development Center at the University of Arkansas; Builders and Backers, a start-up accelerator dedicated to reducing barriers to entrepreneurship; Right to Start Northwest Arkansas, an initiative to engage entrepreneurs from underserved communities; and Tech Summit held by the Greater Bentonville Chamber of Commerce.

Both philanthropies honor the local knowledge and expertise of their partner institutions and use their capital to support these organizations in making strategic investments in the community. Whether it's supporting entrepreneurship or other causes, foundations with deep ties to an area can tailor programming and build the local partners they need to accomplish collective impact. If done with intentionality and inclusion, this can transform a regional economy. But just as there are benefits to a geographic focus, there can also be constraints.

One of the lessons I learned in Tulsa is that a philanthropy's geographic focus can be limiting. Tulsa's immaturity as a tech hub means that there are local limits (for example, limited academic IP to commercialize or start-ups to support). In addition to importing new assets to Tulsa, there are also opportunities across Oklahoma that could directly and indirectly benefit the city if GKFF were able to expand its geographic scope and engage them. But GKFF's focus on northeast Oklahoma prohibits initiatives that function statewide, even if they are designed to drive activity to Tulsa (think of a program that supports academic innovation across the state, but offers commercialization opportunities in Tulsa). For Heartland cities that are unlikely to have all the tech and talent they need, regional philanthropies should consider ways to position their communities as magnets within their state and across their wider region.

What distinguishes GKFF from some of its peers is less the size of its endowment and more its interest in comprehensive economic development and technological innovation. It has a living donor passionate about these subjects. Few foundations are taking as systems-wide an approach to tech-led economic development (or to any other single issue) as GKFF is. As I argued before their board—and TIL later demonstrated—the only way to build an inclusive innovation economy is to create multiple interventions that work in concert. That GKFF has embarked on such an ambitious project is a testament to its enduring commitment to Tulsa and the acknowledgment that tech offers the best opportunities for good jobs and resilient economies.

While GKFF doesn't fund research projects or technology products directly, as its coalition illustrates, the foundation has a strong appetite to support academic innovation and entrepreneurship initiatives that are centered on technology and designed to grow tech start-ups in Tulsa. In T-Town, at least, that interest in tech is unusual. For instance, another Tulsa-based philanthropy, the Lobeck Taylor Family Foundation, prioritizes nontech entrepreneurship. They established Mother Road Market, a food hall on historic Route 66 that allows budding restaurateurs and small business owners to test new food and retail concepts.[10] Mother Road is a pull for locals and the type of amenity tech talent want in their community, complementing GKFF's tech entrepreneurship investments.

To advance the goal of a vibrant tech start-up scene, GKFF deploys capital in creative ways, using both traditional philanthropic dollars (grants) and capital from their endowment (ROI-generating investments)—sometimes combining them to meet the needs of TIL's multifaceted initiatives. This is a relatively new technique for GKFF, pioneered by former chief investment officer Robert Thomas. A good example is the EIC Rose Rock initiative, where GKFF's philanthropic dollars were used to establish a nonprofit accelerator that offers nondilutive grants to start-ups, while GKFF's investment dollars anchored a new venture fund. As I described in the previous chapter, the initiative works because of its interlocking prongs, and they each require their own distinct financing.

GKFF and Tulsa may foreshadow how other philanthropies will invest in similar endeavors in the future, as the need to build inclusive tech-based economies becomes even more urgent. Philanthropy stands to play a leading role, leveraging its third sector status and wealth to bring the public and private worlds together. In fact, philanthropy may be particularly adept at advocating for inclusion in the tech sector and incubating innovation projects with technological, economic, and social benefits. This may be especially true as the next generation of philanthropists are largely going to come from the tech industry. Given philanthropy's ingrained position in cities and their potential to do vast amounts of good, urban leaders will need to learn how to partner with the social sector, leading them in wise and generous directions to fund economic development.

DON'T FOLLOW THE MONEY, LEAD THE MONEY

As I was learning how GKFF operates in Tulsa, one nonprofit leader told me that working with philanthropies is like playing a video game that's impossible to beat; you need a "cheat code" to unlock funding. This sentiment echoes throughout the nonprofit world—philanthropies can be notoriously opaque, hard to engage, and frustrating to secure funding from. Even with my special access, I found it difficult and saw opportunities for greater efficiencies, like more defined procedures and less matrixed decision-making.

My job leading TIL was to figure out a way to navigate those challenges and to raise the money we needed to accomplish our mission—something I had never done before. Yet, in four years, TIL raised about $100 million from GKFF—and another $100+ million from public and private sources. This process was grueling, and each tranche of funding felt like moving heaven and earth, but I discovered some important lessons along the way.

The reality for most Heartland cities, Tulsa included, is that you will need to leverage public, private, and social sector funding for economic development initiatives. By and large, Heartland cities don't have a lot of financial resources, and they struggle to get investment from VCs and the federal government. While most have community foundations, few have a single organization that can—or is willing to—bankroll everything. So how can cities raise money from philanthropy?

Too often, I've witnessed the impulse to design initiatives to match available funding, whether it was philanthropic or govern-mental. This "follow the money" mentality is misguided because it distracts you from your own strategic plan. Cities should take the opposite approach, however counterintuitive it may seem. Don't follow the money: lead the money to you, align on a vision, and then leverage it to unlock additional investment.

There's a common misperception that philanthropies know exactly what they want to fund and have a fixed methodology or approach in mind. I never responded to a request for proposals or a notice of funding opportunity from Tulsa's social sector—the process between TIL and GKFF took place via conversation. Moreover, GKFF never requested a particular outcome from TIL, much less a way to accomplish it. In other words, GKFF didn't bring TIL a solution to develop; TIL brought GKFF a solution to fund. That's why we built TIL in the first place. Many foundations don't have subject-matter expertise and rely on grantees to propose good ideas. Consider how well GKFF received my pitch, which resulted in the formation of Tulsa Innovation Labs.

Philanthropies are also unlikely to issue a solicitation for the exact type of programming you want to do if they issue anything in writing at all. And some competitive grants may be so narrowly scoped that they won't meet your needs. To maximize your opportunities, then, don't just search for the perfect match: develop a solution and then pursue a collaborative and fluid process of partnership that refines that solution. And all of this should come before you submit a proposal.

While it'll depend on the relationship you have and the funder's culture, don't risk going to a funder prematurely. I involved GKFF throughout TIL's initiative-design process, constantly taking their pulse to see if our work was meeting their expectations. But if it's a new relationship, bring the solution to them when it's ready. Here are seven components you should have defined before making an explicit fundraising ask:

STORY: Everyone likes a good story. While PowerPoint slides and financial models are necessary for when funders look underneath the hood, the overall story is what will seize funders' attention.

For the funder, this should be the easiest part to understand, and it should include a description of the problem and how you can work together to solve it.

INTENDED IMPACT: Funders will want to understand the impact you're seeking to make, complete with anticipated metrics, though to what degree could vary widely. Outline what you will accomplish and on what timetable. For example, with the Cyber Skills Center, TIL presented not only intended graduation and job placement rates within the initiative's first three years but also estimates for increased earnings of graduates over their lifetimes.

INITIATIVE DESIGN: The next piece is the how—this is the solution to the problem. Build a model that achieves your desired outcomes. At the New York City Economic Development Corporation, I found that it was helpful to create a comic book–like slide to walk decision-makers through how the project would work, showing the life cycle from the target demographic's point of view step-by-step, breaking down things into constituent parts.

BUDGET: What capital do you need? A reasonable, flexible, and justifiable budget is necessary. Be prepared to show how you plan to make the initiative scalable and sustainable, especially by using other potential funding sources (more on that soon). Also, be able to scale up or down on the budget depending on interest and available funding.

THE ASK: Think carefully about what you're asking for. How much money? Over what period of time? And for what, exactly? Some philanthropies are less inclined to fund real estate, construction, or foundational research but are interested in funding head count and programming, while some may want to fund scholarships or other direct assistance. And some may only want to provide funding for a short period of time. Every foundation has its nuances; learn them and tailor your ask accordingly.

VALUE PROPOSITION: You've communicated the intended impact, but beyond that, articulate a compelling reason why this funder should support your work. How will they benefit? Understand what motivates the funder. Is it national press, local excitement, brand-name partners, financial leverage, mission alignment, or particular impact metrics? Craft your proposal so that it shows strategic alignment.

MENU OF OPTIONS: Many funders desire flexibility, so you shouldn't take a binary—take it or leave it—approach. Rather, the conversation should be about a shared vision and options to achieve it together. Is there a range of funding asks—a high, medium, or low ask that you can present? Prepare a menu of things they can support depending on their interests, but also define what a minimal viable product is to establish a floor of support. Also consider different funding mechanisms, such as a direct grant, matching or challenge grant, forgivable loan, or other instruments. Signaling flexibility and inviting discussion will encourage negotiation and aid in partnership building.

This is all assuming that, before you go to philanthropy with an ask, you've engaged local partners and funders in the ideation process and have been testing and refining along the way, guiding them to the solution you had in mind but open to their ideas. It is vital that you work to make your vision the funder's vision. You'll have also built champions and validators who can lobby the philanthropy on your behalf. Don't forget: Lead philanthropy to you through the strength of your story and the power of your vision. Then meld minds, to the extent possible, marrying your vision with their priorities. The opposite approach—building something from scratch because of a grant opportunity or going in cold with a random ask—will be less likely to meet your city's needs and will suffer because the alignment is forced. If you've done your homework, developed a solution, and tailored your pitch, then the funder should be confident that your proposal will be impactful and that you can deliver on it. But this is only half the battle.

LEVERAGE, NOT IMPACT

Philanthropy has a reputation for being sticklers for impact metrics. Many funders demand of their grantees robust quantitative systems to monitor and track outcomes. In my interactions with philanthropies, however, I've noticed that impact is either taken for granted, assumed, or not really factored into the funding decision at all. This may be a cultural nuance or a feature of place-based foundations and is likely less relevant for nationally or globally operating foundations.

At TIL, I always felt confident in our ability to demonstrate intended impact, but I'd need to use a different approach to get the money to launch an initiative because impact alone wasn't persuasive. And upon reflection, it was naive of me to think that impact and merit were sufficient. To unlock philanthropic dollars, I had to use leverage: How much additional funding can we unlock from the public and private sectors if GKFF were to contribute? One of the most important and valuable powers of philanthropy, if done right, is capital mobilization, and GKFF is effective at this. Leverage is often prioritized because of a risk calculation. More funders mean less risk, less exposure, and less liability for the foundation. Many philanthropies won't take the lead or go it alone, so you'll need to secure additional capital partners. Toward that end, I briefed private sector partners early on, involved them throughout the initiative-design process, and forecasted potential federal funding sources.

Confirming contingent GKFF funding and leveraging it to raise public or private capital was a winning equation. GKFF's support usually came in two general forms: matching grants, where we secured X amount in funding to unlock an equal amount, and challenge grants, where we secured Y amount in funding to unlock Z amount. Having secured a baseline level of support from our philanthropic backer contingent upon additional funds raised, the TIL team then took that opportunity to other prospective funders to try and raise the money we needed to launch the initiative (we also pressed our operating partners, those responsible for the day-to-day of the initiatives, to have skin in the game).

Given our relationship to GKFF, TIL started with the social sector, but depending on your relationships, leveraging funding works across sectors. If you're able to secure a matching grant commitment from a corporation first, you can then take that opportunity to your community foundation and explore ways to secure their support. While there were many days I'd have preferred that GKFF fund the entirety of TIL's needs, I knew that the process of securing additional capital partners made our initiatives stronger, helped secure buy-in from the community, and ultimately led to more robust funding. Besides, for many of TIL's initiatives, private sector contributions were necessary to make the effort work. And on the public side, many federal grant applications require or encourage additional funding partners. (As you'll see in the next chapter, TIL found that pursuing federal grants was a good way to induce funding commitments from philanthropy.)

To demonstrate the power of leverage, here are three quick examples of TIL initiatives and their funding schemes. TIL's energy tech initiative, EIC Rose Rock, required an initial multimillion-dollar commitment from each of three corporations before GKFF would contribute. The Tulsa Regional Advanced Mobility cluster (TRAM), a suite of advanced air mobility initiatives that we'll cover in the final chapter, had a one-to-one match between the US

Economic Development Administration and GKFF (EDA told TIL that GKFF's matching funds were a compelling asset in our successful Build Back Better Regional Challenge [BBBRC] grant application). And the Oklahoma Cyber Innovation Institute also had a one-to-one match between the state of Oklahoma's allocation of American Rescue Plan funds and GKFF grant dollars. For cities looking to raise capital to fund economic development, leverage is the way to go—it encourages coalitions and leads to catalytic funding if everyone chips in.

As funder and capital mobilizer, philanthropy can be the backbone organization in your cross-sector coalition. This can position the social sector as the city's power broker. It's unclear who said it first—Voltaire, Spider-Man's uncle, or RuPaul—but the proverb "With great power comes great responsibility" rings true in the context of philanthropy. Philanthropies not only need to be careful stewards of their wealth but, because that wealth is designated for public good and there are tax benefits and legal requirements associated with it, philanthropies have a special responsibility to engage with and be responsive to their communities—even more so when they're transforming the local economy. As partners with the social sector, governments, grantees, and citizens need to demand that philanthropies hold themselves to the highest standards.

CREATE A CULTURE OF ACCOUNTABILITY

Throughout this book, we've discussed what inclusive growth is and how to achieve it in Heartland cities. We covered specific metrics for inclusive growth in chapter 3 and DEI interventions in chapter 6, for instance. But another component of inclusive growth is the democratization of the economic development process itself. In essence, do engaged citizens get a voice in their city's future? In the Tulsa context, economic development led by philanthropy and not by local government raises fair concerns that should be examined. Doing so can help philanthropy and cities work better together, while holding philanthropy accountable—both for making an equitable impact and doing so in a democratic way.

The truth of the matter is that all the positives and negatives of "Big" (Big Tech, Big Banks, Big Government) can be found in Big Philanthropy itself. The core critiques of philanthropy center on wealth, power, and elitism. For many, philanthropy's founding wealth is the fatal flaw—such extreme wealth should have been taxed and put in public coffers, they contend. Rob Reich, a faculty codirector of the Stanford Center on Philanthropy and Civil Society, argues in his book *Just Giving* that philanthropy can become a "perpetual exercise of power," rather than of social impact, which "fits uneasily, at best, in democratic societies that enshrine the value of political equality."[11] I don't think philanthropy is anathema to a democratic society as some suggest. But I have seen how philanthropy can fit uncomfortably in an urban ecosystem, the proverbial elephant in the room.

GKFF's economic development work in Tulsa reflects some of these concerns. There's no doubt that the foundation is reshaping Tulsa's economy, altering its built environment, and changing its demographics in the process—all without a popular vote. That a philanthropy is taking the lead on what traditionally has been a governmental function throws into relief both social sector critiques and the limitations of government today. Moreover, philanthropic wealth concentrated in a limited area does maximize impact, but it also maximizes the power the foundation has in that city. GKFF enjoys outsized influence in a city Tulsa's size, where other sources of capital are scarce. And as I've seen through TIL's practices, my own leadership, and the GKFF coalition more broadly, stronger community engagement and accountability mechanisms would add value to the historic project underway. For those reasons, the vastness of the Tulsa project and the primacy of philanthropy in it prompts me to wonder how we can be doing better, however altruistic our intent, however positive our impact.

Of course, the very lack of structural accountability is what gives philanthropy the ability to move fast and make an impact—and it's why Tulsa's reset has been relatively rapid. It's why, in part, society created this third sector—to act more quickly and with fewer encumbrances than the public and private sectors can. The result is that "philanthropy is positioned to be society's R&D," as Katherina Rosqueta told me. Rosqueta is the executive director of the Center for High Impact Philanthropy at the University of Pennsylvania.

"The lack of structural accountability is both philanthropy's superpower and blind spot," she explained. "Superpower because, unlike business, which is accountable to its owners to turn a profit, and unlike government, which, in a democracy, is accountable to voters and taxpayers, philanthropy is relatively unaccountable." As a result, she said, philanthropy "can go places that are, frankly, too hot, politically, and where nobody can see a way to make money. That's why philanthropy has always been at the forefront of addressing social issues."[12] Yet the blind spot in this dynamic is donor-directed giving that doesn't engage communities, doesn't meet their needs, and advances the privileged positions of philanthropists more than it fixes flawed systems.

Many philanthropies—GKFF included—know their foibles and work, perhaps imperfectly, to mitigate them. Indeed, a lot of folks who dedicate their lives to social change and who know their institutions best care passionately about improving them. Like the Rockefeller's Rajiv Shah, who calls out philanthropy's predilection for control, Ford Foundation president Darren Walker believes that "the way we [in the social sector] work can easily mirror the imperfect systems that created us and can perpetuate injustice rather than remedy it."[13] In fact, philanthropy began as a way for Americans to contribute to civil society, and for generations most

Americans gave to charity. But as the country and its capitalistic system evolved, wealth disparities increased, leading to less giving by average Americans and the increased power of a few private foundations.

Like with the other "Bigs," the challenge for Big Philanthropy is mitigating the ill effects of extreme, concentrated wealth and leaning into the social mission on which they were founded. They need to live the values they espouse and enable, not skirt, democratic engagement. President Obama said in his 2009 inaugural address, "The question we ask today is not whether our government is too big or too small, but whether it works."[14] The same question goes for philanthropy—does it work, and does it work democratically? Does it engage communities in solution building, or is it a one-way relationship between the "helper" and the "helped"?

With that in mind, I wonder: Can you truly have inclusive growth if philanthropy and not government leads economic development? Anand Giridharadas would likely say no. In *Winners Take All: The Elite Charade of Changing the World,* he argues that the public sector must originate and lead any kind of truly equitable social change: "What is at stake is whether the reform of our common life is led by governments elected by and accountable to the people, or rather by wealthy elites claiming to know our best interests."[15]

But while I'm sympathetic to this argument, I also find it wholly impractical. Elected officials, particularly in Congress, are simply a different flavor of elite, and government continues to be dysfunctional, limiting what it can deliver to the public. At the same time, US tax policy isn't likely to change so dramatically that it'll do away with philanthropy. Giridharadas diagnosed the problem, but it's up to urban leaders to figure out a solution. Acknowledging that capitalism is flawed and that philanthropy encapsulates this imperfect system, society must then work to devise regulations and encourage cultures of accountability to stand guard against overreach and to maximize philanthropy's positive powers. Besides, it's less about who the funder is and more a question whether partners align transparently and whether the ecosystem is being coordinated around a shared vision of inclusive growth. To accomplish that, philanthropy itself will need to change, and how cities work with philanthropy will also need adjusting. There needs to be a new compact between civic organizations and their philanthropic partners.

GUIDING PRINCIPLES FOR PHILANTHROPY TODAY

Fifteen years have gone by since Warren Buffett and Bill Gates launched "The Giving Pledge," a campaign to encourage fellow billionaires to donate the vast majority of their wealth to charity. As of 2023 there are 241 pledgers, including George Kaiser, Elon Musk, and Mark Zuckerberg.[16] The pledge was a good start, but we need new ways to hold philanthropy accountable.

So, can you have inclusive growth if philanthropy, and not government, leads economic development? To me, the answer is yes, with some important caveats. I call these caveats **Guiding Principles for Philanthropy Today**, and I designed them to help philanthropies build a culture of accountability within their institutions:

1. **Systems Strategy (Go beyond piecemeal investments).** Foundations should be dedicated to improving flawed systems, making investments designed to catalyze ecosystem-wide improvements rather than funding one-off projects.

2. **Beneficiaries (Expand the pie).** A significant share of funding should go to support demographics that have historically been most in need: women, children, people of color, and Indigenous populations.

3. **Interventions (Get funding into worthy hands).** A large share of funding should go to direct assistance to individuals, such as through scholarships or fellowships.

4. **Community Engagement (Build solutions together).** Foundations should place a premium on codesigning solutions with the community, which requires a culture of engagement, specific means for doing so, and a commitment to being responsive to local needs.

5. **Geography (Reach "across the tracks").** An appropriate share of funds should go to organizations or projects located in zip codes with median household incomes below the city or national averages.

6. **Competition (Make it a fair game).** A sizable share of funds should be accessible through competitive processes available to local organizations, including avenues for organizations to submit their own ideas. (Here is one way philanthropy would be wise to mimic, with less bureaucracy, governmental grant programs.)

7. **Flexibility (Write checks with no strings attached).** Grants should be given to trusted partners with minimal requirements to encourage autonomy.

8. **Grantee Relations (Treat your partners well).** Foundations should respect and support their grantees and operate in good faith with them, building reciprocal relationships and treating them as indispensable drivers of impact.

9. **Professionalism (Build competent foundations).** Donors should build strong charitable organizations with effective staff to support their grantees.

10. **Goals (Prove your impact).** Foundations should establish quantifiable goals and procedures to monitor progress and share this information with the public to avoid "impact theater."

11. **Conflicts (Keep it kosher).** Philanthropies should build in safeguards to ensure that grant making avoids business and political conflicts of interest.

12. **Sunsetting (Get the money out the door).** Charitable funds should be fully dispensed within twenty-five years of the founder's passing.

Change and accountability are choices, and philanthropies must choose to better democratize their giving. These principles can help build awareness of important concerns and create institutional accountability to mitigate them. A culture of accountability, however, also requires input and collaboration from cities—local governments, nonprofits, and community members alike. What can cities and philanthropy do to create a stronger compact together, one based on mutual respect, shared vision, and a culture of accountability? Consider this an addendum to coordinating your ecosystem, from chapter 3:

COMMUNICATION: Build publicly accessible communications channels and feedback loops, such as office hours at anchor institutions, coffee chats with local leaders, listening sessions, townhall forums, roundtable discussions, visioning sessions, solution sprints, and community festivals. When nonprofits, governments, philanthropies, and communities engage one another, they can learn from one another. Doing so publicly will increase transparency and get economic development out of the shadows and into communities, which can inspire more civic participation and investment.

ALIGNMENT: Align on strategic priorities between the public, private, and social sectors. Create a citywide plan that sets priorities and coordinates timelines, charitable giving, and public projects. Doing so will help unify your ecosystem, get the flywheel spinning, and facilitate collective impact.

TRUST: A culture of accountability—especially nurtured between anchor organizations and partners—must be built on trust. Open communication and strategic alignment are critical to this. They'll ensure stakeholders are on the same page, with clarity on roles and responsibilities. Partners must then continuously remind everyone that the city is united toward a common goal and create a one-team mentality. At the same time, they must keep up their end of the bargain to prove dependability.

OUTCOMES: To foster trust and confidence in the community, it's important that the public and social sector demonstrate results. Together, they should build and adopt a dashboard to monitor their progress, setting citywide goals and tracking performance over time. Multiple parties should be necessary to accomplish these citywide goals, so everyone plays a part. The Economy Forward Framework TIL developed is a good example of a metric system to track inclusive economic growth.

Some civic organizations, governments included, like to keep their work close to their chest, intentionally limiting who is involved. I understand the argument against a community-centered approach. Increasing public engagement has its risks. First, it opens projects up to media scrutiny. But the press is a critical check to power across society even as local news continues to dwindle.

(The Knight Foundation has invested heavily in local journalism throughout the country to correct this trend.) Second, activists can be irritating and gin up trouble. And third, community engagement takes time, energy, and resources. When you're swamped with work and concerned about creating more problems, community engagement is the first thing to go. I know from firsthand experience.

But not engaging citizens on decisions that affect them reveals a power imbalance that, in the words of novelist Saul Bellow, can bring the "right-thinking citizen['s] . . . heart to a boil."[17] Over time, this broken relationship leads to the ingrained distrust we discussed earlier in the book. This is why "instead of making choices for other people, philanthropists must learn to empower individuals," as social sector adviser Mark Kramer and social justice leader Steve Phillips write in the *Stanford Social Innovation Review*. Kramer and Phillips urge philanthropies to give more directly to those in need and empower them to help themselves through community-based solutions. They point to Tulsa's Black Wall Street of the 1900s as proof that minority communities can flourish without "dependency-producing" government or philanthropic programs, which, they contend, can "undermine self-determination."[18] To empower their fellow citizens and create community-centric solutions, every civic leader must do their part to democratize economic development and create a culture of accountability.

WHAT I WOULD HAVE DONE DIFFERENTLY

In retrospect, I optimized for speed and failed to reach out enough to the communities TIL was trying to serve, so I am complicit in taking a private sector–oriented approach to economic development, which limited the inclusiveness of TIL's practices and created too much distance between TIL and the community. If economic development organizations are seen as mere proxies for philanthropy or the private sector, they may not get the buy-in and support from the community they'll need to make initiatives successful. I will also say this isn't unique to philanthropy but is likely indicative of economic development generally; at the New York City Economic Development Corporation, the industry division and the community engagement team were treated as separate, with limited collaboration, and that was a quasi-public agency. This suggests, quite wrongly, that innovation is a top-down industry engagement, with "job fillers" as an afterthought. At both NYCEDC and TIL, I exclusively engaged business and academic leaders, but economic developers lose out in such a narrow approach.

Specifically, if I were to do things differently, I would have handled the development and rollout of TIL's tech-niche strategy in another way. I didn't realize at the time what a massive project this would become, how transformative it would be for Tulsa; nor was I as conscious as I am now about the need to intentionally engage members of the community, not merely the elite. We needed fewer steak dinners with corporate executives at Bull in the Alley and more conversations with engaged citizens. While TIL interviewed more than a hundred local stakeholders as part of our process, I would have also held a series of listening sessions to hear about the pain points everyday Tulsans were encountering as they looked for jobs or sought training in tech. This would have provided greater local insight and context, established broader buy-in, and given our strategy some needed soul.

After we had established the strategy, I would have then promoted it more widely, holding events in Tulsa beyond downtown, not just penning an op-ed or speaking to Tulsa's CEO and chief information officer forums. On college campuses and at community centers, I would have explained what our clusters were and sketched out job and educational opportunities in them that people should explore. I'd have previewed the initiatives TIL was working on to create pathways into those opportunities. Most importantly, I would have solicited input and asked their advice on how to achieve our shared goals and what TIL could do to best support them. This would have been a more democratic and community-centered approach to economic development, akin to how Rick Lowe created his Tulsa Race Massacre arts project—from within the community itself.

For Tulsa, I think there's a healthier balance to strike—an approach that broadens the economic development process to more diverse voices and does so in an organized, methodical, and effective way. Although I know there are limits to what is possible or even ideal, members of the community must be enlisted to help build their own futures. Creating a culture of accountability, where there are sufficient transparency, strategic alignment, trust, and proven results, can do two important things at once: position philanthropy as a valuable and respected community partner, rather than a concentration of wealth and power, and strengthen the democratization of economic development practices, inspiring the community to work toward a shared plan for growth.

As conveners, capacity builders, ecosystem builders, capital mobilizers, and inclusion champions, philanthropies can help invest in American cities, bolster civic engagement, and catalyze inclusive growth. The social sector has the opportunity to drive inclusion in tech and support cities in building innovation economies that benefit all zip codes. But they can't do it alone. In fact, philanthropists and economic developers should take a lesson from grassroots activists, no matter their cause. Those citizens know they can't do it alone, either, and they engage their communities, solicit input, build coalitions, and advocate on behalf of their citizens. This is a great lesson for others: engaged, collaborative work can yield richer, lasting relationships as well as systemic change. If and when this approach is combined with the capital and influence philanthropy can bring, urban reinvention can truly happen.

ACTION PLAN SUMMARY		
REINVENTION *What needs reinventing?*	GROWTH *How do you catalyze growth?*	INCLUSION *How do you advance inclusion?*
Rather than a top-down approach run by an elite partnership of philanthropy and civic organizations, cities need to democratize the economic development process itself to ensure the future is shaped by engaged citizens.	Cities should understand the positive role philanthropy can play in urban place making and economic development and strive to partner with them. To secure funding from the social sector, cities should lead philanthropy to them, merge visions, and then leverage their funding to unlock additional capital.	Together with civic partners, philanthropies need to create a culture of accountability that fosters greater community engagement and drives more equitable outcomes.

CHAPTER 10

STACK HANDS
WITH UNCLE SAM

(FEDERAL FUNDING)

Who would think to put a drone testing facility next to a casino? This curious site isn't the latest attraction in Vegas: it's five miles north of downtown Tulsa. It gets rural fast in Oklahoma, so five miles outside the city means it's in a secluded part of the metro. There, the Osage Casino sits next to the Skyway36 Droneport and Technology Innovation Center. Just a few years ago, it was an empty plot of land, but thanks to a wise investment by the Osage Nation, TIL's strategic vision, and federal grant dollars, Skyway36 is now a fully operational drone port for start-ups, allowing for the testing of unmanned aerial vehicles beyond the visual line of site.

Former assistant chief of the Osage Raymond Redcorn described to me how a Native American tribe came to own and operate a drone port in the first place: "While I was on the [Osage] Congress, we bought the first additional property adjacent to our Tulsa casino, which included an old airstrip. But that airstrip was left over from a long time ago." At the time, the Osage had no interest in emerging technology or a particular plan for the site. They conducted a highest and best use study of the airstrip, which presented several options, including upgrading the airstrip for drone usage. An unlikely innovation champion, Redcorn, whose background is in construction, remembered immediately loving the idea of the drone port. "I don't know how it's anything other than drones," he remembered telling the project team. "It's long enough to fly any airstrip-based horizontal takeoff aircraft. We have great proximity to downtown Tulsa [and its airport] and we have this ranch [around the airstrip], which could be a forty-three-thousand-acre experimental field for unmanned aerial vehicles."[1] The Osage Congress agreed, and shortly thereafter, in 2021, the US Economic Development Administration awarded the tribal government an initial $2.1 million to upgrade the facilities and kick-start the drone port.

When I first toured the site, I was awestruck that this random plot of land was now a drone port. There, outside the city, under the full, expansive sky, you couldn't help but wonder what was possible with tech in northeast Oklahoma. A blue sky of opportunity, indeed. The site at Skyway36 put the "land" in *Heartland*, and I loved the quirkiness of it.

In 2022, I spoke at the Osage Casino when MIT Solve—the university's social innovation organization—hosted their US Equity Summit there. I joked then that it was the only time I'd ever have a gig at a casino. You had to walk through a smoke-filled bar and gaming floor with Lady Gaga blaring overhead to get to a conference room full of social impact professionals. I found the whole thing hilarious. This dichotomy struck me throughout my years in Tulsa: a budding innovation district next to a creaky train track; an entrepreneur who gave me folksy nicknames; and a drone port next to a casino. This was Tulsa's quintessence. This was what innovation looked like in Oklahoma, what reinvention looked like.

And TIL was privileged to serve the region, and I was lucky to be a character in this world.

Skyway36 would later become the linchpin for TIL's regional advanced air mobility strategy. We designed our AAM portfolio to expand the Tulsa region into new parts of the aerospace value chain, an industry that is the second largest in the state, behind only energy. Like similar hardware-intensive parts of the country, Tulsa's low cost of doing business, cheap land and energy, and affordable labor have long made it an attractive place for high-volume, low-tech aerospace manufacturing and maintenance jobs. Anchor sites like American Airlines in Tulsa and Tinker Air Force Base in Oklahoma City, the largest commercial and military manufacturing and maintenance, repair, and overhaul facilities in the world, respectively, have led to an agglomeration of suppliers and contractors that have built a prosperous aerospace ecosystem in Oklahoma. Most aerospace jobs in the state (some 120,000), however, are in maintenance, repair, and overhaul, which makes them accessible to non-college-degree holders but also vulnerable to automation.

Was shifting this legacy industry to tech a pipe dream? For Tulsa, the transition from aerospace to advanced air mobility isn't as much of a gamble as it may seem, for the Heartland has a tradition of innovation in this space. "There is promise in the Heartland and nontraditional tech hubs," explained Daniel Plaisance, TIL's former AAM lead and current graduate student at Harvard's Kennedy School. "Whether it's early airspace innovation in Ohio, corporate excellence in Wichita, or early testing and invention in the Southwest, aerospace has long been geographically distributed. This made the prospect of a Tulsa aerospace innovation hub much more plausible than a generic 'tech hub,' and local partners, national corporates, and federal agencies are noticeably more credulous. In a less hardware-intensive industry or one that was less related to government or defense investments, it might have been a tougher climb to convince people that Tulsa is a viable place to innovate."[2]

To complement the region's legacy base and pivot to tech, TIL leveraged a host of regional assets. These included OSU's Oklahoma Aerospace Institute for Research and Education—run by Jamey Jacob—copious space for manufacturing and testing, and relationships with tribal communities whose lands abut the city, such as the Osage and their facility at Skyway36. This was our key realization: Tulsa's "right to win" in this industry depended on both urban talent and capital density as well as rural industrial assets. No single part of the region would be a contender for this cluster on its own.

As TIL discovered, to catalyze an inclusive innovation economy, midsized cities will need their rural neighbors as partners. Few middleweights can make the transition to a tech-based economy alone. Moreover, regionalism is another important facet of inclusive growth because it helps bridge the urban–rural divide and extend the benefits of growth to outlying communities.

Why is regionalism a wise approach? The first is scale. To be competitive with big cites, it's essential for Heartland metros to have a critical mass of talent and industry. On the volume side, large-scale efforts to attract corporations count on drawing a workforce from a wide radius. And finally, regionalism offers political upside. Oklahoma disproportionately represents rural interests, so building partnerships with rural counties is a smart way to secure state governmental support. Thanks to a major policy shift at the federal level toward place-based economic development, regionalism is also increasingly important to securing federal dollars.

> Cities will need federal funding to scale and sustain economic development. And regions that work to build linkages between urban and rural assets can find themselves competitive for the federal grants necessary to fuel innovation and growth.

But despite the value of regionalism and the government's ability to incentivize urban–rural alliances, hurdles abound in forging partnerships across jurisdictions. Legal and regulatory differences often get in the way, and you may also have to get past political or cultural differences. The initial and steepest hump, however, is mistrust and seeing neighbors as competitors. By taking a regional approach to economic development, with the shared goal of obtaining federal grants, cities can shift from a zero-sum mindset to a more collaborative one.

To execute TIL's regional strategy and to leverage Skyway36 to its fullest potential, we needed more money than GKFF was willing to give on its own. One of the recurring frustrations among Tulsa civic leaders was the paltry amount of federal funding that the city and its universities have received over the past several decades. Game-changing federal funds have not typically gone to places like Tulsa since they often lack high-capacity academic institutions. Instead, these funds have concentrated in a handful of high-performing areas. In 2021, nearly 50 percent of federal R&D funding went to just five states.[3] But that began to change under President Joe Biden and Vice President Kamala Harris's administration.

Thanks to grants from the Economic Development Administration, TIL was able to join forces with OSU, the Osage Nation, the Port of Tulsa, and others to develop a regional advance air mobility cluster. The idea was to create an ecosystem through various initiatives: innovation from R&D at OSU, located in downtown Tulsa, flows outward to be tested at Skyway36, with start-ups growing in Tulsa thanks to OSU talent, while outlying industrial ports provide companies in need of large manufacturing sites with the space to grow—formally linking the urban and the rural.

Here's early evidence of success, a strong green shoot: Skyway36 has attracted an anchor tenant, a Swiss start-up called WindShape, which has created giant wind simulators used by other companies to test drones in various weather conditions, helping ensure drones can fly safely. TIL formally connected its other AAM initiatives to Skyway36 to create a fully functioning AAM ecosystem and drone corridor that unites the region. Simply put, the drone corridor, Skyway36, and TIL's broader AAM portfolio are moving forward because of federal funding.

Of course, the regional coalition that Tulsa built is unique to its environment, but the larger lesson holds true no matter where you are and what assets you have available: every Heartland city needs to work across their region to compete for federal funding. So how did we do it, and how can your city have similar success?

COMPETE FOR FEDERAL GRANTS

Historically, federal R&D spending has been subject to two distinct priorities: ensuring America's continued supremacy in science, innovation, and national security and reinvigorating stagnant sectors of the economy. In certain areas, these incentives converge. The highly publicized effort to onshore the semiconductor supply chain, for instance, has both created thousands of domestic manufacturing jobs and reduced America's reliance on China, limiting vulnerability to disruptions that would have catastrophic economic effects. But more often, they don't align. Federal programs have long favored meritocratic rubrics and neglected to consider community and economic benefits. The bulk of spending has gone to institutions and regions with a proven history of excellence in specific areas (think Palo Alto or Boston/Cambridge). When the sole measure of success is scientific merit, this is logical—the best institutions with the best talent and infrastructure are more likely to produce breakthroughs than elsewhere. But the unintended consequence of this approach is that federal dollars cement the advantages of big coastal cities.

As Jonathan Gruber and Simon Johnson explain in *Jump-Starting America*, federal R&D spending has previously considered economic impacts as spillovers or afterthoughts and not worth truly considering in the grant-making process. The Biden-Harris administration, however, has chartered a new course—thanks to many of the recommendations Gruber and Johnson put forth in their book. To aid recovery from the pandemic and spur innovation-related jobs in underserved parts of the country, the Biden-Harris administration has passed several historic pieces of legislation totaling more than $3 trillion as part of its broader policy shift: the American Rescue Plan, the Infrastructure Investment and Jobs Act, the CHIPS and Science Act, and the Inflation Reduction Act. Together, these bills provided hundreds of millions of dollars in grant money for a more diverse group of cities and regions to invest in innovation infrastructure and ecosystems. Although it will take years for these investments to bear fruit, they mark an encouraging change in federal economic development policy. I am cautiously optimistic that the incoming Trump administration will continue this trend, which has disproportionately helped the Heartland. For example, Trump's Opportunity Zone program in his first term, which offered tax incentives to invest in distressed parts of the country, should be adapted and scaled to support innovation ecosystems in the Heartland.

For the first time in generations, the government is taking a place-based approach to economic development, intentionally seeking to fund projects in communities historically disconnected from the nation's innovation system and in essential industries. They're doing so through a decidedly regional approach. By requiring regional coalitions for major grants, the government is doing more to bring cities and towns together than ever before, and Tulsa has been both a justification of that policy shift and its beneficiary. For Tulsa, federal funding has been a critical validator of and an accelerant to TIL's work and has helped bring the city closer together with its neighbors in northeast Oklahoma and across state lines in Northwest Arkansas. It has also unlocked additional capital necessary to fund major economic development initiatives. By understanding how Tulsa has done this, other midsized cities will be able to replicate the same benefits in their regions.

First, it's worth exploring in greater depth why this change in federal funding happened. The person in charge of many of these grant programs at EDA is Alejandra Y. Castillo, assistant secretary of commerce for economic development. She explained to me that in recent years, EDA has adapted its investment strategies to focus on a "transformational regional approach that builds meaningful economic ecosystems." Castillo said that "economic development knows no boundaries, and so focusing on entire regions—rather than specific localities—helps ensure everyone shares in the economic growth, job creation, and new opportunities equitably." She described how the EDA increasingly designs its regional programs to "meet communities where they are."[4] EDA's Build Back Better Regional Challenge (BBBRC) and the National Science Foundation's Regional Innovation Engines (Engines) are two of the best examples of this new federal approach, empowering communities to develop their economies using existing assets.

Indeed, there has been a palpable shift from top-down to bottom-up development strategy. As part of its shift, which some label "a new era of industrial policy,"[5] the federal government has relied more on challenge grants, rather than formulaic or overly prescriptive grants. This approach doesn't allocate resources solely based on a community's size, capabilities, or the depth of need but rather on a combination of these factors as well as the bold vision laid out by the communities themselves. In addition to balancing the dueling forces of community need, impact, and merit, this structure forces regions to align behind cohesive visions and strategies. The prospect of generational funding caused regions to take a sober assessment of their strengths, weaknesses, and ambitions, develop a strategy for growth and innovation, and identify a workable model for collaboration—much like the effort TIL started in 2020.

These challenge grants are aptly named. Even in cities with strong institutional support in pursuing federal grants, the various functions that create a successful economic development coalition too often stay in silos. As we covered in chapter 3, the flywheel is often splintered, leaving disjointed ecosystems. Organizations specialize in what they're good at and do their best to stay out of one another's way. The design of the BBBRC and Engines programs called on regions to form a coordinated governance plan, testing both their ability to understand the holistic picture of cluster-based strategy and their capacity to collaborate. EDA made it known that they would frown on a region submitting too many disparate and competing applications, forcing regions to coalesce around one or two truly compelling visions.

This approach largely worked in Tulsa. While TIL had spent the better part of two years researching, strategizing, and building partnerships, our vision of a cluster-based strategy had not yet been widely adopted. It took a specific federal funding opportunity that demanded a forward-thinking cluster strategy to truly galvanize support from Tulsa-area partners.

One obstacle emerged while the federal government was cooking up these historic grant opportunities: Tulsa lacked an established organization with the capacity to track these federal grants, much less effectively pursue them. One of the things that struck

Kian Kamas about Tulsa's recent pursuits of federal grants was how much capacity local organizations need to even compete. She said that Tulsa's economic development ecosystem is in a "fairly immature phase of its life cycle," and that, for places like Tulsa, going after large federal funds demands "honesty about [their organizations'] core competencies" and "humility among stakeholders" about what they can deliver.[6] That means figuring out who's on first, who should be leading what, and who should be staying out of the way. Delegating and ceding control is necessary for well-functioning regional coalitions.

The value of fresh perspectives is why both TIL and PartnerTulsa—fairly new organizations—have been taking the lead in seeking federal funds. This new configuration of Tulsa's economic development ecosystem revealed two lessons: first, going after federal grants requires a local institutional leader, and second, it's an ecosystem-wide process that you need to exercise like a muscle. Practice does make perfect. Tulsa isn't quite there yet, despite some initial and impressive wins. But it takes time for that muscle memory to form.

Despite the roadblocks Heartland metros face in securing federal funding versus established coastal players, TIL has raised tens of millions of dollars from federal agencies after we took the wheel for our regional coalition. So how did we do it? It wasn't because my teammates or I were expert fundraisers; we weren't. I attribute our fundraising success to the time and investment we spent on our up-front vision and strategy. TIL's raison d'être, its theory of change, and its tech-niche strategy all predated (and anticipated) federal funding opportunities, meaning that we didn't start the process from scratch or in response to funding opportunities. Moreover, I urged a focused approach to pursuing grants, one that prioritized opportunities based on how well they matched our existing strategy and programmatic needs rather than bird-dogging every open grant, as some outside voices urged TIL to do. When opportunities that were a good fit arose, we were in a competitive position and moved aggressively. We had been executing our strategy for nearly two years before the BBBRC bid was even opened, so we had a head start on our competition and were already implementing projects aligned with EDA's interests.

Examining two federal funding opportunities Tulsa competed for can shed light on how midsized cities can work with rural partners to secure federal funding. TIL's engagement with these programs can also demonstrate many of the other prongs to my action plan for reinvention—from the industry cluster strategy to leadership and ecosystem coordination.

CASE STUDY: EDA'S BUILD BACK BETTER

The Build Back Better Regional Challenge aims to help regions affected by the pandemic develop a transformational growth cluster.[7] In the case of the Tulsa region, the first question of which cluster to focus on proved to be controversial, showcasing the tension between TIL's new approach to economic development and legacy institutions' more traditional approach.

Tulsa's BBBRC coalition primarily comprised the Indian Nations Council of Governments, the city (through PartnerTulsa), OSU, the Tulsa Regional Chamber, the Tulsa Port, and TIL. Among the coalition, TIL was the only organization conducting tech-led economic development. The strength and maturity of our strategy was evident; we had data, plans, initiatives in development, and the staff to execute. We had already diagnosed the region's workforce needs, mapped assets, and compiled most of the materials needed for the application. This confidence, however, came off as arrogant, particularly to our rural partners who took a more understated approach. I needed to be mindful of the cultural and generational gaps between the legacy organization leaders and me and my team.

Despite TIL's "young whippersnapper" attitude (or our good trouble vibe, if you ask me), most of the coalition quickly rallied behind our focus on advanced air mobility. We felt this industry was a particularly good fit for BBBRC because of Tulsa's regional assets. Yet the chamber was advocating for electric vehicles based on their corporate pursuits (which, it's worth mentioning, weren't part of the grant guidelines). Under a traditional economic development mindset, the chamber's logic was sound. The EV industry was booming at the time, and public subsidies were driving massive investment in domestic EV manufacturing. In the best-case scenario, an EV-focused proposal would have helped us attract some companies and a fair share of the industry. But our data found that EVs were a less compelling opportunity for the region than advanced air mobility, and in the EV scenario there was no clear "right to win" for Tulsa—meaning Tulsa's constrained ability to compete for more than just a slice of the pie would limit regional economic impact. Tulsa would always be a second-tier player behind the likes of Detroit. While appealing in the short term, a play for EVs in the long run could make us even more beholden to race-to-the-bottom tax incentives and the decisions of out-of-town executives.

After several intense back-and-forth conversations, TIL and the chamber ultimately forged a compromise focused on the broader advanced mobility cluster, which encompasses both drones and electric vehicles. This is the Concentric Circles Compromise from chapter 3 in action. We called the proposal the Tulsa Regional Advanced Mobility Cluster. TIL considered this a win because TRAM projected a unified coalition to EDA, and the chamber hadn't acted on any initiatives in EVs while TIL had developed a few advanced air mobility projects, so the proposal naturally gravitated toward AAM anyway. By making data-driven arguments and delivering on our responsibilities, TIL quickly demonstrated leadership and established itself as the strategist for the coalition.

The decision to focus on advanced mobility worked, and the EDA named Tulsa one of twenty-one winners across the country (out of 529 applications). It felt like a huge milestone for the area. Four of the six projects we submitted received funding, bringing in $38.2 million to the region and unlocking an additional $30 million from GKFF, the port, and OSU.

Because all four projects were deeply interconnected, we instantly established an AAM corridor connecting the Osage Nation, OSU-Tulsa, and more distant industrial ports. The winning projects that made up the TRAM initiative are: (1) LaunchPad Research & Technology Center, which expands OSU's nationally leading Oklahoma Aerospace Institute for Research and Education to Tulsa, focusing on industry-aligned, later-stage innovation; (2) The Range at Skyway36, a 501(c)(3) collaboration between TIL, the Oklahoma Aerospace Institute for Research and Education, and Osage LLC that develops facilities that will allow companies like WindShape to test new technologies; (3) Port of Inola (less than twenty miles northeast of Tulsa), which involves site improvements that both enable companies to quickly build large-scale manufacturing facilities and prepare two thousand acres of usable land for advanced mobility companies; and (4) Workforce Programs, which equip Tulsans for the next generation of jobs, increasing certificate, degree, and apprenticeship programs and updating curricula for the AAM industry as reflected in chapter 5's upskilling recommendations. This also includes a labor market observatory to track talent supply and demand over time. The cluster's goal is to generate more than thirty thousand jobs and economic activity worth $3.5 billion over the next decade.

EDA's Tech Hubs

Yet BBBRC was just an unofficial pilot of EDA's even more ambitious Tech Hubs program. Tech Hubs invests in regions that have the ten-year potential to "become globally competitive in the technologies and industries of the future—and for those industries, companies, and the good jobs they create, to start, grow, and remain in the United States."[8] Tech Hubs projects are the pipes and future funding is the water: several federal agencies are lining up to funnel money to the Tech Hubs' designees to advance their priorities. Reflecting the greater national security focus of this program, EDA and other agencies identified ten "Key Technology Focus Areas" that the US needs to win in, such as AI, machine learning, semiconductors, robotics, biotech, energy tech, advanced materials science, and cyber.

To meet these imperatives, regional partners drew on both TIL's advanced air mobility and cybersecurity strategies to develop the "Tulsa Hub for Equitable and Trustworthy Autonomy" proposal, with the stated mandate of developing the "technologies and practices that will allow society to realize the maximum benefit of complex autonomous systems without compromising safety, security, privacy, or public trust."[9] The proposal's secure autonomy focus nicely blends TIL's advanced air mobility and cyber portfolios, demonstrating the ideal interconnectedness of a city's tech niche.

Through the BBBRC victory, TIL had gained local credibility and momentum, so TIL became the de facto leader for the Tech Hubs pursuit—a consortium of over seventy-five partners. And we again came out victorious. In the fall of 2023, Tulsa was designated one of thirty-one "Tech Hubs" (out of 378 total applications), making it eligible for tens of millions more federal dollars. A sizable portion of designees are in the Heartland, making good on the federal government's policy shift. And then, in July 2024, EDA announced that Tulsa Innovation Labs was among twelve winners across the nation, awarding us $51 million.

CASE STUDY: NSF'S REGIONAL INNOVATION ENGINES

In 2022, the National Science Foundation launched the Regional Innovation Engines program, which further advanced the Biden administration's shift toward place-based economic development and presented another funding opportunity for Tulsa.

Engines supports new R&D partnerships that drive economic impact in regions that have traditionally not benefited from tech. Speaking for himself, Daniel Goetzel, who leads Engines, said the program wants to "borrow ecosystem-building models from places like Pittsburgh and what they did around robotics and the Research Triangle [in Raleigh-Durham] and what they did around biotech but also provide emerging ecosystems the runway, support, and connections needed to chart their own path." Engines, therefore, funds new models for research translation and economic development in nontraditional regions.

"A meaningful infusion of capital and support at a critical stage in an ecosystem's development can speed up the flywheel effect from what previously took 30+ years to 12–15 years. If we can condense that timeframe in a subset of places (not all of them will be successful), *and* if we can get to many more ecosystems as opposed to just a handful, then we will have meaningfully moved the needle and developed a successful program," Goetzel explained. "If 10 to 15 years from now, the next generation of emerging technologies are all centered in three to five innovation ecosystems, then we (as a program and nation more broadly) have not done enough to shape the new geography of innovation."[10] Reorganizing the geography of innovation would represent a "quantum leap for America and a very high ROI for the American taxpayer," he added.

In this spirit, Engines, like Build Back Better, exemplified TIL's vision for Tulsa. TIL considered working with Oklahoma City on a biotech Engines grant but ultimately decided that Tulsa has better relationships and industry synergies with our friends in Northwest Arkansas.

Just across the Oklahoma–Arkansas state line is the charming town of Bentonville, which locals say is where "Mayberry meets Manhattan." As I outlined in the previous chapter, over the past few years, Bentonville, like Tulsa, has launched entrepreneurial training and upskilling programs. NWA has also made noticeable upgrades to quality of life—from bike paths and parks to hiking trails and museums. While Bentonville is only the ninth most populous city in Arkansas, the community is the birthplace and continual headquarters of Walmart, which brought in more than $570 billion in revenue in 2022 alone.[11] Walmart also gives preferential treatment to suppliers who have an executive or team located in NWA, leading to even more capital flowing through this pocket of the state.

Given the proximity of Tulsa and NWA, the presence of Walmart and other corporations, such as JB Hunt and Tyson, which are category leaders in their own right, and a similarly strong philanthropic sector generally aligned on inclusive growth priorities, the two cities have a lot in common, and Northwest Arkansas warmly received our invitation to join a cross-state effort to pursue Engines. TIL's partners in Arkansas were the Northwest Arkansas Council, an economic development–related nonprofit; Runway Group, a holding company of Steuart and Tom Walton that makes quality of place investments, including in advanced air mobility; and Heartland Forward, the nonprofit advocacy organization for Middle America supported by the Walton Family Foundation.

Despite these commonalities, bringing the two regions together was challenging. Ross DeVol, Heartland Forward's president and CEO, told me that cross-state collaboration "has long been a puzzling question for economic developers because of jurisdictional differences. You find very few situations where economic development officials collaborate across state lines, let alone within state."[12] He pointed to Boston and southern New Hampshire; Philadelphia and Camden, New Jersey; and Kansas City, Missouri, and the eastern suburbs on the Kansas side as examples of effective cross-state partnerships. TIL was proud to work with DeVol and others on creating a new precedent for Tulsa and NWA.

Mike Preston, the former Arkansas secretary of commerce under former governor Asa Hutchinson and current managing partner at a Little Rock–based financial services firm, thinks cross-state collaborations are well worth the effort even with the difficulties they involve. "When attracting economic development projects, it's important to leverage resources. Communities that are close to the border of another state must find a way to reach across state lines to make that happen," he said. "Leveraging resources allows communities that might be smaller or not have all of the needs a company is looking for to make themselves appear larger and more competitive than what's perceived."[13] The challenge is that state governments don't incentivize economic developers to work across state lines. Ultimately, cities and regions need incentives.

Federal grants are those incentives. Despite the challenges in cross-jurisdictional collaboration, TIL and NWA succeeded in building a bridge between the two regions, both economically and politically. A Heartland Forward report explained the opportunity for the collective region TIL and NWA identified: "Although their economic structures are dissimilar in many respects, serendipity was found in the technological advantages of drone use for surveying and reconnaissance in the oil and gas (Tulsa) industry and delivery of consumer packages (Northwest Arkansas). Drone utilization, combined with other corporate investments approaching $1 billion in new technologies in fleet electrification and driverless trucking, hold the promise of building a bridge between Tulsa and Northwest Arkansas. This 412 Corridor superregional innovative cluster approach seems poised to capture a large portion of the future growth in this evolving sector and establish it as world leader."[14] (The 412 Corridor is a commonly used term in the region and refers to the highway that connects Tulsa and NWA, which are about two hours from one other.)

Together, Tulsa and NWA submitted the Future Logistics and Advanced Mobility Engine (FLAME) proposal. FLAME serves as a blueprint for regional economic development for Tulsa and NWA. The plan calls for four elements: (1) Advanced Mobility Research Consortium to align research priorities and projects across the region; (2) Workforce Center of Excellence to expand training opportunities and wraparound services; (3) Technology Integration Hub to spearhead translation efforts at regional universities; and (4) an Industry Council to facilitate industry partnerships across the coalition.

After submitting the proposal, TIL and then Oklahoma secretary of science and innovation Elizabeth Pollard convened a meeting with Oklahoma governor Stitt and then Arkansas Governor Hutchinson at OSU's Helmerich Research Center in Tulsa to sign a memorandum of understanding outlining an advanced mobility cooperation between the two states. It was a symbolic but important step forward in aligning around the regional vision defined in our Engines proposal.[15]

In January 2024, NSF named ten winners, spanning eighteen states—but Tulsa-NWA was not among them. Engines winners included multiple proposals that worked across state lines, including Colorado and Wyoming on climate resilience; Illinois, Ohio, and Wisconsin on water innovation; and North and South Carolina on regenerative medicine.[16] Even though Tulsa-NWA did not make the list, the bid encouraged the two communities to develop an initial collaboration framework. Unfortunately, given the lack of federal funds, the proposal has stalled, and the mega region hasn't developed the governance structure necessary to align efforts and make investments. But I believe in the long-term potential of the partnership.

Win or lose, BBBRC and Engines were hugely important learning experiences for TIL and the Tulsa region. It established TIL as a respected economic development organization, and it brought previously siloed stakeholders together, strengthened the ecosystem, and started exercising Tulsa's federal grants muscle—all of which paid off with the historic Tech Hubs victory. While implementation of the winning projects poses its own distinct challenges, the process of pursuing federal grants should be educational to stakeholders and to regional ecosystems.

FEDERAL GRANTS PLAYBOOK

Through these experiences, I've learned a few recurring lessons in pursuing federal grants, particularly around strengthening regional alignment. I have segmented them according to components of the federal grant pursuit process, because at each stage of applying, cities will encounter different challenges.

Before

Form a Task Force. Even before there's a grant open, you should have an established group of economic development–related entities ready to go. This is a subset of your ecosystem coalition from chapter 3. In the process, you should diversify whom you're thinking of as "economic development leaders." Many organizations critical to success would not identify themselves as such, including universities, technical experts, educators, and corporates. It can be valuable to educate this group on the fundamentals of economic development so they can anticipate their roles as relevant grants surface. Cities should establish a grants task force that includes backbone organizations, intermediaries, strategists, funders, and operators.

Develop an Information-Sharing Function. Assistant Secretary Castillo knows the value of information sharing. She told me how leaders should "continually evolve the ways [they] share information, resources, and research so that the best practices and best minds regularly merge." Two examples are the Ohio Grants Alliance, a state entity, and the Greater Cleveland Partnership. These organizations publish monthly reports on federal grant opportunities and help coordinate state government support for proposals, increasing opportunity transparency and offering technical assistance.

Create a Blueprint. Much of a regional economic development strategy can occur through the Comprehensive Economic Development Strategy process, the formal economic development planning process supported by EDA, in which regions come together to align on strategy and priorities. TIL's strategy focused on cluster development for Tulsa, and the EDA-supported strategy that the Indian Nations Council of Governments had conducted occurred before TIL had identified Tulsa's tech niche. It would have been wise to have developed and leveraged a tech-forward blueprint for *regional* growth before BBBRC opened. This would have enabled the Tulsa metro to anticipate how regional actors could best work together to develop clusters, preparing us for when a grant opportunity arose.

During
Stick to Your Clusters. If midsized cities have identified their tech niche (informed by regional assets) and secured buy-in on specific clusters, then regional coalitions should primarily compete for grants that support the development of those clusters—their guiding vision. TIL and the chamber's debate about BBBRC is a good example of the choice whether to stick to a vetted strategy or to pursue a hot opportunity in the market. Scott Andes was EDA's program lead for Build Back Better and instrumental in its conception. He was previously the executive director of an AI research and policy center at Carnegie Mellon. Andes stressed to me the importance of reflecting a regional vision in federal grant applications. "I'm a huge believer in moving from values to strategies to tactics," he said. "Having a shared vision that translates into an application strategy allows the core team to

say 'no' to things that come up that aren't aligned. . . . This will save a ton of time and limits the risk of a muddled application."[17] Federal grants are an opportunity to build on and accelerate on-going work; if you're starting over on a new technology area or a brand-new cluster or having to create a new vision, you're going to be at a disadvantage.

Secure Executive Buy-In. One obstacle TIL encountered while implementing BBBRC, particularly among our university part-ners, was internal miscommunication. Our main points of contact would agree to something without executive leadership buy-in, and upon staff turnover, the university would have to reeducate itself on their obligations, or, worse, try to renegotiate the deal terms. While the short timeline on grants makes it tempting to by-pass bureaucracy and political sensitivities, having leadership-level familiarity with projects and strong buy-in at the top is essential to success. This level of buy-in will also help maintain continuity and ease implementation so you're not relitigating something or backtracking when you should be in building mode.

Establish a Governance Model. When the grant is sizable and spans multiple years (BBBRC is five years), it is worthwhile to establish a new form of governance up front rather than relying on informal structures or kicking the can down the road. Tulsa couldn't reach alignment on a governance model for its BBBRC proposal, primarily because our diverse and complex partner-ships couldn't agree to one. As a result, we left the governance model vague in the proposal. But—no surprise—when it came to implementation, aligning on roles and responsibilities and data-gathering procedures proved challenging. Don't punt; delaying the governance model will only make things harder down the line.

After

Publicize Efforts. The process of building a diverse coalition and harnessing that energy is an opportunity no matter if you win or not; it brings into clearer focus the breadth of resources and assets that the region has to offer. Let the community in on the grant process. Emphasize that winning the grant would be the "cherry on top," since the collaboration process itself is progress. New connections formed between places and organizations can spark civic pride by demonstrating the capacity of the community and envisioning the future. Sharing that achievement may even inspire new investment and participation from stakeholders.

Conduct a Postmortem. Tulsa's coalition was too exhausted to debrief immediately after submitting the BBBRC application. But after a much-deserved break, partners should reconvene and engage in a formal assessment. What worked? What could we have improved? What are best practices or lessons learned? After identifying these lessons, the coalition should agree on how to codify those procedures going forward. In the spirit of producing a smoother process and better outcome in the future, the coalition should refine strategies or operational tactics.

Maintain Momentum. While large-scale funding opportunities are exhausting, they have an unparalleled ability to galvanize community-wide enthusiasm and command concentrated attention from key leaders. Don't let this go to waste. Between submittal and the funding decision, work on a plan to advance key elements of your proposal or identify a path forward in the absence of federal funding. While investment has increased because of BBBRC, momentum with NWA stalled once the Engines grant didn't come through; we needed to identify next steps in case we lost, a contingency with buy-in from funders and executive leaders that would have kept moving the ball forward.

Besides shared growth, regional economic development can contribute to solving another national problem: the fraying of communities and the polarization of American society.

BRIDGE THE URBAN-RURAL DIVIDE

My time in Tulsa gave me a window into an overlooked world. Working with northeast Oklahoma and Northwest Arkansas exposed me to the challenges and opportunities rural communities face and the goals they share with cities.

I still remember the feeling I had the night of the 2016 election: a profound realization that my understanding of America had been incomplete. Trump's shock win uncovered stark disparities in the geography of opportunity, dragging into the fore urban–rural fractures long in the making. At the national level, generations of underinvestment in regional economies and a city-centered approach to innovation had been exposed as faulty at best. The body politic was ailing, and America needed, at the federal level, to extend opportunities beyond the same cloistered cities to Heartland regions like Tulsa. While the Biden-Harris administration's economic development policies were effective—inflationary pressures notwithstanding—they couldn't alter national political realities. Trump's 2024 win, therefore, came as less of a surprise and, again, highlighted America's worsening urban-rural and class divides. It's little wonder why Americans live in their own opposing worlds.

Research shows increasingly that most Americans live in bubbles of some sort—whether based on race, educational attainment, political persuasion, or other factors. These physical and online bubbles are the cause of political polarization and an unraveling of social cohesion—rooted to a large degree in the gulf of opportunity between the coasts and the Heartland. Limited worldviews, cultural ignorance, and diametrically opposed realities—between the right and the left, the rural and the urban—shake our sense of national identity as well as the fact base on which democracies need to function.

Thanks to Tulsa, I came to appreciate the significance of the urban–rural divide in a way I never did when I lived in DC or New York. In Tulsa, I saw with my own eyes and felt in my personal relationships how the country was changing. Communities are starting to look different from the ones many middle- and working-class Whites grew up in, while technology is making their jobs more obsolete. Many feel their lives are in a state of limbo. As I learned from the pro-Trump members in my own family, these cultural and economic changes produce anxious vulnerability. The future seems scarier by the day. As Tracy Letts writes in his play *August: Osage County*, "Thank God we can't tell the future. We'd never get out of bed."[18]

Unfortunately, some politicians have exploited this dynamic, mining resentment and encouraging people to blame the Other for their troubles. The acclaimed sociologist William Julius Wilson observes in *When Work Disappears*, "During hard economic times, people become more receptive to simplistic ideological messages that deflect attention away from the real and complex source of their problems."[19] That's why extreme populism can be so dangerous. With resilient skills and equitable access to opportunity, however, people can create wealth and embrace the future without fear—and that's as much true for rural residents as it is those who live in cities.

The "cult of agglomeration," Matt Dunne told me, has created the myth that "rural communities can't code." Dunne is the founder and executive director of the Center for Rural Innovation, which, through technical assistance and peer learning networks, helps micropolitans build tech economies across the country. He pointed to the ignorant yet pervasive notion that everything outside a few coastal hubs is a rural wasteland without innovation potential. For decades, rural communities have been dismissed and ignored, while agglomeration economics fed into the dynamism of big cities at an unstoppable rate, leaving rural communities ever isolated.

The forty million Americans who live in rural communities have never recovered from the Great Recession, Dunne said. National crises affect most everyone but hit already vulnerable communities especially hard. I graduated from college in 2008 and remember the uncertainty I felt looking for a job as well as the public anger at Big Banks. I'd regularly walk past Occupy Wall Street protesters when I was living in New York. According to multiple studies, those entering the labor force during that time will earn approximately $60,000 to $100,000 less over their lifetimes,[20] and research found similar losses for those graduating in 2020 or 2021 because of COVID.[21]

For rural communities like the ones Dunne serves, they've been counted out of the nation's innovation system for a while. The result is resentment, disillusionment, drug abuse, and political polarization, symptoms of a pernicious malignancy—the lack of economic opportunity—which has created a slow-motion kind of trauma that leaves enduring scars. It's a rage that fed both 1921 and January 6, 2021. Dunne agrees that "White rural rage" is a big threat to democracy—the premise of Tom Schaller and Paul Waldman's book, *White Rural Rage*, and the subject of an op-ed by Nobel Prize–winning economist Paul Krugman. But unlike Krugman, who admits he has "no good ideas about how to fight [White rural rage],"[22] Dunne sees answers to the challenge of rural economic isolation in tech-led economic development.

To revitalize rural communities and bring their economies into the twenty-first century, automation-prone advanced manufacturing or next-gen agriculture aren't the solution, Dunne asserted, but "wealth creation and entrepreneurship" are. For me, I thought back to the farmer-turned-Uber driver I met in Tulsa and the viability of his farm and his economic future. "You need to have some ownership of production in the age of automation in order to have an economy that works for everybody," Dunne added.[23]

While there are meaningful initiatives like the Center for Rural Innovation that seek to accomplish this, broader DEI efforts utilize rhetoric and target investments largely to urban people of color. There are good reasons for that—as sociologist Matthew Desmond rightly points out, "Poverty is no equalizer. . . . It can be intensified by racial disadvantages or eased by racial privileges."[24] But with that said, it's important to recognize that economic inequality affects Americans of all stripes. Initiatives for inclusion must incorporate wider geography and class dynamics. This includes the White working class, who do not benefit from the lucrative tech jobs and elite educations of many urban and coastal Whites. The rural communities outside Heartland cities like Grand Rapids, Des Moines, and Milwaukee need to be on the national political and policy agenda for both major parties—especially greater support for broadband, which even in 2025 continues to be a serious challenge.[25] Rural communities must be a part of the inclusive-growth coalition, and the federal government must continue to play a role in providing midsized cities and rural communities with the resources they need to invest in innovation, upskill workers into resilient jobs, and promote entrepreneurship.

National leaders need to engage people outside urban centers and the first ring of suburbs. Tulsa gave me the opportunity to do so, and it was eye-opening. I understood the economic anxiety Tulsans experienced. I felt it growing up in Louisiana, watching my own family face the fear of joblessness. My mom was always employed, often working two jobs, yet we felt vulnerable because of the knowledge that a job loss or an illness or a hurricane would take a catastrophic toll on our family. There was no margin for error, much less force majeure.

Getting outside the Acela corridor showed me the large part of the country that goes unseen by policymakers, left struggling by an economy that no longer rewards their skills and communities without the tools to build a brighter future. But at Tulsa Innovation Labs, we are providing the tools and building the ecosystem the northeast Oklahoma region needs to thrive. We're also bringing in the philanthropic and federal funding necessary to achieve our goals. And as I've demonstrated throughout this book, the answer to greater economic prosperity isn't a silo, resentment, or tribalism. It's collective action, community-based investment, and cross-sector partnerships. The answer, in short, is civic reinvention.

ACTION PLAN SUMMARY

REINVENTION	GROWTH	INCLUSION
What needs reinventing?	*How do you catalyze growth?*	*How do you advance inclusion?*
Heartland cities will need to more successfully compete for federal funding than they have in the past. To win, they'll need to do something they're not accustomed to: build a regional coalition that includes partnerships with their rural neighbors. Shifting from a city-centered approach to a regional approach opens new opportunities and strengthens federal grant pursuits.	To scale and sustain economic development, civic organizations should pursue federal grants as a region. Before a particular pursuit, they should form a task force of stakeholders, share information, and develop a blueprint for the region. During the process, they should shape the proposal to drive development of their clusters, secure executive buy-in with partners, and establish a governance model. Following submission, they should publicize their efforts, conduct a postmortem, and align on next steps to maintain momentum.	Just as the coasts and the Heartland represent a divide, so, too, do cities and rural communities. To achieve inclusive growth, geography and class must be considered. And cities would be wise to join forces with rural partners on tech-led economic development. Doing so will make them more competitive for federal grants and help create a more prosperous region.

CONCLUSION

I like to think of my time in Tulsa as the opening snare drum and organ riff in Bob Dylan's "Like a Rolling Stone." We've kicked things off with a bang and set the song in motion, but ultimately, Tulsa's history is yet to be written. And like the music that emerged from this region, the local people themselves will inform it—with their hopes and their dreams.

Tulsa Innovation Labs set a new direction for Tulsa and proved that a midsized city in the Heartland has what it takes to transition to tech and join the innovation economy. Tulsa's positive trajectory resulted from a strategic plan rooted in collaboration—a citywide effort of reinvention that builds from within itself. My job was merely to cause a little bit of trouble and push the city in the right direction. But the concepts, recommendations, and lessons outlined in this book are bigger than any one leader, organization, or city.

While Tulsa's pivot is successfully underway, the city will need to work together over the long haul to realize sustainable outcomes. To meet this challenge, TIL has entered a new phase, focused on continuing the implementation of its initiatives, codifying the principles I advanced throughout the ecosystem, securing adoption of our strategy with new partners, and raising additional funds to scale the work. But at a certain point, my theory of change was no longer a theory, and as Tulsa began this new chapter, it was time for me to move on.

In August 2023, I resigned as TIL's managing director and said goodbye to my beloved team. I was headed for a one-year sabbatical in the City of Angels, where I would write this book as a visiting scholar at UCLA's Luskin School of Public Affairs. My husband, Chris, had matched for fellowship at UCLA's transplant surgery program. He moved from one coast to the other, and I went with him. We would be living together in the same place for the first time since my Tulsa sojourn began.

I still remember the day I left Tulsa. Despite months of succession planning, my exit felt rushed. There were too many people to say goodbye to, countless loose ends to tie up—always more work left to do. When the plane took off for Los Angeles, I closed my eyes and took a deep breath. My shoulders were as light as they had ever been, and my head rested comfortably on the seat as we soared through a pale blue sky.

Although I was physically and emotionally exhausted, I felt a great sense of relief. I had poured my heart and soul into TIL, but the work left me totally spent. The constant travel, stressful fundraising, and typical strains of a long-distance relationship had all taken a toll, and for the first time in my career, I was officially burned out. Yet looking out the window, I saw the whole country below me, and I smiled to myself. Thanks to a leap of faith, a burst bubble, and a shattered myth, I knew flyover country didn't exist. And I felt gratitude to Tulsa for revealing to me America's promise in so many exhilarating and profound ways.

THE YEAR IN Southern California gave me the time I needed to reflect on my Tulsa adventure. As Chris transplanted livers and kidneys, I had the luxury of writing about the Heartland at a museum or at a café by the beach. It wasn't a hardship, to say the least. Under palm trees, I built a mental time machine, traveling both backward and forward to create the action plan for reinvention that gives this book its purpose. I imagined Tulsa's rolling hills, all the wonderful friends I'd made there, and the great work they're doing to improve the city. And I thought about what Tulsa would look like ten years from now, as well as what it really means to reinvent a city.

As I learned through my own personal maturation and professional development in Tulsa, reinvention means growing from within and building on who you are with strategic intention. For me, it meant transitioning to being a leader, while at the same time discovering what inclusive growth meant at the local level and why it's of paramount importance to Heartland cities like the one in which I grew up. For cities, reinvention means adapting to a changing world and investing in themselves to create new opportunities for all their citizens to thrive. It means transitioning to tech and growing inclusively, ensuring opportunities extend to people of color, women, the White working class, and to rural communities alike.

This is a process, I discovered, and it requires civic leaders to guide their communities through this change. Ultimately, reinvention means transforming cities into gathering places of innovation, seeding a culture of entrepreneurship and civic engagement that leads to ever evolving dynamism. And it means making legacy economies go electric, which, as Dylan faced with his transition from the acoustic to the electric guitar, will cause a fair amount of disruption.

No better concept captures reinvention than a city's tech niche. The tech niche is premised on the idea that every midsized city has a place in today's innovation economy and can become their own hub of opportunity. These handful of clusters require ecosystem coordination and collective action to develop. When cities go all in on investing in themselves, they can reinvent their economies and grow in inclusive ways. But this undertaking will take time, and it will certainly require sizable funding.

One important barrier to developing your niche, and to civic reinvention more broadly, is capital. Economic development initiatives cost money, and inclusive growth itself is a matter of financial capital—who has it, where it's going, and how it's getting deployed. It's about capitalism today and how the flow of investment and opportunity are stuck in coastal cities, limiting investment in the Heartland. Concentrations of wealth have corrosive effects, causing capital to function as a "living creature . . . drawing beautiful patterns on its way into realms of increasing abstraction, sometimes following appetites of its own," as novelist Hernan Diaz writes in *Trust*.[1] The flow of capital can either be the lifeblood of the country, empowering people and communities far and wide, or it can continue to be held in a few places by a few hands—like a blocked carotid artery preventing blood from reaching essential parts of the body. In such cases, the nation suffers just like the body does, and the American Dream continues to be personally and systemically elusive.

Jonathan Gruber and Simon Johnson wonder in *Jump-Starting America* about who can "crown" new superstar cities.[2] As I've shown throughout this book, cities need to crown themselves, carving out their own niche in the innovation economy. But we also need to redefine what a superstar city means. Late-stage US capitalism has mistaken growth for success, but to achieve superstar status, we should measure cities by how equitable their economies are. And given the national scale of such a challenge, Big Tech, VCs, and the federal government all have important supporting roles to play in better investing in Heartland cities.

While this book has focused on what cities can do themselves, national partners need to distribute capital in smarter, more equitable, and impactful ways. And the national innovation system itself needs to be reimagined to better incorporate, support, and leverage Heartland cities. This isn't charity; there's an immense return on investment. The federal government needs to continue its place-based economic development policies in subsequent administrations and think even more ambitiously about building diverse talent pipelines in Heartland cities. Venture capitalists need to expand their funnel, refine their investment thesis, and adjust how they evaluate talent to close the investment gap that women and people of color face. While attracting corporations will not be a city's saving grace, Big Tech companies need to recognize the innovation potential Heartland communities can offer and build new outposts and tap new talent. Governments and network operators should work together to invest in stronger broadband, which is still lacking across the Heartland. And, like people, Heartland cities need community. Joining national networks of other cities working on similar challenges can offer peer learning and help identify resources. Local ingenuity and a support system are each necessary for success.

In my case, I worked obsessively to make a better life for myself. But I was never alone. I had a heroic mom who sacrificed everything for my future. A work-study job and teachers who inspired my imagination. Government grants, loans, and scholarships to help pay for college. A fellowship to graduate school. And a friend who helped me get an internship in city government that launched my career. Such support networks are vital. Although individual success stories—of people and cities—inspire our own drive and determination, they shouldn't eclipse societal challenges. Nor should they give us license to stop working to make systems fairer, more supportive, and more inclusive. Together, internal grit and external support can foster resilience to whatever life has in store.

My life has entangled my own individual resilience with the resilience of cities. The work I do with cities isn't just a day job; it's a reflection of my values and experiences. The result is that my personal journey shapes my professional work, providing a perspective that has hopefully enriched this book. It's a perspective that allows me to understand the link between the circumstances of a modern event like Hurricane Katrina and the shameful historical tragedies that still resonate with Tulsa's Indigenous and Black communities. It's a perspective that causes me to see my mother in the hopeful entrepreneurs, researchers, and students my organization served. And it's a perspective that enables me to see a young New Orleans boy dreaming of a better life in a man who flourished in Green Country.

I'm excited and optimistic about Tulsa's future. Not only is Tulsa reinventing itself, but it's also changing how others see the Heartland. The city showed me—and it's showing America—that the Heartland is as full of talent and promise as any place. Tulsa represents the new geography of innovation, and I am filled with pride knowing that the work I did contributed to this important effort. Tulsa gave me a fuller and more optimistic sense of America, and for that I'm thankful. I hope that I gave back to the city as much as it has given me. No matter where my future takes me, I am fortunate that Tulsa is a part of me. I'll be rooting for it. And to all those Heartland cities out there, let your own reinvention begin now.

NOTES

Introduction

1. Bruce Horovitz, "A Plan to Turn New York into a Capital of Cybersecurity," *New York Times*, November 28, 2018, https://www.nytimes.com/2018/11/28/business/a-plan-to-turn-new-york-into-a-capital-of-cybersecurity.html.

2. Damario Solomon-Simmons, "'Running the Negro out of Tulsa': Victims Still Wait for Justice 95 Years After Greenwood Massacre," Oklahoma Policy Institute, June 1, 2016 (updated May 2, 2019), https://okpolicy.org/running-negro-tulsa-victims-still-wait-justice-95-years-greenwood-massacre/.

3. Kelemwork Cook, et al. "The Future of Work in Black America," McKinsey & Company, October 4, 2019, https://www.mckinsey.com/featured-insights/future-of-work/the-future-of-work-in-black-america.

4. Steve Lohr, "Forget Peoria. It's Now: 'Will It Play in Tulsa?'" *New York Times*, June 1, 1992, https://www.nytimes.com/1992/06/01/business/the-media-business-forget-peoria-it-s-now-will-it-play-in-tulsa.html.

5. David Zizzo, "Tulsa Reigns as Most Ordinary U.S. City," *The Oklahoman*, August 8, 1993, https://www.oklahoman.com/story/news/1993/08/08/tulsa-reigns-as-most-ordinary-us-city/62451806007/.

6. Ibid.

7. Daniela Ibarra, "Tulsa Becomes Majority-Minority City," KTUL, September 30, 2021, https://ktul.com/news/local/tulsa-becomes-majority-minority-city. Reporting on 2020 US Census Data: 48.5 percent of Tulsa's population are White, 19.1 percent are Hispanic, 14.6 percent are Black, 4.6 percent are Native American, 3.6 percent are Asian, and 9.5 percent are Other.

8. Richie Bernardo, "Metro Areas That Most and Least Resemble the U.S.," *WalletHub*, June 15, 2016. https://wallethub.com/edu/metro-areas-that-most-and-least-resemble-the-us/6109.

9. "Jonathan Franzen: 2011 Heartland Prize for Fiction," uploaded by Chicago Humanities Festival, December 6, 2011, https://www.youtube.com/watch?v=Yrzcx3la2Xg&t=608s.

10. Kristin Hoganson, *The Heartland: An American History* (Penguin Press, 2019), 302.

11. Robert D. Atkinson, Mark Muro, and Jacob Whiton, "The Case for Growth Centers: How to Spread Tech Innovation Across America," Brookings Institution, December 9, 2019, https://www.brookings.edu/articles/growth-centers-how-to-spread-tech-innovation-across-america/.

12. Amy Liu, "America's Big-Tech Cities Are Thriving, Not Dying," *Washington Post*, October 26, 2023, https://www.washingtonpost.com/opinions/2023/10/25/big-tech-seattle-san-francisco-rebounding/.

13. Raj Chetty, "Chetty on the 'Fading' American Dream," *Washington Post* [Washington Post Live], August 16, 2023, https://www.youtube.com/watch?v=94b0acnV3zI.

14. "Tulsa Metropolitan Statistical Area: 2023 Local Briefing," Oklahoma Employment Security Commission, https://oklahoma.gov/content/dam/ok/en/oesc/documents/labor-market/publications/workforce-briefings/2023/tulsa-msa-workforce-briefing-2023.pdf.

15. Joseph Parilla, "Opportunity for Growth: How Reducing Barriers to Economic Inclusion Can Benefit Workers, Firms, and Local Economies," Brookings Institution, September 28, 2017, https://www.brookings.edu/articles/opportunity-for-growth-how-reducing-barriers-to-economic-inclusion-can-benefit-workers-firms-and-local-economies/.

16. Schaeffer, Katherine. "6 Facts About Economic Inequality in the U.S." Pew Research Center, February 7, 2020. https://www.pewresearch.org/short-reads/2020/02/07/6-facts-about-economic-inequality-in-the-u-s/.

17. Dan Breznitz, *Innovation in Real Places: Strategies for Prosperity in an Unforgiving World* (Oxford University Press, 2021), 4.

18. George Kaiser Family Foundation, 2024.

19. "Tulsa's Path to Inclusive Growth" (with data from McKinsey & Company), Tulsa Innovation Labs, June 2023, 5, https://static1.squarespace.com/static/6390eb779f75186607f90d99/t/64960444dcbfdc6b55c14753/1687553098730/230623_TIL_Report_FA_Digital.pdf.

20. Zora Neale Hurston, *Their Eyes Were Watching God* (HarperCollins, 2004), 53.

Chapter 1

1. Michael E. Porter, "Clusters and the New Economics of Competition," *Harvard Business Review*, November 1998, https://hbr.org/1998/11/clusters-and-the-new-economics-of-competition.

2. Richard Florida, *The New Urban Crisis* (Basic Books, 2017), 8.

3. United States Census Bureau, Median Income, 2022 Data, https://data.census.gov/table/ACSST1Y2022.S1903?q=Tulsa%20median%20household%20income&g=310XX00US46140.

4. "The Paul J. Robbins Interview—Santa Monica, California," March 1965, https://www.interferenza.com/bcs/interw/65-nov08.htm.

5. Jane Jacobs, *The Death and Life of Great American Cities* (Modern Library, 2011 Edition), 585.

6. "ABCD Institute. DePaul University, Chicago," DePaul, 2017, https://resources.depaul.edu/abcd-institute/Pages/default.aspx.

7. G. T. Bynum, email to author, April 4, 2023.

8. Ron Starner, "How Pittsburgh Wrote the Book for TrustBelt Turnaround," *Site Selection Magazine*, October 2018, https://archive.siteselection.com/trustbelt/how-pittsburgh-wrote-the-book-for-trustbelt-turnaround.cfm.

9. Ibid.

10. Michael Machosky, "How Pittsburgh Is Transforming into the Robotics Capital of the World," NEXTpittsburgh, August 31, 2022, https://nextpittsburgh.com/city-design/how-pittsburgh-is-transforming-into-the-robotics-capital-of-the-world/.

11. "About Us," Carnegie Mellon University Robotics Institute, https://www.ri.cmu.edu/about/#:~:text=The%20Robotics%20Institute%20has%20spawned,companies%20employing%20over%201000%20people.

12. Ron Starner, "How Pittsburgh Wrote the Book for TrustBelt Turnaround."

13. https://datausa.io/profile/geo/pittsburgh-pa?redirect=true#:~:text=Poverty%20%26%20Diversity&text=19.7%25%20of%20the%20population%20for,the%20national%20average%20of%2012.6%25.

14. "Making Our Region Work for All," The Pittsburgh Foundation, n.d., https://www.pittsburghfoundation.org/issues.

15. Henry George, Progress and Poverty, Digireads.com Publishing, 2021 ebook edition, page 16.

16. Jason Griess, email to author, February 2, 2024.

17. Ted Chiang, "Will A.I. Become the New McKinsey?" *New Yorker*, May 4, 2023, https://www.newyorker.com/science/annals-of-artificial-intelligence/will-ai-become-the-new-mckinsey.

18. "Tulsa's Tech Niche," Tulsa Innovation Labs, June 2020 (Graphic originally provided by McKinsey & Company).

19. Adam McCann, "Best & Worst States for Health Care," WalletHub, https://wallethub.com/edu/states-with-best-health-care/23457.

20. "Tulsa's Tech Niche," Tulsa Innovation Labs, June 2020 (Data provided by McKinsey & Company).

21. Based on data from McKinsey in the 2020 "Tulsa's Tech Niche" public report.

22. Ibid.

23. Ibid.

Chapter 2

1. Rajiv Shah, *Big Bets: How Large-Scale Change Really Happens* (Simon & Schuster, 2023), 180.

2. US Department of Education, Distribution of Federal Pell Grant Program, 2004.

3. "Economic Diversity and Student Outcomes at Northwestern University," *New York Times*, https://www.nytimes.com/interactive/projects/college-mobility/northwestern-university.

4. Ta-Nehisi Coates, *Between the World and Me* (One World, 2015), 65.

5. Philip Bump, "With Six Words, Michelle Obama Rewires America's Conversation on Race." *Washington Post*, August 21, 2024, https://www.washingtonpost.com/politics/2024/08/21/with-six-words-michelle-obama-rewires-americas-conversation-race/.

6. Cordell Carter, email to author, March 15, 2024.

7. Tom Wolfe, *The Bonfire of the Vanities* (Picador, Kindle Edition), 296.

8. Bruce Katz and Jeremy Nowak, *The New Localism: How Cities Can Thrive in the Age of Populism* (Brookings Institution Press, 2018), 230.

9. Daniel Doctoroff, *Greater Than Ever: New York's Big Comeback* (PublicAffairs, 2017), 352.

10. Kian Kamas, virtual interview with author, December 29, 2023.

11. Kara Goldin, "'I Would Never Hire the Smartest Person in the Room,' Says One CEO—Here's Why," CNBC, August 23, 2019, https://www.cnbc.com/2019/08/22/never-hire-the-smartest-person-in-the-room-says-hint-ceo-kara-goldin.html.

Chapter 3

1. "History," Cain's Ballroom, https://www.cainsballroom.com/venue-info/history/.

2. Judith Rodin, *The Resilience Dividend: Being Strong in a World Where Things Go Wrong* (PublicAffairs, 2014), 4.

3. Ibid.

4. Bruce Katz and Jeremy Nowak, *The New Localism*, 4.

5. Ken Levit, virtual interview with author, November 30, 2023.

6. "Public Trust in Government: 1958–2023," Pew Research Center, September 19, 2023, https://www.pewresearch.org/politics/2023/09/19/public-trust-in-government-1958-2023/.

7. Justin McCarthy, "In U.S., Trust in Politicians, Voters Continues to Ebb," Gallup, October 7, 2021, https://news.gallup.com/poll/355430/trust-politicians-voters-continues-ebb.aspx.

8. Meagan Dooley and Homi Kharas, "How Inclusive Is Growth?" Brookings Institution, November 22, 2019, https://www.brookings.edu/ blog/future-development/2019/11/22/how-inclusive-is-growth/; and C. Carter, R. DeVol, R. Florida, J. Hankins, and N. Lalla, "The Economy Forward Framework," Tulsa Innovation Labs (2022), 5.

9. Ibid.

Chapter 4

1. Ralph Ellison, *Invisible Man* (Second Vintage International Edition, 1995), 577.

2. Richard Florida, "The Rise of the Meta City," *Harvard Business Review*, December 4, 2023, https://hbr.org/2023/11/the-rise-of-the-meta-city.

3. David Wallace-Wells, "American Cities Aren't Doomed After All," *New York Times*, February 16, 2024, https://www.nytimes.com/2024/02/07/opinion/cities-pandemic-urban-doom-loop.html.

4. "Average Rental Price in New York, NY & Market Trends," Zillow Rental Manager, March 8, 2024, https://www.zillow.com/rental-manager/market-trends/new-york-ny/.

5. Michael Overall, "40% More People Living on the Streets in Tulsa, Annual Headcount Finds," *Tulsa World*, May 13, 2022, https://tulsaworld.com/news/local/40-more-people-living-on-the-streets-in-tulsa-annual-headcount-finds/article_cf97efa0-d201-11ec-aee6-efac33e58613.html.

6. Erin Velez, "Annual Point-in-Time Count Shows Increasing Homelessness," Housing Solutions Tulsa, March 22, 2023, https://www.housingsolutionstulsa.org/annual-point-in-time-count-shows-increasing-homelessness/.

7. Kevin Canfield, "Mayor G. T. Bynum Announces Tulsa Housing Challenge During 2022 State of the City Address," *Tulsa World*, December 17, 2022, https://tulsaworld.com/news/local/bynum-provides-more-details-on-500-million-tulsa-housing-challenge/article_fd7637cc-7d6b-11ed-85c5-cf146676de02.html.

8. Prithwiraj (Raj) Choudhury, Emma Salomon, and Brittany Logan, "Tulsa Remote, Moving Talent to Middle America," *Harvard Business School*, October 12, 2021.

9. "Cultivating Community, Driving Innovation," Tulsa Remote, https://23811891.fs1.hubspotusercontent-na1.net/hubfs/23811891/2023%20Tulsa%20Remote%20Economic%20Impact%20Report.pdf.

10. "The Tulsa Remote Program," Tulsa Remote, https://www.tulsaremote.com/.

11. Prithwiraj (Raj) Choudhury, Emma Salomon, and Brittany Logan, "Tulsa Remote, Moving Talent to Middle America."

12. Ibid.

13. Ibid.

14. Ibid.

15. Bill Murphy Jr., "New Data on 2,000 Remote Workers in Tulsa Shows What Happens When People Move to a Low-Cost City," *Inc.*, January 19, 2023, https://www.inc.com/bill-murphy-jr/new-data-on-2000-remote-workers-in-tulsa-shows-what-happens-when-people-move-to-a-low-cost-city.html.

16. Ibid.

17. Ibid.

18. "Cultivating Community, Driving Innovation," Tulsa Remote, https://23811891.fs1.hubspotusercontent-na1.net/hubfs/23811891/2023%20Tulsa%20Remote%20Economic%20Impact%20Report.pdf.

19. Ibid.

20. Prithwiraj (Raj) Choudhury, Emma Salomon, and Brittany Logan, "Tulsa Remote, Moving Talent to Middle America."

21. Justin Harlan, email to author, October 30, 2023.

22. Prithwiraj (Raj) Choudhury, Emma Salomon, and Brittany Logan, "Tulsa Remote, Moving Talent to Middle America."

23. "Tulsa Remote," LinkedIn, March 8, 2024, https://www.linkedin.com/company/tulsaremote/posts/?feedView=all.

24. Ibid.

25. Ibid.

26. "Why Are So Many Remote Workers Moving to Tulsa? We Explain," *The Economist*, Instagram, March 15, 2023, https://www.instagram.com/reel/Cpzp38Gr5Co/?img_index=1.

27. "Lessons from a Leading Remote Work Incentive in Tulsa, Oklahoma," Economic Innovation Group, November 2021, https://eig.org/tulsa-remote/.

28. Ibid.

29. "Cultivating Community, Driving Innovation."

30. Tejas Vemparala, "Solving the Mystery of Millennial and Gen Z Job Hoppers," *Business News Daily*, October 24, 2023, https://www.businessnewsdaily.com/7012-millennial-job-hopping.html.

31. Sawdah Bhaimiya, "Gen Z Workers Change Jobs More Often Than Any Other Generation Because They're Prioritizing Happiness, High Expectations, and Raises," *Business Insider*, January 6, 2022, https://www.businessinsider.com/gen-z-spends-less-time-in-jobs-than-earlier-generations-2021-11.

32. "Oklahoma Supreme Court Rules the Right to Abortion Is Protected in Life-Threatening Situations," Center for Reproductive Rights, March 21, 2023, https://reproductiverights.org/oklahoma-supreme-court-limited-right-abortion/.

33. Prithwiraj (Raj) Choudhury, Emma Salomon, and Brittany Logan, "Tulsa Remote, Moving Talent to Middle America."

34. Ibid.

35. J. H. Cullum Clark, "Immigrants and Opportunities in American Cities," December 8, 2022, https://gwbushcenter.imgix.net/wp-content/uploads/Explainer_Blueprint3_v3.pdf.

36. Greg Iacurci, "Immigration Is 'Taking Pressure Off' the Job Market and U.S. Economy, Expert Says," CNBC, March 2, 2024, https://www.cnbc.com/2024/03/02/immigration-taking-pressure-off-the-job-market-us-economy-expert.html.

37. Pierre Azoulay, Benjamin Jones, J. Daniel Kim, and Javier Miranda, "Immigration and Entrepreneurship in the United States," National Bureau of Economic Research, September 2020, https://www.nber.org/papers/w27778.

38. Michael Roach and John Skrentny, "Why Foreign STEM PhDs Are Unlikely to Work for US Technology Startups," PNAS, August 5, 2019, https://www.pnas.org/doi/full/10.1073/pnas.1820079116.

39. Alicia A. Caldwell, "To Become a Tech Hub, Tulsa Recruits Ukrainian Workers," Interview by Zoe Thomas, April 19, 2023, https://www.wsj.com/podcasts/google-news-update/to-become-a-tech-hub-tulsa-recruits-ukrainian-workers/2740c515-3030-4a6a-ab48-7670a902d27d.

40. Andrii Skorniakov, virtual interview with author, November 7, 2023.

41. Tom Huddleston Jr., "Millennials and Gen Zers Do Want to Buy Homes—They Just Can't Afford It, Even as Adults," CNBC, June 12, 2022, https://www.cnbc.com/2022/06/12/millennials-and-gen-zers-want-to-buy-homes-but-they-cant-afford-it.html.

42. "Boston Housing Market: House Prices & Trends," Redfin, https://www.redfin.com/city/1826/MA/Boston/housing-market.

43. Gayla Cawley, "Boston Commute 5th Worst in US, Study Says," *Boston Herald*, February 4, 2023, https://www.bostonherald.com/2023/02/04/boston-commute-5th-worst-in-us-study-says/.

44. "People Feel Lonelier in Crowded Cities—but Green Spaces Can Help," World Economic Forum, March 7, 2023, https://www.weforum.org/agenda/2022/01/lonely-study-green-space-city/.

45. Chrissy Molzner, "Urban Loneliness: The Dark Side of Living in a Big City," The Roots of Loneliness Project, https://www.rootsofloneliness.com/urban-loneliness-isolation.

46. Kurt Vonnegut, Commencement Address, 1974, https://www.hws.edu/news/transcripts/vonnegut.aspx.

47. Lynn Greenberg, email to author, November 6, 2023.

48. Mike Dorning, "WFH Federal Employees Have Republicans, Some Dems Demanding Return to Office," *Bloomberg*, March 9, 2023, https://www.bloomberg.com/news/features/2023-03-09/wfh-federal-employees-have-republicans-some-dems-demanding-return-to-office.

49. Ella Fertitta, "Annual Urban Land Institute, PwC Report Outlines 'The Great Reset' a New Era in Real Estate," ULI Americas, October 31, 2023, https://americas.uli.org/emerging-trends-in-real-estate-2024/?utm_source=linkedin&utm_medium=social-media.

50. "Lessons from a Leading Remote Work Incentive in Tulsa, Oklahoma," Economic Innovation Group, November 2021.

Chapter 5

1. Fred Lambert, "Elon Musk on Tesla Cybertruck: 'The Goal Is to Kick Most Amount of Ass Possible with This Truck,'" Electrek, August 3, 2020, https://electrek.co/2020/08/03/tesla-cybertruck-elon-musk-kick-most-ass/.

2. Tom Krisher, "Tesla Picks Austin, Tulsa as Finalists for New US Factory," AP News, May 16, 2020, https://apnews.com/general-news-0a9fd1530e5cb8ddcd94143eae641248.

3. Sabine Muller, "Austin Is Home to 20 Unicorns, with More in the Paddock," dealroom.co, August 3, 2022, https://dealroom.co/blog/austin-startup-ecosystem#:~:text=A%20city%20of%20tech%20giants%2C%20unicorns%E2%80%A6&text=But%20as%20far%20as%20homegrown,tech%20cities%20in%20the%20country.

4. Aaron Gordon, "'Last Stages of Desperation': Inside Tulsa's Courtship of Elon Musk," *Vice*, February 15, 2022, https://www.vice.com/en/article/jgmbp3/last-stages-of-desperation-inside-tulsas-courtship-of-elon-musk.

5. Kirsten Korosec, "TechCrunch Is Part of the Yahoo Family of Brands," *TechCrunch*, July 22, 2020, https://techcrunch.com/2020/07/22/tesla-picks-austin-for-its-next-u-s-factory-to-build-cybertruck-semi-truck-model-y/.

6. Fred Lambert, "Tesla Reveals Unbelievable Employment Numbers at Giga Texas," *Electrek*, September 22, 2023, https://electrek.co/2023/09/22/tesla-reveals-unbelievable-employment-numbers-giga-texas/.

7. Riley Edwards, "Breaking Down the Amazon HQ2 Deal," Citizens Budget Commission of New York, November 21, 2018, https://cbcny.org/research/breaking-down-amazon-hq2-deal.

8. Robert McCartney, "Amazon in Seattle: Economic Godsend or Self-Centered Behemoth?" *Washington Post*, 2019, https://www.washingtonpost.com/local/trafficandcommuting/amazon-in-seattle-economic-godsend-or-self-centered-behemoth/2019/04/08/7d29999a-4ce3-11e9-93d0-64dbcf-38ba41_story.html.

9. Bob Bryan, "Amazon's HQ2 Deal with New York Is Officially Off—and It Means the State and the City Could Lose Out on $27.5 Billion in Tax Revenue," *Business Insider*, February 14, 2019, https://www.businessinsider.com/amazon-hq2-leaving-new-york-city-would-mean-tax-revenue-loss-2019-2.

10. John Byrne, "Chicago's Secret Weapon in Amazon HQ Bid: Captain Kirk," *Chicago Tribune*, May 31, 2019, https://www.chicagotribune.com/2017/10/25/chicagos-secret-weapon-in-amazon-hq-bid-captain-kirk/.

11. Mark Anthony Thomas, email to author, October 14, 2023.

12. Connie Chen, "Amazon's New NYC Office Opens, Building on Commitment to New York," Amazon, September 13, 2023, https://www.aboutamazon.com/news/amazon-offices/amazon-opens-hank-office-at-lord-and-taylor-building-in-nyc.

13. "Amazon Career Choice," The City University of New York, https://www.cuny.edu/about/administration/offices/ocip/students/amazon-career-choice/.
14. Kian Kamas, virtual interview with author, December 29, 2023.
15. "Population Overview," Austin Chamber of Commerce.
16. Chris Hachtman, Paul Kolter, and Steven Smith, "Uniquely Austin: Stewarding Growth in America's Boomtown," McKinsey, Apri 18, 2023, https://www.mckinsey.com/featured-insights/sustainable-inclusive-growth/future-of-america/uniquely-austin-stewarding-growth-in-americas-boomtown.
17. "The Racial Wealth Divide in Austin," Austin Community Foundation, 2019, 3, 8, https://www.austincf.org/wp-content/uploads/2020/01/RacialWealthDivide-Profile-Austin.pdf.
18. "Program Enrollments and Degrees," University of Texas at Austin Cockrell School of Engineering, https://cockrell.utexas.edu/about/facts-and-rankings/program-enrollments-and-degrees.
19. "TU Fast Facts," University of Tulsa, https://utulsa.edu/about/why-tu/tu-fast-facts/.
20. "Program Rankings," University of Texas at Austin Cockrell School of Engineering, https://cockrell.utexas.edu/about/facts-and-rankings/program-rankings.
21. John Berkowitz, virtual interview with author, March 19, 2024.
22. Noel Tichy, "No Ordinary Boot Camp," *Harvard Business Review*, April 2001, https://hbr.org/2001/04/no-ordinary-boot-camp.
23. Composite based on Tulsa Innovations and O*NET.
24. Ibid.
25. Ibid.
26. "15 Careers in Cybersecurity," Indeed, April 18, 2024, https://www.indeed.com/career-advice/finding-a-job/career-in-cyber-security.
27. "11 Jobs You Can Do with a Business Analytics Degree," Indeed, April 18, 2024, https://www.indeed.com/career-advice/finding-a-job/what-do-with-business-analytics-degree.
28. "What Does a Software Engineer Do?" Coursera, March 29, 2024, https://www.coursera.org/articles/software-engineer.
29. "7 Skills Every Data Scientist Should Have," Coursera, April 5, 2024, https://www.coursera.org/articles/data-scientist-skills.
30. "15 Essential Skills for Cybersecurity Analysts in 2024," Coursera, March 15, 2024, https://www.coursera.org/articles/cybersecurity-analyst-skills.
31. Sydney Lake, "The Cybersecurity Industry Is Short 3.4 Million Workers—That's Good News for Cyber Wages," *Fortune Education*, October 20, 2022, https://fortune.com/education/articles/the-cybersecurity-industry-is-short-3-4-million-workers-thats-good-news-for-cyber-wages/.

32. Martha Ross and Mark Muro, "How Federal, State, and Local Leaders Can Leverage the CHIPS and Science Act as a Landmark Workforce Opportunity," Brookings Institution, January 4, 2024, https://www.brookings.edu/articles/how-federal-state-and-local-leaders-can-leverage-the-chips-and-science-act-as-a-landmark-workforce-opportunity/.

33. Libby Ediger, email to author, January 23, 2024.

34. "Tulsa Metropolitan Statistical Area: 2023 Local Briefing," Oklahoma Employment Security Commission, https://oklahoma.gov/content/dam/ok/en/oesc/documents/labor-market/publications/workforce-briefings/2023/tulsa-msa-workforce-briefing-2023.pdf.

35. Lauren Andersen, email to author, March 28, 2024.

36. Tejus Kothari, phone interview with author, December 7, 2023.

37. "Talent Action Team," Michigan Economic Development Corporation, https://www.michiganbusiness.org/talent-action-team/.

38. Hector Daniel Mujica, email to author, January 4, 2024.

39. "Census Bureau Releases New Educational Attainment Data," United States Census Bureau, February 24, 2022, https://www.census.gov/newsroom/press-releases/2022/educational-attainment.html.

40. Zeynep Ton, *The Good Jobs Strategy: How the Smartest Companies Invest in Employees to Lower Costs and Boost Profits* (New Harvest, Houghton Mifflin Harcourt, 2014), 10.

41. "Tulsa's Path to Inclusive Growth" (with data from McKinsey & Company), June 2023, 6, https://static1.squarespace.com/static/6390eb779f75186607f90d99/t/64960444dcbfdc6b55c14753/1687553098730/230623_TIL_Report_FA_Digital.pdf.

42. Alexis Gable, et al., "The Workforce Almanac Report: A System-Level View of U.S. Workforce Training Providers," Harvard Project on Workforce, November 2023, https://www.pw.hks.harvard.edu/post/workforce-almanac-2023.

43. Pete Selden, email to author, November 19, 2023.

44. Eunice Tarver, email to author, September 28, 2023.

45. Sarah Kessler, Ephrat Livni, and Michael J. De La Merced, "Tech Fears Are Showing Up on Picket Lines," *New York Times*, September 16, 2023, https://www.nytimes.com/2023/09/16/business/dealbook/uaw-strike-tech-ai-unions.html?smid=nytcore-ios-share&referringSource=articleShare.

46. Jane Oates, interview with author, November 21, 2023.

47. Frank Herbert, *Dune* (ACE, ebook, 2010), 504.

Chapter 6

1. "Channing Gerard Joseph," Whiting, https://www.whiting.org/content/channing-gerard-joseph#/.

2. Emily Martin, "From Police Raids to Pop Culture: The Early History of Modern Drag," *National Geographic*, June 2, 2023, https://www.national

geographic.com/history/article/drag-queen-drag-balls-early-history-pop-culture.

3. Melissa Callahan, "Dewey's Lunch Counter Sit-In," Encyclopedia of Greater Philadelphia, March 16, 2022, https://philadelphiaencyclopedia.org/essays/deweys-lunch-counter-sit-in/.

4. Carl Romer and Kristen Broady, "The Black and Brown Activists Who Started Pride," Brookings Institution, June 29, 2021, https://www.brookings.edu/articles/the-black-and-brown-activists-who-started-pride/.

5. Ronald K. Porter, "A Rainbow in Black: The Gay Politics of the Black Panther Party," *Counterpoints* 367 (2012): 364–75, http://www.jstor.org/stable/42981419.

6. Chelsey Boyle, "Why Is David White? The Entwinement of Race and Sexuality," University of Notre Dame, April 4, 2021, https://sites.nd.edu/jamesbaldwin/2021/04/04/why-is-david-white-the-entwinement-of-race-and-sexuality/.

7. Louie Napoleone, text message to author, December 5, 2023.

8. M.V. Lee Badgett, Andrew Park, and Andrew Flores, "Links between Economic Development and New Measures of LGBT Inclusion," The Williams Institute, March 2018, https://williamsinstitute.law.ucla.edu/wp-content/uploads/Global-Economy-and-LGBT-Inclusion-Mar-2018.pdf.

9. Jay H. Bryson and Nicole Cervi, "The "Secret Sauce": The LGBTQ+ Community & State Economic Growth Rates," Wells Fargo, June 1, 2023, https://wellsfargo.bluematrix.com/links2/html/09715269-77b0-4c34-a1fc-9181b8ae131e.

10. Ella Ceron, "Despite Backlash, Companies Still Benefit from Being Pro-LGBTQ," *Bloomberg*, October 6, 2023, https://www.bloomberg.com/news/articles/2023-10-06/lgbtq-spending-power-outweighs-hate-campaign-risk-for-businesses.

11. Richard Florida and Charlotta Mellander, "There Goes the Neighborhood: How and Why Bohemians, Artists and Gays Effect Regional Housing Values," March 2007, https://citeseerx.ist.psu.edu/document?repid=rep1&type=pdf&doi=d6ad06152389846babf3320acbc560a70d24a320.

12. Richard Florida, *The Rise of the Creative Class—Revisited: Revised and Expanded* (Basic Books, 2014), 410.

13. "MEI 2023: See Your Cities Scores," Human Rights Campaign, https://www.hrc.org/resources/mei-2023-see-your-cities-scores?_ga=2.72023632.2113715705.1699738964-535954575.1699237728.

14. Ibid.

15. "2023 Municipal Equality Index Scorecard—Tulsa, Oklahoma," Human Rights Campaign, https://hrc-prod-requests.s3-us-west-2.amazonaws.com/MEI-2023-Assets/MEI-2023-Tulsa-Oklahoma.pdf.

16. Hannibal B. Johnson, *Black Wall Street 100: An American City Grapples with Its Historical Racial Trauma,* Illustrated Edition (Eakin Press, 2020), 41.

17. Ibid., 41–42.
18. Scott Ellsworth, *The Ground Breaking: An American City and Its Search for Justice* (Dutton, 2021), 32.
19. Scott Ellsworth, *The Ground Breaking*, 32–33.
20. Victor Luckerson, *Built from the Fire: The Epic Story of Tulsa's Greenwood District, America's Black Wall Street* (Random House, 2023), 100.
21. Ibid., 102.
22. Alex Albright, et al., "After the Burning: The Economic Effects of the 1921 Tulsa Race Massacre," *NBER Working Paper Series*, National Bureau of Economic Research, June 23, 2021, https://scholar.harvard.edu/files/nunn/files/tulsa.pdf.
23. Sam Anderson, *Boom Town* (Crown, 2018), 193.
24. Mary Pattillo, "Black Advantage Vision: Flipping the Script on Racial Inequality Research," *Issues in Race & Society*, 2021, https://sociology.northwestern.edu/documents/faculty-docs/faculty-research-article/pattillo-black-advantage-vision-2021.pdf.
25. Hannibal Johnson, phone interview with author, March 14, 2024.
26. Lisa Camner McKay, "How the Racial Wealth Gap Has Evolved—and Why It Persists," Federal Reserve Bank of Minneapolis, October 3, 2022, https://minneapolisfed.org/article/2022/how-the-racial-wealth-gap-has-evolved-and-why-it-persists.
27. Thomas Piketty, *Capital in the Twenty-First Century*, 746.
28. Talmon Joseph Smith and Karl Russell, "The Greatest Wealth Transfer in History Is Here, with Familiar (Rich) Winners," *New York Times*, May 23, 2023, https://www.nytimes.com/2023/05/14/business/economy/wealth-generations.html.
29. Chris Metinko, "VC Dollars to Black Start-Up Founders Fell More Than 50% in 2022," *Crunchbase News*, February 22, 2023.
30. Jasmine Browley, "This Woman Is Leading the Charge for the Second Coming of Black Wall Street in Tulsa," *Essence*, August 15, 2023, https://www.essence.com/news/build-in-tulsa-ashli-sims/.
31. Tyrance Billingsley II, virtual interview with author, November 1, 2023.
32. "Darrien Wilson," LinkedIn, accessed March 18, 2024, https://www.linkedin.com/in/darrien-watson-7ab648a1/.
33. "Edna Martinson," LinkedIn, accessed March 18, 2024, https://www.linkedin.com/in/edna-martinson-0513b63b/.
34. Kathryn Finney, "Inside Chicago's New Black Entrepreneurial Renaissance," *Inc.*, August 4, 2021, https://www.inc.com/kathryn-finney/inside-chicagos-new-black-entrepreneurial-renaissance.html.
35. Nalin Patel and Jordan Rubio, "The World's Top Start-Up Cities," *PitchBook*, April 18, 2024, https://pitchbook.com/news/articles/pitchbook-global-vc-ecosystem-rankings.

36. Jared Council, "How Chicago Emerged as a Hotbed of Diverse-Owned Start-Ups—Hint: There's a Billionaire Involved," *Forbes*, April 10, 2023.

37. TechRise, "Three Year Impact," https://techrise.co/.

38. "1871 BLKtech Founders Program," https://1871.com/blktech-founders/.

39. Revitalizing Innovation: Models of Equitable Entrepreneurship Across the U.S., 2024 by Nasdaq Entrepreneurial Center, page 42.

40. Kaanita Iyer, "Oklahoma Governor Signs Executive Order Defunding DEI Efforts in Public Colleges," CNN, December 15, 2023, https://www.cnn.com/2023/12/15/politics/oklahoma-dei-office-defund-reaj/index.html.

41. Hannibal Johnson, phone interview with author, March 14, 2024.

42. "Transforma: New Orleans 2005–2010," https://www.transformaprojects.org/.

43. Simon Vozick-Levinson, "Poetry and Jazz Meet in a Vision of Tulsa's Past and Future," *Rolling Stone*, May 7, 2021, https://www.rollingstone.com/music/music-features/fire-in-little-africa-shining-tulsa-song-review-1166767/.

44. Brentin Mock, "The Wakanda Reader," *Bloomberg*, February 18, 2018, https://www.bloomberg.com/news/articles/2018-02-22/what-you-can-learn-about-the-future-of-cities-from-wakanda.

Chapter 7

1. Nick Hazelrigg, "Reorganizing Away the Liberal Arts," *Inside Higher Ed*, June 5, 2019, https://www.insidehighered.com/news/2019/06/06/cuts-leave-concerns-liberal-arts-tulsa.

2. Ibid.

3. Sacha Litman, et al., "A Turnaround for Higher Ed in the US," Boston Consulting Group, April 26, 2023, https://www.bcg.com/publications/2023/higher-ed-transformation-in-the-us.

4. Lauren Fisher, "How a Radical Restructuring Plan Fractured a Campus and Fueled a No-Confidence Vote," *Chronicle of Higher Education*, November 14, 2019, https://www.chronicle.com/article/how-a-radical-restructuring-plan-fractured-a-campus-and-fueled-a-no-confidence-vote/.

5. Nick Hazelrigg, "Reorganizing Away the Liberal Arts."

6. Snemona Hartocollis, "Slashing Its Budget, West Virginia University Asks, What Is Essential?" *New York Times*, August 21, 2023, https://www.nytimes.com/2023/08/18/us/west-virginia-university-budget-cuts-deficit.html.

7. Nick Hazelrigg, "Reorganizing Away the Liberal Arts."

8. Paul Togh, "Americans Are Losing Faith in the Value of College. Whose Fault Is That?" *New York Times*, September 5, 2023, https://www.nytimes.com/2023/09/05/magazine/college-worth-price.html.

9. Sacha Litman, et al., "A Turnaround for Higher Ed in the US."

10. Ibid.

11. Ibid.

12. Willa Cather, *The Song of the Lark* (Houghton Mifflin, 1915), 443.

13. Erwin Gianchandani, email to author, October 18, 2023.

14. Orin Herskowitz, email to author, October 15, 2023.

15. "TU Cyber Corps to Receive $6.3M from National Science Foundation," University of Tulsa, September 7, 2022, https://utulsa.edu/news/cyber-corps-national-science-foundation/.

16. "Higher Education Research and Development (HERD) Survey: 2022," National Center for Science and Engineering Statistics, November 2023, https://ncses.nsf.gov/surveys/higher-education-research-development/2022#data.

17. Ross DeVol, Joe Lee, and Minoli Ratnatunga, "Concept to Commercialization: The Best Universities for Technology Transfer," Milken Institute Center for Jobs and Human Capital, April 2017, https://milkeninstitute.org/sites/default/files/reports-pdf/Concept2Commercialization-MR19-WEB_2.pdf.

18. Brad Carson, email to author, December 22, 2023.

19. Tom Wavering, email to author, October 23, 2023.

20. Richard R. Nelson, *National Innovation Systems: A Comparative Analysis* (Oxford University Press, 1993), 513.

21. Ibid.

22. "Purdue Recognized as National Innovation Leader: 4th Among US Universities in US Patents Received," Purdue University Research Foundation News, September 12, 2023, https://www.purdue.edu/newsroom/releases/2023/Q3/purdue-recognized-as-national-innovation-leader-4th-among-us-universities-in-us-patents-received.html.

23. Ross DeVol, Joe Lee, and Minoli Ratnatunga, "Concept to Commercialization."

24. "Boilermaker Research Demonstrates Excellence at Scale: Purdue Ranks in Top 5 in U.S. for U.S. Patents Received," Purdue University News, February 15, 2024, https://www.purdue.edu/newsroom/releases/2024/Q1/boilermaker-research-demonstrates-excellence-at-scale-purdue-ranks-in-top-5-in-u.s-for-u.s-patents-received.html.

25. "A Place for Technologies to Launch," Discovery Park District, https://www.discoveryparkdistrict.com/tech-discovery-park-district/.

26. "Available Technologies," Purdue Office of Technology Commercialization, https://inventions.prf.org/.

27. "Heartland BioWorks," US Economic Development Administration, https://www.eda.gov/funding/programs/regional-technology-and-innovation-hubs/2023/Heartland-BioWorks.

28. "What Is the Ohio I.P. Promise?" InnovateOhio, https://innovateohio.gov/priorities/resources/the-ohio-ip-promise/what-is-ohio-ip-promise/.

29. "Stats and Rankings: Ohio IP Promise," University of Cincinnati, 1819 Innovation Hub, https://innovation.uc.edu/ideas-and-innovations/the-ohio-ip-promise/Stats_rankings_Ohio_IP_Promise.html.

30. "University of Cincinnati Available Technologies," University of Cincinnati, 1819 Innovation Hub, https://uc.technologypublisher.com/.

31. "Life Sciences Business in Cincinnati," REDI Cincinnati, December 18, 2023, https://redicincinnati.com/industries/life-sciences/.

32. "Wichita State Rises to No. 2 in National List for Industry-Funded Engineering R&D," Wichita State News, January 8, 2024, https://www .wichita.edu/about/wsunews/news/2024/01-jan/research_3.php.

33. "B-1 Increases Contract Ceiling with NIAR to $200M; Expands Partnership to Include Repair Prototyping," Wichita State News, January 25, 2024, https:// www.wichita.edu/about/wsunews-releases/2024/01-jan/b1contract_3.php.

34. "Matchmaking Program Gives Entrepreneurs a Chance at Commercializing WSU Technologies," Wichita State News, March 28, 2022, https://www .wichita.edu/about/wsunews/news/2022/03-march/matchmaking_program _4.php.

35. "China Leads US in Global Competition for Key Emerging Technology, Study Says," Reuters, March 1, 2023, https://www.reuters.com/technology /china-leads-us-global-competition-key-emerging-technology-study -says-2023-03-02/.

36. Bruce Katz, Milena Dovali, and Victoria Orozco, "The Defense Dividend and What It Means for Cities—the New Localism," The New Localism, October 19, 2023, https://www.thenewlocalism.com/newsletter/ the-defense-dividend-and-what-it-means-for-cities/.

37. Ibid.

38. Shoshanna Solomon, "Israeli Universities Churn Out Start-Ups as Ties with Tech Industry Grow," Times of Israel, April 23, 2023.

39. Dan Senor and Saul Singer, The Start-Up Nation: The Story of Israel's Economic Miracle (Twelve, 2009).

40. Nadav Zafrir, email to author, December 20, 2023.

Chapter 8

1. Kenny A. Franks, "Petroleum Industry," Oklahoma Historical Society, https://www.okhistory.org/publications/enc/entry.php?entry=PE023.

2. "Tulsa City, Oklahoma," US Census Bureau, Census Bureau QuickFacts, https://www.census.gov/quickfacts/fact/table/tulsacityoklahoma/ PST045219.

3. Kenny A. Franks, "Petroleum Industry."

4. "Inflation Rate Between 1927–2024: Inflation Calculator," https://www .officialdata.org/us/inflation/1927?amount=40000.

5. Kenny Franks, The Osage Oil Boom (Oklahoma Heritage, 1989), 111.

6. Kenny A. Franks, "Petroleum Industry."

7. David Grann, Killers of the Flower Moon: The Osage Murders and the Birth of the FBI (Doubleday, 2017), 28.

8. "Industry (1901–1945)," Tulsa Preservation Commission, https://tulsapreservationcommission.org/resources/tulsa-history/industry/.

9. Ibid.

10. Ibid.

11. "Designing Tulsa: Oil Capital Architects," Tulsa Historical Society & Museum, https://www.tulsahistory.org/exhibit/designing-tulsa-oil-capital-architects/.

12. Daniel Yergin, *The Prize: The Epic Quest for Oil, Money & Power* (Free Press, 2008), xvi–xvii.

13. "2021 Cleantech Innovation Hubs Survey White Paper," Saoradh Enterprise Partners, 13.

14. Jim Kunstler, "An Interview with Jane Jacobs, Godmother of the American City [reprint]," *Metropolis*, May 4, 2016, https://metropolismag.com/profiles/jane-jacobs-godmother-of-the-american-city/.

15. David Hall, email to author, October 26, 2023.

16. "Michigan Central Launches with Newlab Opening in Reimagined Book Depository," Michigan Central, April 24, 2023, https://michigancentral.com/michigan-central-launches-with-newlab-opening-in-reimagined-book-depository/.

17. Matt Banholzer and Sid Ramtri, "Three Essentials of Successful Corporate Venture Capital," McKinsey & Company, November 2, 2023, https://www.mckinsey.com/capabilities/strategy-and-corporate-finance/our-insights/three-essentials-of-successful-corporate-venture-capital.

18. Sean Brown, et al., "Collaborations Between Corporates and Start-Ups," McKinsey & Company, May 10, 2021, https://www.mckinsey.com/capabilities/strategy-and-corporate-finance/our-insights/collaborations-between-corporates-and-start-ups.

19. Matt Banholzer, John Levene, and Sid Ramtri, "How to Make Investments in Start-Ups Pay Off," McKinsey & Company, November 9, 2022, https://www.mckinsey.com/capabilities/strategy-and-corporate-finance/our-insights/how-to-make-investments-in-start-ups-pay-off.

20. Michael Brigl, et al., "After the Honeymoon Ends: Making Corporate-Startup Relationships Work," BCG Global, July 1, 2021, https://www.bcg.com/publications/2019/corporate-startup-relationships-work-after-honeymoon-ends.

21. Simone Bhan Ahuja, "Why Innovation Labs Fail, and How to Ensure Yours Doesn't."

22. David Clouse, email to author, November 6, 2023.

23. Brian Hlavinka, email to author, October 25, 2023.

24. Garrison Haning, email to author, October 31, 2023.

25. Kastle Jones, email to author, February 29, 2024.

26. Octavia E. Butler, *Parable of the Sower* (Grand Central Publishing, 1993), 147.

27. "World Energy Transitions Outlook: 1.5°C Pathway," *IRENA*, International Renewable Energy Agency, 2021, https://www.irena.org/-/media/Files/IRENA/Agency/Publication/2021/Jun/IRENA_World_Energy_Transitions_Outlook_2021.pdf.

28. Devashree Saha, Rajat Shrestha, and Phil Jordan, "How a Clean Energy Economy Can Create Millions of Jobs in the US," World Resources Institute, September 14, 2022, https://www.wri.org/insights/us-jobs-clean-energy-growth.

29. "Oklahoma State Profile and Energy Estimates," US Energy Information Administration, June 15, 2023, https://www.eia.gov/state/analysis.php?sid=OK.

30. Carmen Forman, "Enel to Build $1 Billion Solar Panel Plant at Tulsa Port of Inola," Tulsa World, May 22, 2023, https://tulsaworld.com/news/local/enel-to-build-1-billion-solar-panel-plant-at-tulsa-port-of-inola/article_05ea9a06-f675-11ed-a564-4f503f10ca71.html#:~:text=OKLAHOMA%20CITY%20—%20An%20international%20green,development%20project%20in%20state%20history.

31. Michael Berkowitz, virtual interview with author, December 18, 2023.

32. Laura Fox, email to author, March 4, 2024.

33. David Hall, email to author, October 26, 2023.

Chapter 9

1. Kevin Canfield, "Five Years After Opening, Gathering Place Continues to Awe Visitors, Attract New Residents," Tulsa World, September 8, 2023. https://tulsaworld.com/news/local/gathering-place/article_08fa88ac-4c18-11ee-b62a-87ccobbf9e3d.html.

2. Ken Levit, virtual interview with author, November 30, 2023.

3. Diana Tittle, *Rebuilding Cleveland: The Cleveland Foundation and Its Evolving Urban Strategy* (Ohio State University Press, 1992), ix, https://archive.org/details/rebuildingcleveloootitt/mode/2up?q=dead+hand.

4. "Our Grantmaking," Cleveland Foundation, https://www.clevelandfoundation.org/grants/our-grantmaking/.

5. "Consolidated Financial Statements: The Cleveland Foundation (Years Ended December 31, 2022 and 2021)," Ernst & Young LLP, https://www.clevelandfoundation.org/wp-content/uploads/2012/08/The-Cleveland-Foundation-Audited-Financial-Statements-_2022.pdf.

6. "Pulling Together for Cleveland's Future: Editorial," Cleveland.com, March 3, 2022, https://www.cleveland.com/opinion/2022/03/pulling-together-for-clevelands-future-editorial.html.

7. "Economic & Workforce Development," Cleveland Foundation, https://www.clevelandfoundation.org/grants/impact-areas/economic-development/.

8. "Cleveland Innovation Project Announces Initiatives to Propel Region's Growth," Cleveland Foundation, October 14, 2020, https://www.clevelandfoundation.org/news_items/cleveland-innovation-project/.

9. "Walton Family Foundation Inc.," ProPublica, https://projects.propublica.org/nonprofits/organizations/133441466.

10. "Lobeck Taylor Family Foundation," https://www.lobecktaylor.org/mother-road-market.

11. Rob Reich, *Just Giving: Why Philanthropy Is Failing Democracy and How It Can Do Better* (Princeton University Press, 2018), 7–8.

12. Katherina Rosqueta, virtual interview with author, April 5, 2024.

13. Darren Walker, *From Generosity to Justice: A New Gospel of Wealth* (Disruption Books, 2023), 6.

14. Barack Obama, "Inaugural Address," Washington, DC, January 20, 2009, https://obamawhitehouse.archives.gov/realitycheck/the-press-office/president-barack-obamas-inaugural-address.

15. Anand Giridharadas, *Winners Take All: The Elite Charade of Changing the World* (Knopf, 2018), 10.

16. "About," The Giving Pledge, https://givingpledge.org/about.

17. Saul Bellow, *Herzog* (Viking Press, 1964), 51.

18. Mark Kramer and Steve Phillips, "Where Strategic Philanthropy Went Wrong," *Stanford Social Innovation Review* (Summer 2024), https://ssir.org/articles/entry/strategic-philanthropy-went-wrong.

Chapter 10

1. Raymond Redcorn, phone interview with author, November 16, 2023.

2. Daniel Plaisance, email to author, November 6, 2023.

3. "Federal Obligations for Research and Experimental Development, by State or Location, Agency, and Performer: FY 2021," Data set, *Survey of Federal Funds for Research and Development: 2021–2022*, National Science Foundation, December 2023, https://ncses.nsf.gov/surveys/federal-funds-research-development/2021-2022#data. (According to Table 44 of the same survey, only twelve mostly coastal states had university-affiliated research centers that received federal R&D.)

4. Alejandra Y. Castillo, email to author, December 15, 2023.

5. Jeanne Whalen, "A New Era of Industrial Policy Kicks Off with Signing of the Chips Act," *Washington Post*, August 9, 2022, https://www.washingtonpost.com/us-policy/2022/08/09/micron-40-billion-us-subsidies/.

6. Kian Kamas, virtual interview with author, December 29, 2023.

7. "Notice of Funding Opportunity," US Economic Development Administration, January 2022, https://www.eda.gov/sites/default/files/2022-01/ARPA-BBBRC-NOFO.pdf.

8. "Regional Technology and Innovation Hubs (Tech Hubs)," US Economic Development Administration, https://www.eda.gov/funding/programs/regional-technology-and-innovation-hubs.

9. "Tulsa Hub for Equitable Trustworthy Autonomy," US Economic Development Administration, https://www.eda.gov/sites/default/files/2023-11/Tulsa_Hub_for_Equitable_Trustworthy_Autonomy.pdf.

10. Daniel Goetzel, email to author, March 4, 2024.

11. Blake Morgan, "Walmart vs. Amazon: Who Wins the Retail Battle in 2023?" *Forbes*, July 10, 2023, https://www.forbes.com/sites/blakemorgan/2023/07/10/walmart-vs-amazon-who-wins-the-retail-battle-in-2023/?sh=1d9c888b68fe.

12. Ross DeVol, virtual interview with author, November 15, 2023.

13. Mike Preston, email to author, December 11, 2023.

14. Ross DeVol and Dave Shielder, *Regional Collaboration Drives Economic Development: Tulsa and Northwest Arkansas's FLAME Proposal*, Heartland Forward, May 11, 2023, 4, https://heartlandforward.org/case-study/regional-collaboration/.

15. "Governors Stitt, Hutchinson Partner to Create Super Region for Advanced Mobility in the Heartland," OCAST, August 18, 2022, https://oklahoma.gov/ocast/about-ocast/news/governors-stitt--hutchinson-partner-to-create-super-region-for-a.html.

16. "Interactive NSF Engines Award Data," US National Science Foundation, https://new.nsf.gov/funding/initiatives/regional-innovation-engines/interactive-nsf-engines-award-data.

17. Scott Andes, email to author, May 23, 2024.

18. Tracy Letts, *August: Osage County*, Act I, Scene 4 (Theatre Communication Group, 2008), 54.

19. William Julius Wilson, *When Work Disappears: The World of the New Urban Poor* (Vintage, 1997), 192.

20. Janet Nguyen, "How Much Are We Earning Almost a Decade After the Great Recession?" *Marketplace*, May 23, 2018, https://www.marketplace.org/2018/05/23/wages-college-graduates/.

21. John Friedman, "Lifetime Earnings Effects of the COVID-19 Recession for Students," *Opportunity Insights*, February 2, 2021, https://opportunityinsights.org/wp-content/uploads/2021/02/Oi_StudentEarnings_analysis.pdf.

22. Paul Krugman, "The Mystery of White Rural Rage," *New York Times*, February 26, 2024, https://www.nytimes.com/2024/02/26/opinion/white-rural-voters.html.

23. Matt Dunne, virtual interview with author, March 18, 2024.

24. Matthew Desmond, *Poverty, by America* (Crown, 2023), 22.

25. Nicol Turner Lee, "Closing the Digital and Economic Divides in Rural America," Brookings Institution, https://www.brookings.edu/articles/closing-the-digital-and-economic-divides-in-rural-america/.

Conclusion

1. Hernan Diaz, *Trust* (Riverhead Books, 2022), 16.
2. Jonathan Gruber and Simon Johnson, *Jump-Starting America: How Breakthrough Science Can Revive Economic Growth and the American Dream* (PublicAffairs, 2019), 147.

ACKNOWLEDGMENTS

One of the great joys in writing this book was that it reminded me of all the wonderful people in my life. The book not only brought together a talented team of professionals to work on the project, but it also served as a happy excuse to reconnect with many old friends and colleagues—for interviews, feedback sessions, or simply to catch up. Along the way, writing the book helped me make new friends as well. Encapsulated in these pages, then, are the people who have shaped my life and the life of the book. I am thankful to every one of them—especially to my core book team.

First and foremost, thank you to my executive editor, Tim Burgard, at HarperCollins, for his enthusiastic support. I'm grateful to Tim for his ability and willingness to see the bigger American story in Tulsa and for challenging me to widen my ambition to share that story with readers.

Thank you to my literary agent, Sabrina Taitz, at William Morris Endeavor. Sabrina's early championing of the book helped turn my dream into a reality. Her close engagement throughout the process made every step easier, and her wise counsel and regular therapy sessions kept me grounded and moving forward.

Like air-conditioning, editors are a godsend, and I was lucky to have a smart and diligent one to help give this book narrative shape and structure. To Kevin Lincoln, thank you for showing me how to be conscious of readers' needs and how to build the Tulsa world *within* the book. Your documentary film background lent itself well to sculpting this story about a city in the Heartland, and you elevated the entire project in the process.

To Marcie Bianco, thank you for your rigorous editorial guidance. You strengthened my arguments by pushing me to think deeper, challenging my assumptions, questioning my premises, and by excising my many unnecessary tangents.

This book—and my experience writing it—benefited greatly from the foundation established in the book proposal, built alongside Zach Gajewski. His hard work not only helped produce a comprehensive and winning proposal, but it also resulted in an outline that served me well as I turned to writing.

I was also fortunate to have two strong research assistants who contributed mightily to the project. To Adam Lipsey, thank you for your diligent digging; the data and comparative examples you compiled gave the book further depth. And to Daniel Te, my former TIL colleague, thank you for your research briefs, which showed sensitivity and insight into local communities.

And to my strategic adviser, Daniel Plaisance, who I have had the pleasure of working with from NYCEDC to Tulsa Innovation Labs, thank you for being such a great teammate and friend and for providing such insightful perspective.

AN ARMY OF additional supporters contributed to *Reinventing the Heartland*—from refining the book's initial concept to being interviewed on-the-record to providing input on chapters.

When I first had the idea for the book, I took it to Marco Greenberg, who was then representing TIL through his public relations firm Thunder11. Through conversations with him and Liel Leibovitz, I was able to put what was happening in Tulsa within broader national and global contexts and realize the core story in Tulsa's reinvention. I'm thankful for Marco's continued wisdom.

Thank you to my friend Cody Min, who first introduced me to Sabrina Taitz and who has served as my formal and informal design consultant over the years. Cody's firm, Astronaut Monastery, developed TIL's brand, built my website, and contributed to the book proposal and cover design.

To ensure my ideas were sound, identify potential blind spots, and refine my thinking, I relied on multiple outside readers to lend me their perspectives. Thank you to the following individuals for their constructive feedback on select chapters: Lauren Andersen, Madeline Brozen, Kate Daley, Conor Godfrey, Brigit Goebelbecker, Tejus Kothari, Justin Kreamer, Alison Lands, Michael Manville, Marc Norman, Chris Rhie, and Buzz Rubenstein.

Special thanks go to those who reviewed multiple chapters and provided extensive feedback: Lena Gloeckler, Sara Hammerschmidt, Karyn Lacy, Brian Ratajczak, and Ian Veidenheimer.

Thank you to all those who were interviewed for the book: Sean Alexander, Lauren Andersen, Scott Andes, John Berkowitz, Michael Berkowitz, Tyrance Billingsley II, Mayor G. T. Bynum, Brad Carson, Cordell Carter, Alejandra Y. Castillo, David Clouse, Ross DeVol, Matt Dunne, Libby Ediger, Laura Fox, Erwin Gianchandani, Daniel Goetzel, Jason Griess, Lynn Greenberg, David Hall, Garrison Haning, Justin Harlan, Orin Herskowitz, Brian Hlavinka, Hannibal Johnson, Kastle Jones, Kian Kamas, Tejus Kothari, Ken Levit, Andrew Lowenthal, Hector Mujica, Louie Napoleone, Mike Neal, Jane Oates, Daniel Plaisance, Mike Preston, Raymond Redcorn, Katherina Rosqueta, Pete Selden, Andrii Skorniakov, Eunice Tarver, Mark Anthony Thomas, Tom Wavering, and Nadav Zafrir.

The following individuals also provided valuable assistance: Zach Beecher, Ryan Birchmeier, Michael Carney, Meghan Chandler, Steven Collens, Matthew Creegan, Jake Cronin, Josh deLacy, Aaron Dubin, Jeff Farr, Kenan Fikri, Christopher Fletcher, David Gilford, Jennifer Holk, Patrick Hosford, Shawna Khouri, Caitlin Lewis, Jared Lipsey, Sacha Litman, Linda Lopez, David McNeill, Todd Rufo, Dave Shideler, Steven Smith, Steven Strauss, Robert Thomas, Chris Valentine, Alison Williams, and Lauren Yayboke.

And thank you to Fortier Public Relations, in particular Mark Fortier and David Wolpert.

ALL THE WORK depicted in this book is highly collaborative. And as the culmination of two decades of working as an urbanist, this book—not to mention me—have benefited from my professional communities and colleagues, so there are many people to thank.

To the UCLA community, thank you for welcoming Chris and me into your esteemed institution. I'm grateful to the Luskin School of Public Affairs and the Lewis Center for Regional Policy Studies for their sponsorship of me while I was a visiting scholar, especially Helmut Anheier, Evelyn Blumenberg, and Anastasia Loukaitou-Sideris.

Thank you to my former colleagues at Tulsa Innovation Labs, including Sahee Abdelmomin, Abisoye Ajayi-Akinfolarin, Oscar Guillén Arauz, Joanna Jeffries, Justin Kits, Robert O'Gara, Precious Okoruwa, Alejandra Palomo, Jessica Remer, Carrigan Tillman, and Kayla Valencia.

Thank you to TIL's advisory council, including Aaron Bean, Jennifer Bennett, Bob Blakely, Jamey Jacob, Bharat Kejriwal, Jerome Loughridge, Sid McNally, Rick Muncrief, Mayor Tom Murphy, Vi Nguyen, Vinit Nijhawan, Simeon Sessley, Steve Smith, Sharon K. Sputz, and Nicol Turner-Lee.

To my Tulsa community, thank you for showing me such kindness and warmth, especially: Sean Alexander, Grant Bumgarner, Cody Davis, Libby Ediger, Mary Fencl, Will Gray, Steve Higgins,

Andrew Howard, Kian Kamas, Louie Napoleone, Max Nobel, Karen Pennington, Reid Spears, Tracy Spears, Megan Thomas, and Robert Thomas.

Thank you to my former colleagues at the New York City Economic Development Corporation, including Gideon Abramowitz, Kristin Bell, Sophia Cacciatore, Alex Costas, Sander Dolder, Ericka J. Garcia, Eric Goodnight, Danielle Hamilton, Liat Krawczyk, Hudson Leung, Wilson Lin, Kokei Otosi, James Patchett, Nicole Spina, Josh Stephens, Doug Thiede, Mark Anthony Thomas, Stacey Weismiller, Jasper Steele Wilson, and Carlo Yuvienco.

Thank you to the Urban Land Institute and my former colleagues there: Gayle Berens, Carolyn Brennan, Kathleen Carey, Caroline Dietrich, Tom Eitler, Maria Fiore, Alison Johnson, Brendan McEneaney, Patrick Phillips, Lynn Ross, Adrienne Schmitz, Brett Widness, and Jess Zimbabwe.

Thank you to the City of New Orleans—Ashleigh Gardere and Mayor Mitch Landrieu. And to Jared Munster and Brandon Robb.

And to my partners across various roles, thank you to: Alan Armstrong, Mia Bartlett, René Bastón, Ben Borodach, Robert Burns, George Coyle, Mridula Damodaran, Fiona Darmon, Francesca Fiore, Richard Florida, Kathryn Fox, Guy Franklin, Jeremy Goldberg, Daniel Goldstein, Christian Gonzales, Sara Holoubek, Youssef Kalad, Andrew Lackner, Erel N. Margalit, Nelson Peacock, John Pyrovolakis, Jonathan Roberts, Roger Roberts, Uzi Scheffer, Ramona Schindelheim, Seema Shah, Jeff Shulman, Kevin Skillern, Yoav Tzruya, Phil Venables, and Eric Vieira.

I am also indebted to the mentorship and friendship of Kate Daley, Alison Lands, Mark Anthony Thomas, and Robert Thomas.

EDUCATION HAS TRANSFORMED my life, and I have been blessed with amazing teachers whose lessons and wisdom stay with me to this day.

Thank you to Cornell University and its Africana Studies and Research Center, especially Margo Crawford and Riché Richardson, for developing me as a thinker.

My life changed when I entered Northwestern University, and I'd like to thank Katharine Breen, Susan Dun, Mary Pattillo, and Julia Stern for guiding me during this formative time in my life.

And to my teachers at De La Salle High School in New Orleans, thank you for nurturing me as a teenager: Kathleen Calder, John Fuchs, Peggy St. John, and Tom Waguespack.

NONE OF THIS would be possible if not for the love and support of my family and friends.

Thank you to my dear husband, Chris. And to my mom, brother Alex, and Grandma Bette. As a kid, Grandma Bette would tell me, "I know you have a book in you." She must be so proud. Thank you also to Aunt Debbie, Aunt Jeannie, Aunt Josie, Aunt Kathleen, cousin Katie, and Uncle Billy for their lifelong support.

Finally, thank you to my friends, especially Paul Courtney, Jarett Gross, Sara Hammerschmidt, Ariella Lis, Marion Liu, and Jessica Orgeron. And to Stephanie Bischoff, Nelson Chan, Jinx and Fio Challa, Jon Jacques, Tyler Roe, Bonnie Steen, Brandon Watts, and Aaron Jay Young.

I hope this book can have a similar effect on you: that it brings you together with new and old friends to think about, discuss, and collaborate on the reinvention of cities.

INDEX

BIOGRAPHY

NICHOLAS LALLA is an urbanist and social entrepreneur, working at the intersection of economic development and emerging technology. He partners with cities to build strategies and initiatives that catalyze inclusive growth. Lalla founded Tulsa Innovation Labs, an organization deploying more than $200 million to build northeast Oklahoma's innovation economy. He previously led Cyber NYC for the New York City Economic Development Corporation, a cybersecurity initiative the *New York Times* called "among the nation's most ambitious." Earlier in his career, at the Urban Land Institute, he launched a national resilience program for cities combatting the effects of climate change. Lalla has written for *Newsweek*, *Fast Company*, *Stanford Social Innovation Review*, and *Next City*, among other outlets. He can be found online at nicholaslalla.com.

Nicholas Lalla is available for select speaking appearances through BrightSight Speakers. To inquire, please contact Tom Neilssen at Tom@BrightSightSpeakers.com.